Oracle Certified Linux Expert Exam Cram:

OCE Exam: 1Z0-046: Managing Oracle on Linux Certified Expert

Hubert Savio

This book is dedicated to all the creators of Linux, UNIX and Oracle for without their work, IT would be quite boring.

Hubert Savio

Oracle Certified Linux Expert Exam Cram:
OCE Exam: 1Z0-046: Managing Oracle on Linux Certified Expert

By Hubert Savio

Printed in the United States of America.
Published in Kittrell, North Carolina, USA.
Oracle In-Focus Series: Book 38
Series Editor: Donald K. Burleson
Production Manager: Robin Rademacher
Production Editor: Valerre Aquitaine
Cover Design: Janet Burleson
Printing History: December 2010 for First Edition

ISBN 10: 0-9844282-1-6
ISBN 13: 978-0-9844282-1-2
Library of Congress Control Number: 2011921295

Table of Contents

Using the Online Code Depot

Purchase of this book provides complete access to the online code depot that contains sample code scripts. Any code depot scripts in this book are located at the following URL in zip format and ready to load and use:

rampant.cc/oracle_linux_oce.htm

If technical assistance is needed with downloading or accessing the scripts, please contact Rampant TechPress at rtp@rampant.cc.

Conventions Used in this Book

It is critical for any technical publication to follow rigorous standards and employ consistent punctuation conventions to make the text easy to read. However, this is not an easy task. Within database terminology, there are many types of notation that can confuse a reader. For example, some Oracle utilities such as STATSPACK and TKPROF are always spelled in CAPITAL letters, while Oracle parameters and procedures have varying naming conventions in the database documentation. It is also important to remember that many database commands are case sensitive, and are always left in their original executable form, and never altered with italics or capitalization. Hence, all Rampant TechPress books follow these conventions:

- Parameters: Database parameters will be *lowercase italics.* The exception is parameter arguments that are commonly capitalized (KEEP pool, TKPROF), which will be ALL CAPS.
- Variables: Procedural language (e.g. PL/SQL) program variables and arguments will also remain in *lowercase italics* (i.e. *dbms_job*). However, since this book deals with Linux, certain variables such as *$ORACLE_HOME* must be kept as capitalized italics in the code depot and so they will remain that way in the text.
- Tables & dictionary objects: Data dictionary objects are referenced in lowercase italics (*dba_indexes*, *v$sql*), including *v$* and *x$* views (*x$kcbcbh*, *v$parameter*) and dictionary views (*dba_tables*, *user_indexes*).
- SQL: All SQL is formatted for easy use in the code depot and displayed in lowercase. Main SQL terms (select, from, where, group by, order by, having) will appear on a separate line.
- Programs & Products: All products and programs that are known to the author are capitalized according to the vendor specifications (CentOS, VMware, Oracle, etc). All names known by Rampant TechPress to be trademark names appear in this text as initial caps. References to UNIX are always made in uppercase.

Acknowledgements

This type of highly technical reference book requires the dedicated efforts of many people. Even though I am the author, my work ends when I deliver the content. After each chapter is delivered, several Oracle DBAs carefully review and correct the technical content. After the technical review, experienced copy editors polish the grammar and syntax.

The finished work is then reviewed as page proofs and turned over to the production manager, who arranges the creation of the online code depot and manages the cover art, printing distribution, and warehousing.

In short, the author plays a small role in the development of this book. First, I would like to thank all the contributors from the Open source community, UNIX and Linux makers and also Oracle for bringing stable and amazing software to IT specialists. My sincere thanks also to the Oracle exam team for making it possible for us to take the Oracle credentials and challenge us with the certifications.

This book would not have been possible without the awesome support of the people of Rampant and my family. Special thanks goes to Denis Canty, database consultant and OCP, for his advice and reviews during the redaction of this book - it was an amazing support. Thanks also to Constantine Shulyupin for his excellent work on the Linux Kernel diagram and for the various advices provided by Robert Williams from CertGuard on certifications and book publications.

I would like to thank all my teachers and working colleagues from the past and present, especially the ones who inspired, guided and helped me during my career. Thanks to Christiane Humm, Arne Møller, Mikael Notté, Renaud Velter, Philippe Thomas, Harald Hammerhoi, Tom Aasted Jensen, all the Kenneths and all the others I have in mind.

Next is a list of the people from Rampant who made this book possible:

Robin Rademacher for production management including the coordination of the cover art, page proofing, printing, and distribution.

Valerre Q Aquitaine for help in the production of the page proofs.

Janet Burleson for exceptional cover design and graphics.

John Lavender for assistance with the web site and for creating the code depot and the online shopping cart for this book.

With my sincerest thanks,

Hubert Savio

Preface

Foreword

Dear Reader,

Thank you for choosing this book to prepare for the Oracle Certified Expert exam. The OCE exam is meant to be a validation of your expertise in a specific area not covered by the classical exams OCA and OCP.

Rampant TechPress is a distinctive publishing paradigm targeted at IT professionals who need fast and accurate working examples of complex issues. Rampant TechPress books are unique because they have a focused agenda and quickly provide IT professionals with what they need to solve their problems. Rampant TechPress books are designed for the practicing IT professional and are an affordable way for all IT professionals to get the information they need, and get it fast.

Feedback on this book is quite important. If any errors are discovered, please send a short email to rtp@rampant.cc so other readers can be informed and to help increase the publication quality.

Best of luck on preparation for the exam.

The Rampant Oracle Series Edition Team

Reasons to Certify

Before beginning the process of certification, it may be worthwhile looking at the advantages that certification can have. First, the certification process, i.e. studying and practicing the subject matter, will help the DBA to become more confident with the technology. It will also prove to an employer, colleagues, customers and community peers that sufficient knowledge has been learned to perform certain tasks. Not least, certification will increase the potential to get a new job or a new function in the same company.

Certmag's (http://www.certmag.com/) Salary Survey made in 2003 states the following:

- Respondents with specialization in Database Administration had a higher average annual salary.
- 76% of respondents reported that certification gives them a higher level of confidence in the work they do.
- 70% said that being certified earns them more respect from managers and peers.
- 61% have seen a greater demand for their skills since becoming certified.
- 64% said certification has improved their problem solving skills.
- 60% believe certification has contributed to increased productivity.

The salary survey of 2008 conducted by Certmag still shows that the Oracle Database Administrator has a higher salary than other DBAs. Oracle offers to certified professionals the following advantages:

- Access to the OCP members-only website
- Use of the Oracle Certification Program logo for endorsement of the user's proven skill by Oracle Corporation
- Open line of communication with Oracle
- Special discounts and offers

It would be advisable to ask what support the DBA's company offers in regards to the training course, books, time to study and cost of the test trails. Perhaps the company is an Oracle Partner already and this entitles employees to considerable savings on training courses and tests. Or perhaps the company is willing to become an Oracle Partner and will, therefore, need to have a minimum number of qualified, i.e. certified, people. This contributes to a DBA becoming a more valuable asset to the company.

Certification Tracks

Oracle offers a lot of certification tracks on their products at the database, middleware, application and Linux level. The entire list of certifications can be found on the following webpage: www.oracle.com/education/certification.

OCA/OCP/OCS/OCM, but what is OCE?

OCA (Oracle Certified Associate), OCP (Oracle Certified Professional), OCS (Oracle Certified Specialist) and OCM (Oracle Certified Master) are the classical certifications for Oracle databases that need at least two exams to be passed to get the professional title. Oracle introduced the Oracle Certified Expert (OCE) exams in 2007 with beta-exams on the topics of SQL, Linux, tuning and Real Application Cluster. The OCE exams are now in production and are assessing your knowledge on these areas.

The Oracle Certified Expert exam is a credential that recognizes competency in specific technologies, architectures or domains not currently covered in the path-based Certified Associate and Certified Professional certifications.

Some characteristics of the Expert certifications are:

1. Credentials are separated from the current OCA, OCP, OCS and OCM hierarchies.
2. They validate a specific product or technology knowledge.
3. It is a single comprehensive exam instead of a series of exams.
4. Expert program levels are created to prove the DBA's mastery of advanced technologies.
5. It is an additional validation of specific knowledge not covered by the classical OCA and OCP exams which can be preparation for the OCM certification.

If the reader is a 10g or 11g Oracle Certified Associate or Professional, he/she is not required to take the Oracle Training Course about Oracle under Linux.

If the reader does not have any prior Oracle certification, the following training course will be needed: Oracle Database 10g - Managing Oracle on Linux for Database Administrator. This is because the hands-on form given by Oracle at the end of the training course needs to be submitted. This book is an excellent companion to prepare for the exam if there is a need for the Oracle training course.

Where to Find Official Information

The official information about the Oracle certification can be found on the Oracle certification website, www.oracle.com/education/certification. In case there are questions about the certifications, get in touch with Oracle via ocpexam_ww@oracle.com or on the Oracle Technical Network Forum at http://forums.oracle.com in the following section: Forum Home » Technology Network Community » Certification. In the OTN forum, both Oracle users and Oracle employees can be communicated with who are Certification Program Managers.

Why This Book and Not Another

All the people that are interested in taking the exam will benefit from this book as it will provide the knowledge needed to pass the exam. It was written by people that are giving Oracle training courses, who have taken the beta exam and have practical experience with Oracle products under Linux.

What This Book Covers

This book covers all the requirements to prepare and pass the exam Oracle Database 10g - Managing Oracle on Linux for Database Administrators. It will also help people after the exam as a useful reference book for Linux and Oracle.

If many more details are needed on the Linux OS fundamentals that are not covered by this book, then it would be helpful to read the following book (see http://www.rampant-books.com/ book_0501_linux_commands.htm for more information):

Easy Linux Commands: Working Examples of Linux Command Syntax, Jon Emmons & Terry Clark

ISBN: 0-9759135-0-6
ISBN 13: 978-0975913505
Library of Congress Number: 2005901265
220 pages
Perfect bind - 9x7 Publication
Date: October 2006

Also consult the Redhat manuals at http://www.redhat.com/docs/manuals/enterprise/.

The Structure of the Book

This book has three parts: the first and the second part are about the exam requirements while the third part gives advice on the daily work as an Oracle DBA. Note that nearly every chapter offers exercises and questions to help prepare for the exam.

Part I: Linux

- CHAPTER 1: What is Linux?

Level: Beginner

This chapter gives a short story on Linux and introduces all the Linux basics needed to pass the exam. If Linux has been worked with for several years, just answer the questions and make sure that more than 80% are answered correctly.

- CHAPTER 2: Linux Level 2

Level: Beginner, Intermediate

This chapter provides information on Linux users, file permissions, processes, semaphores, shell limits of kernel sessions and how to perform user management. As with Chapter 1 and all other chapters, if the reader thinks they have the necessary knowledge to skip this chapter, then at least take the sample exam to be sure that more than 80% of the questions are answered correctly.

- CHAPTER 3: Linux Level 3

Level: Intermediate

This section offers an overview of file systems, init modes, and OS patches.

- CHAPTER 4: Linux Measurement and Scheduling Tools

Level: Intermediate

This chapter describes the measurement and scheduling tools available in Linux and also contains exercises and questions to be equipped with the necessary knowledge on that topic.

- CHAPTER 5: The Linux Text Editors

Level: Beginner

This chapter does not contain exam topics, so it does not include questions as this is not required during the Linux OCE exam. If the desire is to be more confident with the vi or emacs editor, then read this chapter. The vi or emacs editor is an essential tool that should be used in daily work.

Part II Oracle Under Linux

- CHAPTER 6: Preparing Linux for Oracle

Level: Intermediate

This chapter helps with preparing the Linux systems to perform the installation of Oracle. After reading the theoretical part, do the exercises and answer the questions.

- CHAPTER 7: Install Oracle Under Linux

Level: Intermediate

This section will be a guide to perform the installation of the Oracle binaries and give a list to control how the installation shall be performed.

- CHAPTER 8: Managing Storage

Level: Intermediate

This chapter covers all the aspects related to the Linux storage and its relation with Oracle. Perform the exercises and answer all the questions in order to evaluate knowledge on this exam topic.

- CHAPTER 9: ASM

Level: Intermediate

The reader will learn about ASM, be able to perform exercises and answer practical exam questions related to ASM in this chapter.

- CHAPTER 10: Create an Oracle Database

Level: Beginner

In this section, commands will be given to perform a database creation using both the graphical way and the text based commands.

- CHAPTER 11: Customizing Oracle on Linux

Level: Beginner

This chapter explains all the elements needed to perform customizing on Oracle under Linux.

- CHAPTER 12: Managing Memory with Oracle

Level: Beginner

This chapter covers the memory management of Oracle in a Linux environment.

- CHAPTER 13: Debugging Oracle 10g on Linux

Level: Beginner

Oracle 10g under Linux is not bug–free, and therefore it is important for the DBA to know how he/she can perform the debugging of Oracle and what information and elements shall be provided by Oracle support.

PART III Oracle Post Certification Knowledge

- CHAPTER 14: Post Certification Information

Level: Intermediate

The chapter is a post-exam chapter that can be read after the exam is passed. It contains on-the-job advice, PL/SQL scripts and mandatory readings for the Oracle DBA. Backup and restore of Oracle database is an important topic for the Oracle DBA. Monitoring of the Oracle database is also quite important. This chapter gives an idea on how monitoring can be done on the database.

Exam Objectives and Requirements

As stated previously, the reader will need either the training or prior certification on Oracle OCP 10g or 11g to continue on the path of managing Oracle on Linux. If a 10g or 11g Oracle OCP has not be acquired, then take the training course Oracle Database 10g - Managing Oracle on Linux for DBAs. Test results will be given upon completion of the test.

There are 105 minutes allowed to answer about 70 questions and as of this writing, the passing score is 65%. Please note that this is subject to change and it is recommended that the exercises and example questions be practiced before taking the exam. This information can be found on www.oracle.com/education/certification in the exam section Exam list -> Exam number: 1Z0-046.

Exam Topics

Introduction

The following exam topics were published in 2008 on the Oracle certification website.

- Interpret Linux kernel version information

- Identify a tainted kernel
- Use common Linux commands
- Write a simple bash shell script

Preparing Linux for Oracle

- Use the package manager to determine and update package support
- Set up the operating system environment for Oracle Database
- Create the necessary groups and users for Oracle Database

Installing Oracle on Linux

- Describe the Linux file system security
- Install multiple versions of Oracle Database software on the same server
- Accommodate multiple Oracle homes on one database server

Managing Storage

- Distinguish the differences between certified and supported file systems
- Select a file system

Automatic Storage Management

- Install and initialize Automatic Storage Management Library Driver (ASMLib)
- Mark disks for ASMLib
- Create an Automatic Storage Management instance

Creating a Database

- Create an Oracle database that uses ASM
- Identify the location of various Oracle files
- Implement OS authentication

Customizing Oracle on Linux

- Create automated startup/shutdown scripts
- Automate tasks using scheduling tools
- Configure Linux startup and shutdown sequence

Managing Memory

- List the memory models available in Linux kernels
- Implement hugepages
- Describe */proc/meminfo* contents
- List the implications of Linux memory configuration on an Oracle Database
- Identify the issues regarding 32-bit OS versus 64-bit OS

Using Linux Measurement Tools

- Use Linux monitoring tools
- Interpret memory measurements
- Interpret I/O measurements

Tuning Performance

- Evaluate file systems
- Tune supported file systems
- Configure initialization parameters
- Implement asynchronous input/output (I/O)
- Implement advanced memory management techniques

Debugging Oracle 10g on Linux

- Install and configure OS Watcher
- Use Oracle Support's Remote Diagnostics Agent

- Trace programs and processes with *strace*
- Gather required information for resolving *ORA-600* and *ORA-7445* errors

Free Test and Sample Questions

Official free sample questions can be obtained from Oracle on http://www.oracle.com/global/us/education/certification/sample_questions /exam_1Z0_046.html. Oracle recommends also using Self Test Software (http://www.selftestsoftware.com) or Transcender (http://www.transcender.com/) practical tests providers to prepare for Oracle certifications. For the moment, they do not have tests for the OCE exams.

Exam Information

Before taking the exam, be certain that the exam can be passed. To verify readiness, correctly answer most of the questions for each chapter. The Oracle exam can be taken in a Pearson VUE testing center or at an Oracle University.

If the user has never taken a Pearson VUE exam before, make sure to create a web account with them to be able to sign up for exams. Be sure to record the login information for future Oracle exam appointments.

For taking the exam at an Oracle University location, contact the local Oracle University. Also, more information can be found at http://education.oracle.com.

Arriving at the Pearson VUE Testing Center

- Have at least two forms of identification. A government-issued photo identification card is a must. Both forms of identification must contain the examinee's signature.
- Bring all the voucher information (numbers, candidate information, etc.) to the test appointment. Present this voucher to the proctor prior to testing.
- Be sure to arrive at the testing center at least 15 minutes before the exam begins. If the tester arrives more than 15 minutes late, the testing center personnel may choose not to seat the tester as this disturbs the other examinees in the testing room.

- It is not possible to bring papers, books, bags, computers, personal organizers, or calculators into the testing room. There will be writing paper offered by the test proctor for use while testing. All those papers will be collected and destroyed by testing center proctors at the end of the exam.
- Before taking the exam, there is a non-disclosure form of the Oracle Certification Candidate Agreement that must be signed before the test starts. This agreement can be viewed prior to arriving at the testing center by viewing this web page: http://www.oracle.com/global/us/education/downloads/certification/certagreement.pdf.

Never Taken an Oracle Certification Exam Before?

If an Oracle exam has never been taken before, try the non-proctored exams on the website http://wsvprd1a.pearsonvue.com/oracle. These exams can be taken from home. The following exams are available:

- 1Z0-007 Introduction to Oracle9i SQL®
- 1Z0-051 Oracle Database 11g: SQL Fundamentals I
- 1Z0-200 11i E-Business Suite Essentials for Implementers
- 1Z0-204 Oracle E-Business Suite R12: E-Business Essentials

The non-proctored exams cost about $125 each and might give an impression on how the exam interface is working and how it takes place. These exams are not preparation for the Oracle under Linux exam topics.

Advice for Taking the OCE Exam

When taking the OCE exam, try to follow this advice:

- Stay calm and do not panic during the test. Do not be stressed by time and do not study late into the night prior to the exam day.
- Carefully read both the questions and the possible answers before answering too fast.
- Answer first the questions which one is confident of the answer.
- Do not get stuck: Just move onto the next question as time is limited.

- Try to eliminate the wrong or incorrect answers to limit the choice of the correct answer.
- Use the mark feature on the questions that are not able to be answered immediately so that the marked questions can be revisited after answering the easier ones. By doing this, no time will be wasted.
- Do not let any question go unanswered as incorrect answers have no negative score on this kind of certification, but an unanswered question is automatically wrong.
- Some questions give answers that may help answer other questions.
- Use time wisely after answering all the questions to make sure that no question was left unanswered and that all questions are answered correctly to the best of the tester's ability. If there is still time left, do not submit the exam; instead, take all the questions in a reverse order from the end to the beginning.

How to Use This Book

This book will help with the required topics, provide exercises and list questions which will help in evaluating whether the tester is ready to take the exam or needs to study more on specific topics.

- Make a reasonable schedule to study at least one chapter a day, but do not read too many chapters at once. Do not hurry to study all chapters. Instead, try to understand each chapter thoroughly step by step.
- Find a quiet place to study the chapters, perform the exercises and answer the questions. By doing regular work with this book, one should be able to pass the certification.
- Evaluate the acquired knowledge first with the knowledge assessment test that can be found in this preface. After studying each chapter and performing the exercises, take a coffee break and then try to answer the questions at the end of the chapter.
- The HINTs are included for each answer in the test question sections. The information in the HINT guides the reader to the appropriate section of the book to review if the wrong answer has been chosen.
- Take some short notes on the points that are judged to be important and also use the exam advice giving throughout the book

- Use the exam topic checklist to follow up on the chapter, exercises performed and results of the tests.
- Evaluate whether the chapter information has been absorbed with the questions at the end of the chapters. If all the questions were not answered correctly, use the HINT to find out which section in the chapter should be read again. Ask friends and colleagues to help by making a Q&A session with this book. Ask them to make questions on a chapter that was read before, give a response and explain what the technology is about or why this option is chosen.
- Get a dedicated computer or virtual machine with Linux in order to do the exercises and necessary practice to help during the learning sessions. It is possible to use VMware, Sun Virtual Box or Oracle's VM in order to have a virtual environment to do the exercises and tests. The virtual servers are also suitable after the exam for the tests of procedures or changes before applying them on the real environments.
- Build flashcards based on the exam advice and on the topics that need special attention and use those flashcards on both sides. On one side, put a question and put the response on the other side. Get through all the flashcards by doing this on all the difficult topics to memorize.
- Use mind maps to prepare the exam. It is possible to build mind maps and an example will be given next.

Mind Maps

Mind maps are an excellent tool to memorize and build a structure that will aid in organizing and preparing the exam.

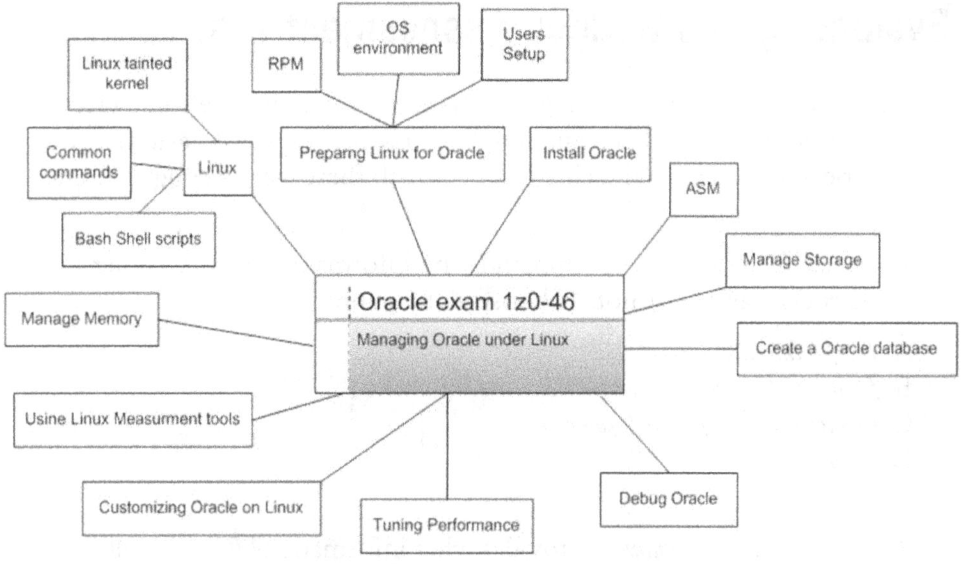

Figure P.1: *Example of Mind Map*

If the Exam is Not Passed

Do not be discouraged by not passing the exam the first time! Certification exams are quite difficult and it is not easy to pass them the first time. Try again after the list of topics in the "Item Feedback" has been obtained and those topics are better understood. By doing this, the exam can definitely be passed.

If the Exam is Passed

Congratulations on passing the exam! It is the author's hope that this book contributed to that success. The next step is to find other challenges like passing the Oracle Certified Master or another Oracle Certified Expert exam. Consult Part III of this book to get some on-the-job advice.

Evaluating Knowledge: Assessment Test

This test will help in evaluating and assessing the examinee's knowledge. After all the questions have been answered, review the responses, evaluate the results and specifically review the chapters on which there were wrong answers.

1. What file contains or commands the information as to whether the Linux kernel is tainted or not? (Choose all that apply)

A. */etc/taintor.txt*
B. */proc/sys/kernel/tainted*
C. *lsmode /var/opt/kernel_color.conf*
D. *lsmod*

2. The command *uname -r* provides what information? (Choose all that apply)

A. List all the users connected on the system
B. Enables viewing the kernel information
C. Gives the information about the last reboot
D. Provides the version number of the kernel with the fields *(<Base>-<Errata>.<Mod><Type>)*

3. The command *alias* provides what information?

A. Create a directory
B. Define command *macro*
C. Gives the alias name of the Linux users
D. List of the pseudo commands

4. Analyze the shell script in the exhibit and answer what is missing in the script. (Choose all that apply)

```
case "$1" in
    'start')
        # Start your Oracle databases:
        su - $USER -c "$ORACLE_HOME/bin/lsnrctl start"
        su - $USER -c $ORACLE_HOME/bin/dbstart
        ;;
    'stop')
        # Stop your Oracle databases:
        su - $USER -c $ORACLE_HOME/bin/dbshut
        su - $USER -c "$ORACLE_HOME/bin/lsnrctl stop"
        ;;
esac
```

A. Nothing is missing - the script will work without any issues
B. Script is missing the variables *$USER* and *$ORACLE_HOME*
C. The following line shall be added in the beginning: *#!/bin/sh*
D. *esac* should be written in that script

5. The linux utility command *rpm* can be use to ... (Choose all that apply)

A. Determine what packages are installed
B. list the errors in */var/adm/messages*
C. Install the RPM packages
D. Remove packages

6. What is the correct file in this list that contains the persistent system kernel parameters?

A. */etc/system*
B. */etc/default*
C. */etc/sysctl.conf*
D. */etc/services*

7. What are the semaphores doing in Linux?

A. Semaphore is a method to control the access to critical resources (i.e. shared memory, processes)
B. Semaphore is a process that controls the disk usage
C. Semaphore is a security parameter to control users' accesses
D. Semaphore is used in network protocols

8. What are the Linux groups that shall be allocated to the Oracle user in order to install Oracle? (Choose all that apply)

A. system: For the system and database administrator
B. oinstall: For the Oracle inventory
C. dba: For the database administrator privileges (SYSDBA)
D. oper: For the database administrator privileges (SYSOPER)

9. What is the command *groupadd dba* doing?

A. It adds a new user in the memory
B. It creates a new semaphore group
C. It creates a dba group in the file */etc/group*, and the command must be executed as root
D. It create a dba group in the file */etc/group*, and the command must be executed as oracle

10. When the *id* command is used with the Oracle account, what should be the correct output in order to install Oracle?

A.
```
$ id
uid=502(oracle) gid=503(oinstall)
groups=503(oinstall),504(dba),506(oper)
```
B.
```
$ id
oracle      pts/1        Dec 26 14:30     (tty1)
```
C.
```
$ id
oracle 27511     1  0   Dec 16 ?         10:09 ora_dbw0_ORCL
```
D.
```
$ id
Dec 26 15:05:18 oracle-srv su: [ID 810491 auth.crit] 'su root' failed for
oracle on /dev/pts/1
```

11. What is the *rpm* command doing with those options *rpm –Uvh my_package_i686.rpm* ? (Choose all that apply)

A. U means Uninstall the RPM package called *my_package_i686.rpm*
B. U stands for Upgrade the RPM package *my_package_i686.rpm*
C. V stands for Print verbose information
D. H means Print 50 hash marks as the package archive is unpacked.

12. Set the following description of a Linux file with the following *drwxrwxrwx* in the proper combination with the capital letter and lowercase letter that explains the purpose of this:

A. d stands for:
B. First group rwx means:
C. Second group rwx stands for:
D. Third group rwx means:

a. Group
b. Other
c. Owner
d. directory

13. What are *setiud* and *setgid* bits used for?

A. *setiud*: Sets user identity and *setgid*: Sets group identity
B. *setiud* and *setgid* are used to control login access
C. *setiud* and *setgid* are network commands to control protocols
D. *setiud* and *setgid* commands only exist on Windows

14. Which of the following shells exist under Linux? (Choose all that apply)

A. Bash: Bourne again shell
B. KSH: Korn shell
C. C: C Shell
D. SAS: Secure Advance Shell

15. What are the correct options of the *umask* command? (Choose all that apply)

A. To view the user mask in symbolic format: *umask -S*
B. To delete the user mask: *umask -d*
C. To set the user mask *umask -S u=rwx,g=rx, o=rx*

D. Output in a form that may be reused as input: *umask -p*

16. What does OFA means?

A. Output Function Application
B. Option Features Automatic
C. Optimal Feature Architecture
D. Optimal Flexible Architecture

17. Is it possible to run multiple versions of Oracle on the same server, and what is important in that configuration? (Choose all that apply)

A. This is impossible because there needs to be a server dedicated to each version of Oracle
B. Multiple versions of Oracle can run on the same server, but there must be different *$ORACLE_HOME* set in order to make that possible
C. *oraenv* script must be used to change the *$ORACLE_SID* value. It will prompt for a SID unless *ORAENV_ASK* is set to *N*.
D. Multiple versions of Oracle can run on the same server, but there must be different *$ORACLE_BASE* set in order to make that possible

18. What are the tasks that Jack, a junior database administrator, performs to install Oracle on the server? (Choose all that apply)

A. Make sure that all the needed RPM packages to install Oracle are present
B. Make sure that the semaphore's values are correct
C. Set all the needed Oracle variables before performing the installation
D. Make sure that the server has enough memory, mount points and the oracle user and groups exist
E. Issue the command *runInstaller* to start the Oracle Universal Installer

19. When should the Oracle *opatch* utility be used?

A. Get a list of all the temporary patches installed
B. Apply temporary patches
C. Start/stop the Oracle database
D. Rollback temporary patches

20. What are the correct *relink* commands? (Choose all that apply)

A. *relink all*: All the Oracle executables will be relinked
B. *relink aemagent*: Agent will be relinked
C. *relink network*: Listener, cman and names will be relinked
D. *relink utilities*: SQL*Loader, rman, impdp, expdp, imp and exp will be relinked

21. What are the criteria for choosing a particular file system? (Choose all that apply)

A. Reliability
B. Memory allocation
C. Security
D. Performances

22. What does OCFS means?

A. Oracle Clouds File Sercurity
B. Oracle Cloning File System
C. Oracle Cluster File System
D. Oracle Clarion File System

23. In the given list, what are the file systems that are certified by Oracle? (Choose all that apply)

A. ext1
B. ext2
C. ASM (Automatic Storage Management)
D. OCFS (Oracle Cluster file system) and OCFS2
E. reiserfs
F. jfs2

24. What is correct about the Automatic Storage Management Library Driver? (Choose all the apply)

A. It can only be installed on UNIX and Windows, not Linux
B. Eliminates the need for binding the raw devices
C. It works only on a standalone server
D. It can be downloaded as *rpm* from http://www.oracle.com

25. How can the Automatic Storage Management Library Driver be installed?

A. With *runInstaller*
B. By uncompressing a tarball
C. With *rpm*
D. Only with *dpkg*

26. In the following list, what is considered best practice when using ASM? (Choose all that apply)

A. Get ASM and the RDBMS installed in different *$ORACLE_BASE*
B. Install ASM and the RDBMS in the same *$ORACLE_HOME*
C. Create one ASM instance per node
D. Get ASM and the RDBMS installed in different *$ORACLE_HOME*

27. Select the best practices for disk groups in this list. (Choose all that apply)

A. Create only one disk group that contains both the database and the binaries
B. Use different kinds of disk performances to obtain better performances
C. Create disk groups using large numbers of similar type (same size and performance characteristics)
D. Create at least two disks groups for the database and the flashback areas

28. What utility or command enables the creation of a database? (Choose all that apply)

A. *netca*
B. *dbca*
C. *netmgr*
D. *create database*

29. In Oracle 10g, where are the dump and trace files (audit, background process, coredump and user dumps) usually located?

A. *$ORACLE_BASE/admin/$ORACLE_SID*
B. *$ORACLE_SID/admin/$ORACLE_HOME*
C. *$ORACLE_HOME/admin/$ORACLE_SID*
D. *$HOME/admin/$ORACLE_SID*

30. What does the *portlist.ini* file contain?

A. List of ports used by Linux
B. Information used by *tnsnames.ora*
C. All the port number information for Oracle related applications like iSQL*Plus and Enterprise Manager
D. Parameter settings for the database startup

31. What does *LOCAL=YES* means when some Oracle processes are being listed with the Linux command *ps –efd | grep –i oracle*?

A. It means that the *sqlplus* session was started without service name specified
B. It means that the *sqlplus* session was started with service name specified
C. It means that the *rman* session was started without the target specified
D. It means that the *rman* session was started with the target specified

32. What is the proper order to create a database using ASM?

A. Get the database created and then create the ASM database
B. Create the ASM database first and then create the database
C. Create both the database and the ASM database at the same time
D. Create only the database and ASM will be installed automatically

33. What can be used to start and stop Oracle under Linux? (Choose all that apply)

A. *init 6*
B. *dbstart*
C. *oracle_start_script*
D. *dbshut*

34. Which of the following are the proper descriptions of different Linux run level modes? (Choose all that apply)

A. Run level 0: Halt the server
B. Run level 20: Super user single mode with network
C. Run level 1: Single user
D. Run level 5: Multi user with X11

35. Confirm what is the correct formatting in the file */etc/oratab* where the name of the database is *PRD*, the *$ORACLE_HOME* is */u01/app/oracle/product/10.2.0/db_1* and is not started automatically:

A. *N:PRD:/u01/app/oracle/product/10.2.0/db_1*
B. */u01/app/oracle/product/10.2.0/db_1:N:PRD*
C. *PRD:/u01/app/oracle/product/10.2.0/db_1:N*
D. *PRD:/u01/app/oracle/product/10.2.0/db_1:Y*

36. In the given list, what are the OS Scheduling tools? (Choose all that apply)

A. *super-crontab*
B. *cron* and *anacron*
C. *at* and *batch*
D. Linux Task Scheduler

37. What are the benefits of using *spfile*? (Choose all that apply)

A. Must not be edited manually but within the database via *alter system set* commands
B. Allows for making dynamic changes to parameters that are persistent
C. Can be taken in RMAN backups
D. Scope cannot be specified in the *alter system* command parameters with those values *memory*, *spfile* and *both* since only *pfile* enables that

38. What are the correct options for backing up Oracle databases? (Choose all that apply)

A. User managed backup while the database is open with OS tools (cp, tar, etc.)
B. User managed backup with third-party tools (i.e. Oracle database agent backup module)
C. User managed backup while the database is shutdown with OS tools (cp, tar, etc.)
D. Using RMAN to perform the backups

39. What is the purpose of the swap space?

A. To make a better network connection and ensure failover connections
B. To enhance the memory protection area called MMU

C. To make more memory available to the system even when the RAM memory is limited
D. To ensure that all users get an account on the server

40. Dan is a junior DBA and Linux system administrator, and he needs to configure the swap on three different servers:

- Server 1 : has 12 GB RAM memory
- Server 2 : has 5 GB RAM memory
- Server 3 : has 1 GB RAM memory

Help Dan find out what are the correct configurations of the swap size in the list hereunder. (Choose all that apply)

A. Server 3 will have 150 % of the RAM size, so 1.5 GB swap space (<= 2 GB is 150 % of your RAM size)
B. Server 1 will have 12 GB swap space (after 8 GB RAM size, there must be the same size for the chosen swap area)
C. Server 2 will have 5 GB swap space (among 2 GB and 8 GB, the swap size is equal to the RAM size for the swap size)
D. Server 1 will have 9 GB swap space (after 8 GB RAM size, there must be 75% of the RAM size for the swap size)

41. In this list, what is correct memory terminology in Linux? (Choose all that apply)

A. PAE (Page Address Extensions)
B. Hugepages
C. Page table
D. Max address space (virtual size)

42. What are the standard measurement tools under Linux? Select all the correct answers.

A. *iostat*
B. *top*
C. *memx_stats*
D. *sags*
E. *sar*
F. *topas*
G. *prtstat*

H. *vmstat*

43. Select the sentences that are the most accurate for analyzing the CPU bottlenecks: (Choose all that apply)

A. How many CPU are there in the server?
B. How the network card is performing?
C. What is the load factor?
D. What is the load average?
E. How is the graphic card configured?

44. What is the ideal block size for an OLTP (Online Transaction Processing) database?

A. *DB_BLOCK_SIZE*=1 KB (on raw device)
B. *DB_BLOCK_SIZE*=2 KB (on jfs2)
C. *DB_BLOCK_SIZE*=4 KB (on ext3)
D. *DB_BLOCK_SIZE*=8 KB (on reiserfs)

45. What is the ideal block size for a DSS (Decision Support) database?

A. *DB_BLOCK_SIZE*=8 KB (on reiserfs)
B. *DB_BLOCK_SIZE*=16 KB (on ext3)
C. *DB_BLOCK_SIZE*=1 KB (on raw device)
D.*DB_BLOCK_SIZE*=4 KB (on ext3)

46. What can help to increase the performances of high data manipulation language (DML)? (Choose all that apply)

A. Increase the swap size
B. Increase the value of the *log_buffer* parameter
C. Increase the memory of the server
D. See the performances on the waits on the redologs

47. What are the initialization parameters on Oracle under Linux that can affect performance on Linux? (Choose three)

A. *pre_page_sga*
B. *db_writer_process*
C. *max_dump_file_size*

D. *dbwr_io_slaves*

48. What are the benefits of using ASMM (Automatic Shared Memory Management)? (Choose all that apply)

A. Automatically adapts the needs of memory in the SGA
B. Enables Linux to auto-tune the memory values on both the RAM and the SWAP
C. Helps to maximize the memory utilization
D. Get rid of all out-of-memory errors in the SGA

49. Enumerate all the Oracle tools available on Linux to perform debugging operations. (Choose four answers)

A. asmone
B. RDA (Remote Diagnostics Agent)
C. topas
D. OS Watcher
E. *alert log* and trace files with the messages *ORA-xxxxx*
F. strace

50. Give the action that can be performed to solve an *ORA-7445 error.* (Choose all that apply)

A. Open a Service Request in Metalink
B. Ignore this error as it is only a warning that is not critical
C. Use the Oracle Search Tool in Metalink for the *ORA-7445* error to find some workarounds
D. Collect all the traces related to that error and add it to the Service Request

Answers

1. B. */proc/sys/kernel/tainted* and D. *lsmod* are the correct answers. Consult Chapter 1 for more information.

2. B. Enables seeing the kernel information and D. Provides the version number of the kernel with the fields *(<Base>-<Errata>.<Mod><Type>)* are correct. Read Chapter 1 for more information.

3. B. Define command *macro* is the only correct answer. Consult Chapter 1 for more information.

4. B. Script is missing the variables *$USER* and *$ORACLE_HOME* and C. The following lines shall be added in the beginning: *#!/bin/sh* are correct. See Chapter 1 for more information.

5. A. Determine what packages are installed, C. Install the RPM packages and D. Remove packages. Consult Chapter 1 for more information.

6. C. */etc/sysctl.conf* is the only correct answer. Consult Chapter 2 for more information.

7. A. Semaphore is a method to control the access to critical resources (i.e. shared memory, processes) is the only correct answer. Refer to Chapter 2 for more information.

8. B. *oinstall*: For the Oracle inventory, C. *dba*: For the database administrator privileges (SYSDBA) and D. *oper*: For the database administrator privileges (SYSOPER) are needed and shall be allocated to perform the installation of Oracle. Look up Chapter 6 for more information.

9. C. It creates a dba group in the file */etc/group*, and the command must be executed as root is the only correct choice. Check in Chapter 2 for more information.

10. Only A. `$ id uid=502(oracle) gid=503(oinstall) groups=503(oinstall),504(dba),506(oper)` is correct. Consult Chapter 2 for more information.

11. B. U stands for Upgrade the RPM package *my_package_i686.rpm*, C. V stands for Print verbose information and D. H means Print 50 hash marks as the package archive is unpacked. Consult Chapter 1 for more information.

12. The correct combination is:

A. d stands for: d. directory
B. First group rwx means: c. Owner
C. Second group rwx stands for: a. Group
D. Third group rwx means: b. Other

Read Chapter 2 for more information.

13. A. *setiud*: Set user identity and *stegid*: Set group identity. Refer to Chapter 2 for more information.

14. A. Bash: Bourne again shell, B. KSH: Korn shell and C. C: C Shell. Consult Chapter 1 for more information.

15. A. To view the user mask in symbolic format: umask -S, C. To set the user mask umask -S u=rwx,g=rx, o=rx and D. Output in a form that may be reused as *input : umask -p* are the correct answers. Consult Chapter 2 for more information.

16. D. Optimal Flexible Architecture is the only correct answer. Consult Chapter 7 for more information.

17. B. Multiple versions of Oracle can run on the same server, but there must be different *$ORACLE_HOME* set in order to make that possible and C. *oraenv script* must be used to change the *$ORACLE_SID* value. It will prompt for a SID unless *ORAENV_ASK* is set to *N* are correct. Consult Chapter 7 for more information.

18. All the answers are correct. Consult Chapters 6 and 7 for more information.

19. A. Get a list of all the temporary patches installed, B. Apply temporary patches and D. Rollback temporary patches. Consult Chapter 7 for more information.

20. A. *relink all*: All the Oracle executables will be relinked, C. *relink network*: Listener, cman and names will be relinked and D. *relink utilities*: SQL*Loader, rman, impdp, expdp, imp and exp will be relinked. Read Chapter 7 for more information.

21. A. Reliability, C. Security and D. Performances are correct. Go to Chapter 8 for more information.

22. C. Oracle Cluster File System is the only correct answer. Consult Chapter 8 for more information.

23. B. ext2, C. ASM. Automatic Storage Management and D. OCFS (Oracle Cluster file System) and OCFS2 are the correct answers. Consult Chapter 8 for more information.

24. B. Eliminates the need for binding the raw devices and D. It can be downloaded as *rpm* from http://www.oracle.com are correct. Consult Chapter 9 for more information.

25. C. With *rpm* is the only correct answer. Consult Chapter 9 for more information.

26. C. Create one ASM instance per node and D. Get ASM and the RDBMS installed in different *$ORACLE_HOME*. Read Chapter 9 for more information.

27. C. Create disk groups using large numbers of similar type (same size and performance characteristics) and D. Create at least two disks groups for the database and the flashback areas are the correct answers. Refer to Chapter 9 for more information.

28. B. *dbca* and D. *create database* are the correct answers. Consult Chapter 10 for more information.

29. A. *$ORACLE_BASE/admin/$ORACLE_SID* is the only correct answer. Read Chapter 10 for more information.

30. C. All the port number information for Oracle related applications like iSQL*Plus and Enterprise Manager is the only correct answer. Consult Chapter 10 for more information.

31. A. It means that the *sqlplus* session was started without service name specified is the only right answer. Consult Chapter 10 for more information.

32. B. Create the ASM database first and then create the database is the correct answer. Consult Chapter 10 for more information.

33. B. *dbstart* and D. *dbshut* are the administrative scripts to start up and shutdown an Oracle database. Consult Chapter 11 for more information.

34. A. Run level 0: Halt the server, C. Run level 1: Single user and D. Run level 5: Multi user with X11. Read Chapters 3 and 11 for more information.

35. C. *PRD:/u01/app/oracle/product/10.2.0/db_1:N* is the only correct answer. Consult Chapter 11 for more information.

36. B. *cron* and *anacron*, C. *at* and *batch* and D. Linux Task Scheduler are correct. Refer to Chapter 4 for more information.

37. A. Must not be edited manually but within the database via *alter system set* commands, B. Allows for making dynamic changes to parameters that are persistent and C. Can be taken in RMAN backups are the answers. Consult Chapter 11 for more information.

38. B. User managed backup with third-party tools (i.e. Oracle database agent backup module), C. User managed backup while the database is shutdown with OS tools (cp, tar, etc.) and D. Using RMAN to perform the backups.

39. C. To make more memory available to the system even when the RAM memory is limited is the only correct response. Consult Chapters 3, 4 and 12 for more information.

40. A. Server 3 will have 150 % of the RAM size, so 1,5 GB swap space. (<= 2GB is 150 % of the RAM size), C. Server 2 will have 5 GB swap space. (Among 2 GB and 8GB the swap size is equal to the RAM size for the swap size) and D. Server 1: will have 9 GB swap space. (after 8 GB RAM size there must be 75% of the RAM size for the swap size). Consult the chapter 6 for more information.

41. A. PAE (Page Address Extensions), B. Hugepages and C. Page table are all correct memory terminology in Linux. Read Chapter 12 for more information.

42. A. *iostat*, B. *top*, E. *sar* and H. *vmstat* are the correct answers. Refer to Chapter 13 for more information.

43. A. How many CPU is there in the server?, C. What is the load factor? and D. What is the load average? More information can be found in Chapter 13.

44. C. *DB_BLOCK_SIZE*=4 KB (on ext3) is the correct answer for Linux OS. See Chapter 12 for more information.

45. B. *DB_BLOCK_SIZE=16 KB* (on ext3) is the only correct answer as DSS needs the larger blocks to reduce the overhead (16KB is the largest block size on Linux). Read Chapter 12 for more information.

46. B. Increase the value of the *log_buffer* parameter and D. See the performances on the waits on the redologs are the correct answers. Consult Chapter 13 for more information.

47. A. *pre_page_sgq*, B. *db_writer_process* and D. *dbwr_io_slaves* are the three correct solutions. Consult Chapter 13 for more information.

48. A. Automatically adapts the needs of memory in the SGA, C. Helps maximize the memory utilization and D. Get rid of all out-of-memory errors in the SGA. More details are in Chapter 13.

49. B. RDA (Remote Diagnostics Agent), D. OS Watcher, E. *alert log* and trace files with the messages *ORA-xxxxx* and F. strace are the four correct answers. Read more in Chapter 13.

50. A. Open a Service Request in Metalink, C. Use the O*racle Search Too*l in Metalink for the *ORA-7445* error to find some work-arounds and D. Collect all the traces related to that error and add it to the Service Request are the correct answers. See Chapter 13 for more information.

Introduction to Linux

CHAPTER

This chapter covers the following exam objectives:

1. Introduction
1.1. Interpret Linux kernel version information
1.2. Identify a tainted kernel
1.3. Use common Linux commands
1.4. Write a simple bash shell script

What is Linux?

Linux is an operating system family based on a Linux Kernel that is UNIX-like. Unlike UNIX, Linux is based on open source software development that can be freely used, modified and distributed with the GNU GPL licenses (GNU General Public License originally written by Richard Stallman).

Linux can be recompiled and installed on a wide variety of computer hardware ranging from embedded devices, mobile phones, laptops, and netbooks to supercomputers. The name Linux comes from the Linux kernel, originally written in 1991 by Linus Torvalds.

History of Linux and UNIX

UNIX history began in the 1960s and was officially released in 1970. The operating system was easily ported onto different hardware platforms. This resulted in wide distribution in universities, academic institutions and businesses. IBM distributed their AIX (Advanced Interactive eXecutive) in 1981 and Sun (Stanford University Network) distributed SUN OS, now called Solaris, in 1982. They are the most popular commercial UNIX releases.

In 1987, Andrew S. Tanenbaum released MINIX, a UNIX-like system intended for academic use. Linus Torvalds, a student at the University of Helsinki in 1991, began to work on a non-commercial successor to MINIX. It resulted in the Linux kernel. Originally, Torvalds used the name Freax ("free" and "x" as an allusion to UNIX) for the OS, but Ari Lemmke, a student and co-worker at the same university, called the project Linux as he did not like the name Freax. Linus Torvalds later accepted the new name.

It all started with this message on comp.os.minix when Linus Torvalds wrote the following lines on his i386:

```
"Linus Benedict Torvalds
     More options Aug 26 1991, 7:12 am
Newsgroups: comp.os.minix
From: torva...@klaava.Helsinki.FI (Linus Benedict Torvalds)
Date: 25 Aug 91 20:57:08 GMT
Local: Sun, Aug 25 1991 9:57 pm
Subject: What would you like to see most in Minix?

Hello everybody out there using Minix -

I'm doing a (free) operating system (just a hobby, won't be big and
professional like gnu) for 386(486) AT clones.  This has been brewing since
April, and is starting to get ready.  I'd like any feedback on things people
like/dislike in Minix, as my OS resembles it somewhat (same physical layout
of the file-system (due to practical reasons) among other things).

I've currently ported bash(1.08) and gcc(1.40), and things seem to work.
This implies that I'll get something practical within a few months, and I'd
like to know what features most people would want. Any suggestions are
welcome, but I won't promise I'll implement them :-)
                Linus (torva...@kruuna.helsinki.fi)
PS.  Yes - it's free of any Minix code, and it has a multi-threaded fs. It
is NOT portable (uses 386 task switching etc), and it probably never will
support anything other than AT-harddisks, as that's all I have :-(.  "
The code in Linux is usually written in C, about 71%, but other languages
have also used: C++, assembly language, Fortran, Python, Perl, and various
shell scripting languages. The Linux kernel contains 2.4 million lines of
code. LMI (Linux Mark Institute) is an organization in charge of
administrating the Linux trademark on behalf of Linus Torvalds. The
organization is in charge of clarifying the usage of the Linux trademark on
software, services, implementation and documentation of Linux products.
```

Oracle and IBM contributed also to the success of Linux by adapting their products to Linux and also distributing code of some major products, i.e. the file system from IBM JFS. Currently, IBM has 15,000 Linux customers and supports 500 software programs on the platform.

Hewlett-Packard, Dell and Intel are beginning a drive to promote Linux as an alternative to Windows on the desktop. Oracle has contributed to Linux with Oracle Cluster File System, which is now part of the Linux kernel and Oracle-driven OSS projects: http://oss.oracle.com/projects. Figure 1.1 illustrates the family history of a GNU GPL document.

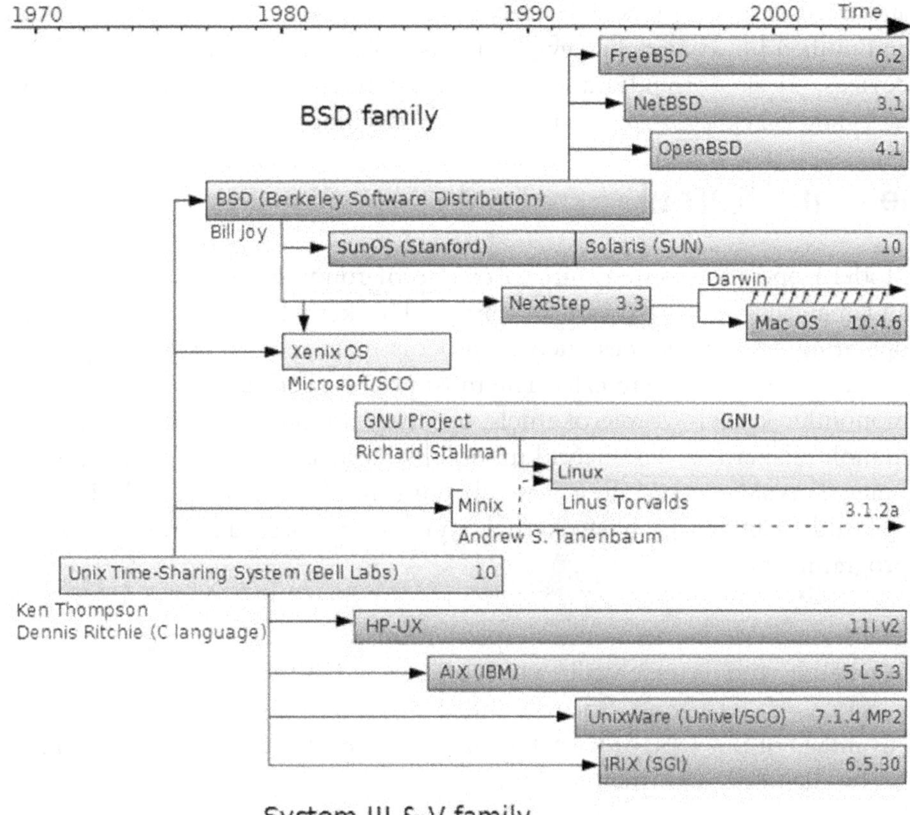

Figure 1.1: *Summary of the History of UNIX-like OS Source GNU GPL Document*

The sales of PCs running Linux reached $10 billion by 2008, following IDC predictions. Linux was used on about 17 million Linux PCs in 2008, bringing the total installed base to 42.6 million. Market share of new and used PCs running Linux grew from 3% in 2003 to 7% in 2008.

"Linux on desktop is a tough road. It is really about installed base momentum," Al Gillen, research vice president of system software at IDC said. "It is growing and we're expecting Linux on the desktop to gain through 2010 but it's going at a 30 to 40 percent compound growth rate."

The main advantages of UNIX and Linux operating systems are that they provide a multi-user, multi-tasking with protected memory, multiprocessing and multi-threading OS. The OS provides Access controls, advanced security and unified file system, i.e. everything is a file: data, programs, and all physical devices. It also provides a lot of small utilities and commands to do specific tasks and is available on a wide variety of machines.

The Linux Kernel

Modern operating systems are in charge of running applications for the user and managing the hardware resources. The kernel is responsible for all the operating system services such as process management, scheduling, memory management and system calls. The most popular kernel architectures are either monolithic kernels or microkernels, but there are other kernel types like hybrid monolithic kernels. The hybrid monolithic kernels are the type used by Linux. Linus Torvalds and Andrew Tanenbaum started a debate in early 1992 that is still quite active on what kernel type is the best and most flexible for programmers.

The monolithic kernel is the simplest form of kernel. It is based on a single executable and is essentially used on many UNIX systems such as earlier versions of AIX and Solaris, and Linux, MS DOS and Windows. The advantage of this type of kernel is that data does not need to pass several layers to be handled and memory management is relatively simple. The major disadvantage, however, is that the entire kernel has to be rebuilt whenever there is a need to fix an issue or add new drivers.

Applications	Shell(s)
System Calls interfaces	
Kernel (Monolithic)	
Hardware	

Figure 1.2: *Architecture of a Monolithic Kernel*

The kernel used in Linux is a UNIX-like kernel. It is licensed under the GNU General Public License version 2 (GPLv2) and has contributions from developers and programmers from all over the world. The architecture of the Linux kernel is layered into distinct subsystems where all the basic services are in the kernel, meaning monolithic. It is quite different from microkernel architecture where the kernel provides only basic services such as communication, I/O, memory, and process management. Additional services and drivers are plugged into the microkernel.

This inherit modularity was not originally part of the monolithic kernel architecture. A monolithic kernel runs as a single image, whereas a microkernel kernel uses multiple server images like file systems and device drivers that communicate with the kernel through Inter Process Communication (IPC). However, the Linux kernel is still very stable and quite efficient both in CPU and memory usage. Due to this flexible kernel architecture and its size, it can be ported easily to new platforms and the number of people supporting the community contributes also to the stability and the success of the platform. Nowadays, Linux is compiled on a huge number of processors and platforms, each with different architectural constraints and needs. On certain hardware platforms, it can be run on processors with a memory management unit (MMU) as well as those that provide no MMU.

Since 1995, the Linux Kernel includes Loadable Kernel Modules that allows the kernel to be adapted with drivers for the user's hardware devices. Loading new modules essentially added some of the modularity that was inherent in microkernel. Modules are dynamically linked into the running kernel without the need to rebuild the kernel. By doing this, the specific hardware can be adapted to the Linux installation.

Note: One way to taint a kernel is to add proprietary kernel modules. Tainted kernels will be covered later in this chapter.

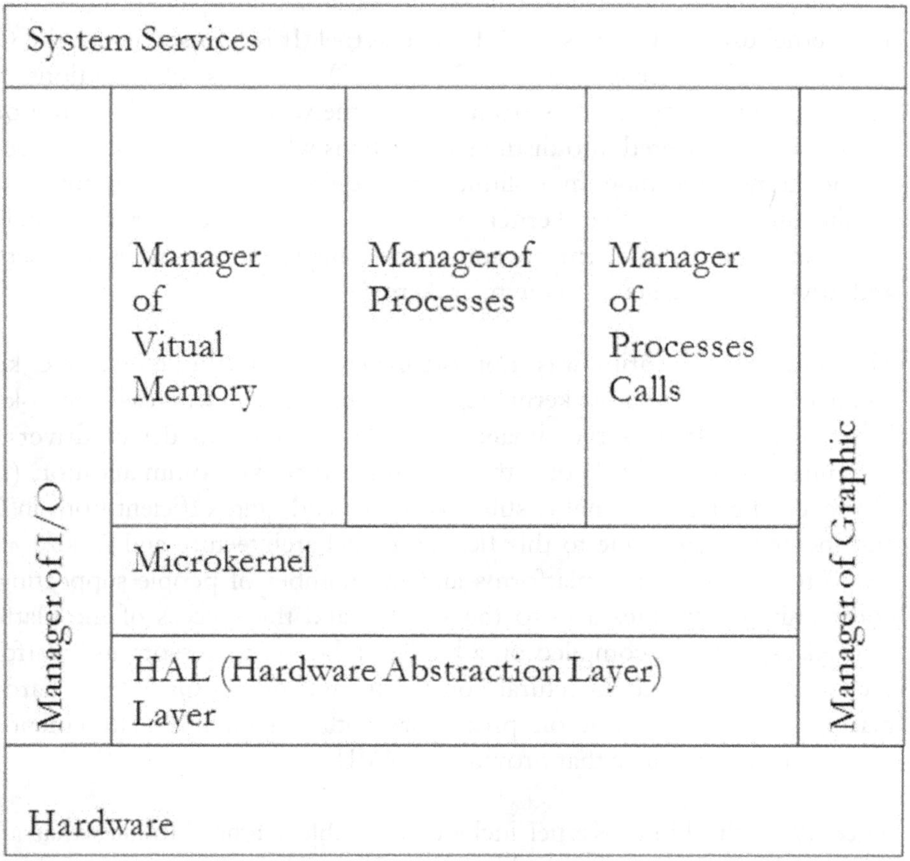

System Services

Manager of I/O

Manager of Vitual Memory

Managerof Processes

Manager of Processes Calls

Manager of Graphic

Microkernel

HAL (Hardware Abstraction Layer) Layer

Hardware

Figure 1.3: *Architecture of a Microkernel*

The following diagram (Figure 1.4) shows in detail how the Linux kernel is structured:

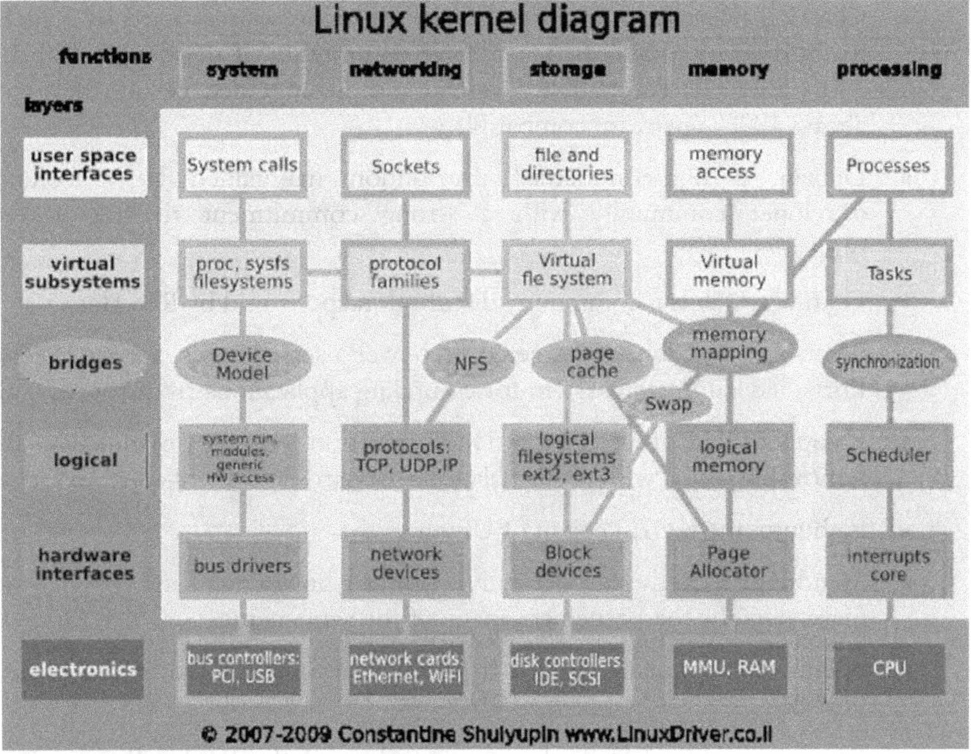

Figure 1.4: *Linux Kernel Structure Diagram*

It is recommended that the administrator consult the following excellent sites for obtaining much more information about the Linux kernel: http://kernelnewbies.org/ and http://www.kernel.org/.

The Linux kernel is the heart of the operating system, which means it can easily be configured and can be patched, recompiled and customized infinitely, making Linux a very flexible OS that can be adapted to the user's needs.

The Different Distributions of Linux

Following is a list of the various distributions that can be found in Linux:

- Archlinux, a distribution based on the KISS principle with a rolling release system.

- CentOS, a distribution derived from the same sources used by Red Hat, maintained by a dedicated volunteer community of developers with both 100% Red Hat-compatible versions and an upgraded version that is not always 100% upstream compatible.
- Debian, a non-commercial distribution maintained by a volunteer developer community with a strong commitment to free software principles.
- Fedora, which is a community distribution sponsored by Red Hat.
- Gentoo, a distribution targeted at power users, known for its FreeBSD Ports-like automated system for compiling applications from source code.
- Knoppix, The first Live CD distribution to run completely from removable media without installation to a hard disk. Derived from Debian.
- Kubuntu, the KDE version of Ubuntu
- Mandriva, a Red Hat derivative popular in France and Brazil, today maintained by the French company of the same name.
- openSUSE, originally derived from Slackware, sponsored by the company Novell.
- Pardus, developed in Turkey as a product of the Pardus Project. It was named after the Anatolian Leopard.
- PCLinuxOS, a derivative of Mandriva, grew from a group of packages into a popular, community-spawned desktop distribution.
- Red Hat Enterprise Linux, which is a derivative of Fedora maintained and commercially supported by Red Hat.
- Slackware, one of the first Linux distributions, founded in 1993 and since then actively maintained by Patrick J. Volkerding.
- Ubuntu, a popular desktop distribution derived from Debian, maintained by Canonical.
- gOS and other netbook operating systems

Consult the excellent website DistroWatch for more information (http://en.wikipedia.org/wiki/DistroWatch) as it maintains a popularity ranking of distribution information on its website using primarily page views. However, this is not considered to be a reliable measure of distribution popularity.

How is Linux Structured?

Linux distributions are based on two parts: the kernel (and kernel modules) and RPM packages (for Redhat-like distributions). When an installation of Linux is performed, choose all the necessary packages that will be present on the server. A Linux package can be composed of source codes, patches, configuration files, manuals or binaries. A RPM (Redhat Package Manager) package can be built from source files or patches. Oracle requires specific RPM packages to be installed in order to perform an installation of the Oracle software. Those requirements will be covered in Chapter 6, Preparing Linux for Oracle.

The Linux directory structure

```
/            Root (starting point of your directory structure)
|---root              Home reserved for root user
|---etc               Configuration files specific to the machine.
|---etc/inittab       describes processes to be started /stopped
|---etc/fstab         descriptive information about the file systems
|    and their mount points
|---etc/passwd        contains information for user account
|
|---home              Contains the user's home directories
|---bin               Commands needed during start-up
|---sbin              Commands run by system administrators
|---proc              This mount point is virtual
|---usr      Contains all commands, libraries, man pages and
|    static files
|---usr/doc           Documentation for the user apps
|---usr/src            Code sources files for the system's software,
|    contains also Linux kernel
|---usr/include       Header files for the C compiler
|---usr/X11R6         X Window System directory
|
|---boot              Files used during boot, LILO (vmlinuz Kernel
|                     images can be stored).
|---lib               Shared libraries needed by the programs on the
|                     root filesystem
|---dev               Device files for devices such as disk drives,
|                     serial ports, etc.
|
|---var               Contains files that change for mail, log files,
|                     man pages, temp files
|---mnt               Mount points for temporary mounts by the system
|                     administrator.
|---tmp               Temporary files.
|---lost+found        Contains files to restores after a system crash
|                     or partition not un-mounted before a system
|                     shutdown
```

Why Oracle on Linux?

Linux that is running Oracle offers the following advantages:

- Lower costs via GPL licenses and suppresses additional license costs for the OS
- Stable OS and a huge community for support
- Higher availability, flexible and scalable
- Excellent support from Oracle on Linux

Therefore, Linux and Oracle is an outstanding choice to support the IT systems.

Linux has a long history at Oracle Corporation. The first commercial version started in 1998 and developed so well that Oracle provided a code level support on Linux and had an 80% share of the market. All key Oracle products are run under Linux. Oracle itself runs all the following business applications only on Linux: Oracle.com, Oracle financial system, Oracle demo system and Oracle On Demand.

Oracle RDBMS systems require from an operating system the following characteristics:

- Asynchronous I/O management that enables I/O to be handled without waits as the processing continues, thus avoiding I/O bottlenecks. With synchronous I/O, the requests are submitted to the OS and the writing processes are blocked while they wait until the write is confirmed as completed.
- Memory support, more than 4 GB to be allocated
- Ability to run on servers with multiple processors so tasks can be dedicated to two or more processors
- Support cluster technology
- Large support of hardware platforms and components such as network cards, disk controllers and such
- Robust I/O support; for example, RAID, SAN or NAS controllers

All those needs are covered by Linux, and especially in the newest kernel, the support of multiprocessing is further enhanced.

What is the Oracle Unbreakable Linux Program?

Oracle Unbreakable Linux Program is an initiative driven by Enterprise customers' requirements. Oracle provides specific server deployments with patches and three levels of Linux support: Network Access, Basic and Premier. More information about the Oracle Unbreakable Linux Program can be found on http://www.oracle.com/technologies/linux/index.html. Another place for more information is from the document ID: 264040.1 Subject: The Oracle Unbreakable Linux Program in Metalink.

Potential Users of Linux and Oracle

Linux started in the internet arena as a platform for web servers and other internet applications running the web server Apache. Linux is now on its way to replacing all UNIX servers and it is a strong competitor of Microsoft Windows.

The following organizations and people are using Linux for their IT systems:

- Small enterprises and personal users who are willing to have cheap IT systems and standard solutions to support their small businesses. They need accounting, email, spreadsheets and word processors. All those applications exist under Linux and furthermore, Oracle can be used as repository storage for the information.
- Medium enterprises that are looking for simple and efficient IT systems to support the business and are willing to buy designed software. The IT people in those corporations have a general knowledge of IT systems.
- Corporations and service providers, like power suppliers and hospitals, are big users of IT systems; they have critical systems that need to be up seven days a week and 24 hours a day. With solutions based on Oracle and Linux, they will be able to get those IT systems up to that level.
- Universities, education and research institutions that need a platform for administrative work but also need a platform for scientific computing or research. Obviously, the benefit of a free-of-charge OS and a database that is stable and efficient is a must-have solution.

Hardware Supported by Linux OS

Oracle gives support on x86, x86-64, and ia64 architecture-based hardware running Linux. All hardware platforms that are certified by Red Hat for RHEL3, RHEL4 and RHEL5 for x86, x86-64, ia64 (starts with Release 4 Update 6) architectures are supported by Oracle.

Oracle certifies the following Linux distributions as Oracle RDBMS 10g-supported. For the Oracle Database Enterprise Edition 10g on Linux, there is the following support matrix:

Linux OS Supported	**x86**	**x86-64**	**Itanium**
SLES-9	ORACLE Certified	ORACLE Certified	ORACLE Certified
SLES-10	ORACLE Certified	ORACLE Certified	ORACLE Certified
Red Hat Enterprise AS/ES 5	ORACLE Certified	ORACLE Certified	ORACLE Certified
Red Hat Enterprise AS/ES 4	ORACLE Certified	ORACLE Certified	ORACLE Certified
Red Hat Enterprise AS/ES 3	ORACLE Certified	ORACLE Certified	ORACLE Certified
Linux OS Supported	x86	x86-64	Itanium
Oracle Enterprise Linux 5/Oracle VM	ORACLE Certified	ORACLE Certified	
Oracle Enterprise Linux 4/Oracle VM	ORACLE Certified	ORACLE Certified	
Asianux Server 3	ORACLE Certified	ORACLE Certified	

Asianux 2.0	ORACLE Certified	ORACLE Certified	
Asianux 1.0	ORACLE Certified		

Table 1.1: *Linux OS-Supported Distributions*

Oracle supports the Asianux-based distribution from Miracle Linux release 4.0 and higher (www.miraclelinux.com) and Red Flag DC server 5.0 and higher releases.

For more information on supported Linux distributions and the updated certification list, consult Metalink in the certify section and also read the note 266043.1 with the subject Support of Linux and Oracle Products on Linux.

Oracle does not certify hardware, but only OS platforms or drivers that the OS vendor supports, as announced previously. However, some details can be found on the hardware configurations that are certified or compatible with Enterprise Linux by consulting the website http://linux.oracle.com/hardware. On the same site there is also information about the Support of Oracle Virtual Machine and all hardware systems considered certified or compatible by Red Hat Incorporated.

The following table, 1.2., gives a list of the Oracle certified Linux distributions and the sites where they can be downloaded:

Linux OS Supported	**Site to download**
SLES-9	http://en.opensuse.org/Download ftp.suse.com
SLES-10	http://en.opensuse.org/Download ftp.suse.com
Red Hat Enterprise AS/ES 5	https://www.redhat.com/apps/download/
Red Hat Enterprise AS/ES 4	https://www.redhat.com/apps/download/
Red Hat Enterprise AS/ES 3	https://www.redhat.com/apps/download/
Oracle Enterprise Linux 5/Oracle VM	http://edelivery.oracle.com/linux
Oracle Enterprise Linux 4/Oracle VM	http://edelivery.oracle.com/linux
Asianux Server 3	http://www.asianux.com/downl_list.php
Asianux 2.0	http://www.asianux.com/down_list.php

Asianux 1.0	http://www.asianux.com/down_list.php

Table 1.2: *Linux Distribution Download Sites*

Tainted Kernels

As has already been shown, the kernel is the heart of the operating system, and therefore it is important that the state of the kernel is known and controlled. Since it is possible to modify the kernel with LKM (loadable kernel modules), then it is also possible to place the kernel in an unknown or unreliable status. When this happens, the kernel is said to be 'tainted'.

The taint status of the kernel is maintained by a set of flags and when no flags are set, the kernel is reliable, or untainted. When the kernel becomes tainted, a kernel error message is raised and a single character flag is set to indicate what caused the tainted status. Some, but not all of the flags, are listed below.

- P: This means that the kernel has a Proprietary license loaded. It could be a module that is not under GNU General Public License (GPL) or a compatible license.
- G: All modules loaded were licensed under the GPL or a license compatible with the GPL, but something else has tainted the kernel. This will be indicated in a different flag.
- F: This is a module that was loaded using the Force option *-f* of *insmod* or *modprobe*, so versioning information cannot be checked.
- M: This is a Machine Check Exception (MCE) triggered by hardware to indicate a hardware related problem.

Once the tainted status has been set, the status is permanent. Even if whatever caused the taint has been corrected, the flag remains set until the kernel is restarted. The DBA can control if a kernel is tainted or not by checking the /proc/sys/kernel/tainted virtual file.

```
$ cat /proc/sys/kernel/tainted
```

```
0
```

If the output is 0, the kernel is not tainted, and when the output is other than zero, then kernel is tainted. Alternatively, use the following command to perform the same check:

```
/sbin/lsmod
```

As result of the lsmod command, a header line appears that should include the text 'Not tainted', as in the following output:

```
oracle2@linux-mlpb:~> lsmod
Module Size Used by Not tainted
vmsync                     10016  0
vmmemctl                   14104  0

(...)
```

In the file */proc/modules*, all the information can be found about the modules loaded in the kernel. The content of that file varies depending on the Linux distribution used and the configuration. The content of the file */proc/modules* can be viewed like a text file with the *cat* or *less* command. The number of lines in the output hereunder is reduced for length reasons.

```
oracle@linux-mlpb:~> cat /proc/modules
vmsync 10016 0 - Live 0xf8c48000
vmmemctl 14104 0 - Live 0xf8c5f000
vmblock 20516 3 - Live 0xf8c58000
binfmt_misc 15752 1 - Live 0xf8c53000
(...)
scsi_transport_spi 29184 1 mptspi, Live 0xf883d000
scsi_mod 156020 7
sr_mod,sg,sd_mod,libata,mptspi,mptscsih,scsi_transport_spi, Live 0xf8d64000
thermal 27164 0 - Live 0xf8826000
processor 53552 1 thermal, Live 0xf882e000
```

With the root user, more information can be obtained about the modules loaded by using the command *modinfo* and the name of the module that was found in */proc/modules.* This example shows the information about the processor modules.

```
linux-mlpb:~ # modinfo processor
filename:       /lib/modules/2.6.25.5-1.1-
default/kernel/drivers/acpi/processor.ko
alias:          processor
license:        GPL
description:    ACPI Processor Driver
author:         Paul Diefenbaugh
srcversion:     F22498BC60F67547B41B9F1
alias:          acpi*:ACPI0007:*
depends:
supported:      yes
vermagic:       2.6.25.5-1.1-default SMP mod_unload 586
parm:           ignore_ppc:If the frequency of your machine gets
wronglylimited by BIOS, this should help (uint)
```

```
parm:           max_cstate:uint
parm:           nocst:uint
parm:           latency_factor:uint
```

It is possible to get specific information by using specific shortcut switches from the *modinfo* command on the license with *modinfo -l* and about the parameter with *modinfo –p*. Other switches that are *-a -d –n* are informing the user respectively about the author, description and the file name.

```
linux-mlpb:~ # modinfo -l  processor
GPL
linux-mlpb:~ # modinfo -p  processor
ignore_ppc:If the frequency of your machine gets wronglylimited by BIOS,
this should help
```

It is possible to remove modules with the command *rmmod.* This command must be used as the user root. An autoclean function can be invoked to delete unused modules with the command *rmmod -a.*

 Exam Advice: Be able to explain what a tainted kernel is, what command can be used and how to interpret the result.

Note: Oracle may or may not support the user's installation if Linux is tainted. If the modules OCFS and EMC powerpath drivers are installed, then Oracle supports the installation. (Metalink note 284823.1 Subject: Linux Kernel Support - Policy on Tainted Kernels).

Defining User's Linux Version

For Oracle Enterprise Linux and Red Hat, information can be found by viewing the content of the file */etc/redhat-release.*

```
$ cat /etc/redhat-release
  Red Hat Enterprise Linux ES release 4 (Nahant Update 3)
```

On SuSE Linux , see the file */etc/SuSE-release.*

To get the kernel release information, execute the following command:

```
$ uname -s -r
Linux 2.6.25.5-1.1-default
```

With the option *–a*, all the information related to the chosen system appears:

```
$ uname -a
Linux linux-mlpb 2.6.25.5-1.1-default #1 SMP 2008-06-07 01:55:22 +0200 i686
i686 i386 GNU/Linux
```

Version information from the */proc* (virtual file system) can also be obtained by doing the following command:

```
$ cat /proc/version
Linux version 2.6.25.5-1.1-default (geeko@buildhost) (gcc version 4.3.1
20080507 (prerelease) [gcc-4_3-branch revision 135036] (SUSE Linux) ) #1 SMP
2008-06-07 01:55:22 +0200
```

The Linux kernel version number is composed of four numbers, though previously it was a three-number versioning scheme. It can be explained with the following information:

```
<Base>-<Errata>.<Mod><Type>
i.e.  2.6.25.5-1.1
```

The number sections are:

1. Base: This is the base kernel version with three or four integers split by a period. The first two (i.e. 2.6 was first available in 2003) do not change very often.
2. Errata: This is a version that is about the fixes after the base version was released. The errata consist of errors that were fixed or minor enhancements on the kernel.
3. Mod: This section depends on the Linux used; it is used to give the source modifier on the kernel. Sometimes developers use their nicknames or initials. On Redhat distributions, they often use EL for Enterprise Linux.
4. Type: This is used to describe the hardware architecture for which the kernel is designed. The value can be blank for monoprocessor architecture, smp for SMP up to 16 GB and hugemem for SMP up to 64 GB.

Processes and Threads in Linux

In Linux, there are many applications and programs running at the same time on the system. To handle all these operations, the operating system uses processes. Processes have their own virtual memory space and are running independently. There may be hundreds of processes running at any one time on the system and each of these is competing for CPU time.

To handle this, Linux has a task scheduler that is in charge of scheduling all the processes that are running on behalf of the users. Each process is allowed a small amount of time to run before another process is loaded in the CPU. Each time a process is loaded/unloaded in the CPU, the system saves/restores all the important information such as program counters and registers about the process.

This switching in and out of processes in the CPU is called task switching or context switching. The task scheduler is also in charge of the processes' priorities. In the kernel, the processes are represented by random numbers, data, stack variables, I/O information, priorities and signal tables.

Threads are a concurrent set of instructions that are running in a single process. It is like having concurrent programs in a single large application. The benefits of threads are that they reduce the costs of the context switches, or task switches, by allowing a group of processes to share the same information.

Devices in Linux

The Linux Operating System consists of many different devices. Devices can be seen in the OS as a file whose purpose is to handle inputs and outputs. There are two types of devices in Linux: raw (character) and block devices. Oracle normally uses block device file systems.

- Character devices (raw devices): This handles data in a sequential manner; user processes are usually transferring the data directly. The character devices can be accessed by programs that normally are using block devices. Oracle uses raw devices for data storage. If the need is to use character devices to store data, they must be accessed via the block interface of the character devices.

- Block devices: Buffered I/O are able to handle specific requests for data and they can be accessed randomly. Block devices are able to receive different size requests, whereas character devices are unable to get different sizes. Examples of block devices can be RAM disks, SCSI disks devices and DVD-ROM.

File and File Systems

Everything in Linux is a file. Some files can be hardware components and others can be software components. File systems are in charge of the storage and organization of data. They provide an easy way to find and access the data. File systems can use many data storage devices such as CD/DVDs and hard disks. In Chapter 8, Managing Storage and Chapter 9, Automatic Storage Management, more about the file systems that might be used with Oracle databases will be examined.

Bash Shell

Bourne-Again Shell is a GNU free licensed program. It got its name from the UNIX Bourne shell (sh) originally written by Stephen Bourne in UNIX 7 (1978). The syntax of Bash is a superset of the sh, but it also includes some of Korn shell's (ksh) and C shell's (csh) features such as command line history, editing, POSIX commands and $PPID variables. Bash is able to perform redirections of standard output (stdout) and standard error (stderr) simultaneously by using > operator. Bash supports regular expression in the release with nearly the same syntax as Perl.

Commands and Programs in Linux

The following Linux commands, with a brief description of each, comprise a short list of commands that any developer must know. The man pages can be used to get a more detailed description of the commands and the command options, switches, and examples.

Command	Purpose and Function
alias	Create an alias, aliases allow a string to be substituted for a word
awk	Replace and Find text strings
anacron	Runs commands periodically
bash	GNU Bourne-Again SHell
bg	Send a program after a crtl-z to background
cal	Show a calendar, with the argument *2009,* the calendar of 2009 appears
cat	Display the contents of a file without page breaks
cd	Change Directory
chgrp	Change group ownership
chmod	Change access rights
chown	Change owner of files and groups
cksum	Print CRC checksum and byte counts of the file
clear	Clear terminal display screen
cmp	Compare two files
compress	Compression of files
cp	Copy one or more files to another location
crontab	Scheduling a command to run at a later time
date	Display or change the system date and time
dc	Decimal Calculator
dd	Convert and copy the standard input to the standard output, write disk headers, boot records
df	Command that shows the Disk Free on all the mount points
diff	Display the differences between two files
dmesg	Print or control the kernel ring buffer
du	Disk usage on the file system
dumpe2fs	Dumps superblocks on the file system ext2 and ext3
echo	Set and print environment variables
env	Show all environment variables
eval	Evaluate several commands/arguments
exit	Exit the actual shell session
export	Set an environment variable
fdisk	Partition table manipulator for Linux
fg	Sends the program after a crtl-z to foreground
file	Gives the file type
find	Commands helps to find the files with specific criteria
for	*For* loop is a programming language statement which allows code to be repeatedly executed
free	Display memory usage

fsck	File system consistency check and repair of mount points
grep	Search file(s) for lines that match a given pattern
groupadd	Add new groups
groups	Print the group names a user is member of
gzip	Compress or decompress named file(s)
halt	Command to Halt the Linux system
head	Output the first part of file(s)
history	History of all the previous executed commands
hostname	Print or set system name
id	Print the actual user and group ids
if	Conditionally perform a command
ifconfig	Configure a network interface
insmod	Simple program to insert a module into the Linux kernel
ipcs	Print report on inter-process communication (IPC) message queues, shared memory segments, and semaphore arrays
kill	Kill processes by giving PID (Process ID number)
killall	Kill all processes by name
last	Display all the users login session and timestamps
less	Display output one screen at a time
ln	Makes links between files (can be physical or logical)
locate	Locate files
logname	Prints the current login name
logout	Exit an actual active shell
ls	List information about file(s)
lsof	List directory contents
lsmod	Program to show the status of modules in the Linux kernel
make	Recompile a group of programs
man	Manual pages to get details on all the commands in that
mkdir	Create new folder(s)
mkfs	Create new file system
modprobe	Program to add and remove modules from the Linux kernel
more	Display output one screen at a time
mount	Mount a file system
mv	Move or rename files or directories
nice	Execute a utility with an altered scheduling priority
nohup	Run a command immune to hang-ups
nslookup	Query the DNS servers interactively
open	Open a file in its default application
passwd	Change a user password
printenv	Yet another command to print the environment variables

ping	Test a network connection
ps	Report a snapshot of the current processes
pwd	Print Working Directory
rcp	Remote Copy files between two machines
reboot	Reboots the Linux the system
renice	Alter priority of running processes
rm	Remove files or directories
rmdir	Remove directories
rmmod	Simple program to remove a module from the Linux kernel
rsync	Remote file copy (Synchronize file trees)
screen	Multiplex terminal, run remote shells via ssh
scp	Secure copy (remote file copy)
sed	Stream Editor
sftp	Secure File Transfer Program
shutdown	Command that enables Shutdown or restart of the Linux system
sleep	Delay for a specified time
slocate	Find files
sort	Sort text files
ssh	Secure Shell client (remote login program)
stat	Information on the inodes
strace	Trace system calls and signals
su	Substitute user identity
sudo	Execute a command as another user
sum	Display file checksums and block counts
sync	Force completion of pending disk writes (flush cache)
tail	Displays the last part of a file
tar	Tape Archiver that enables one to put files and directory in one file
tee	Read from standard input and write to standard output and files
test	Evaluate a conditional expression
time	Run programs and summarize system resource usage
touch	Change file access timestamps
top	List processes running on the system
type	Describe a command
ulimit	Limit user resources
umask	Mask for the Users file created
umount	Unmount file systems
unalias	Unset an alias
uname	Print system information
uptime	Display how long the server was running after startup
useradd	Add a new user on the server

usermod	Modify a new user on the server
useradd	Add a new user on the server
vi	Text Editor
vmstat	Report virtual memory statistics
watch	Execute a program periodically, showing output full screen
wc	(Word Count) print the number of newlines, words, and bytes in files
which	Locate a program file in the user's path
while	Execute commands
who	Print all usernames currently logged in
whoami	Print the current user id and name (`id -un')
xargs	Execute utility, passing constructed argument list(s)
.	Run a command script in the current shell
&	Runs the commands in background

Table 1.3: *Common Environment Variables for Linux and Oracle*

Navigation in the file system in Linux is similar to other OS like UNIX or MSDOS, also using the command *change directory cd* and *pwd*. The forward slash, /, is used as a separator to navigate in the Linux directory, i.e. going to */root/tests/logs/*, type *cd /root/tests/logs/*.

With the *ls* command, the content of the directory can be displayed. There are some shortcuts that enable the user to go back to the user home directory just by typing *cd*, or use *cd ~myusername*, i.e. *cd ~oracle*, to do the same. It is possible to use *cd -* to come back to the previous directory.

Environment Variables

Environment variables are variables that are set in the shell and can be accessed by the programs. The programs will need to get values about an example of the Oracle home or SID; therefore, the ability to set environment variables is needed.

In Bash, environment variables can be set by using the *export* command:

```
export DISPLAY=10.20.302.55:0.0
```

The variable can be referenced by using the variable name preceded by a $. Example: *echo $display*

A list of all the variables set in the shell can be found by using the env or printenv commands. When keeping the values stored and usable for the next shell session is required, the values should be kept in the file *.bash_profile*, which is located in the user's *$home* directory.

Variables	Definition
$HOME	User Home directory value
$PATH	A colon-separated list of directories used by Bash shell to lookup the commands.
$PS1	Primary prompt string
$PS2	Secondary prompt string
$DISPLAY	Use to identify the display used by the X11 sessions
$EDITOR	Use to setup the favorite editor like vi or emacs
$LD_LIBRARY_PATH	Use to indicate the library directories
$PWD	This variable indicates the working directory and is maintained by Linux
$USER	The value of the current username
$TERM	The variable enables setting of the terminal values
$SHELL	With that variable , the SHELLcan be set in the environment

Table 1.4: *Linux Variables*

Variables	Definition
$ASM_HOME	Is the value of the Automatic Storage Management root directory (Value is optional)
$ORACLE_BASE	Is the value of the oracle root directory (Value is optional)
$ORACLE_HOME	This variable helps to specify the Oracle home for all the binaries, libraries, and more
$ORACLE_SID	variable that gives the name of the actual the database instance
$CRS_HOME	Value is only necessary when Cluster Ready Service is being used with RAC
$AGENT_HOME	Value is only necessary when grid controller agents are being used
$ORA_NLS10	Can be used with multiple versions of Oracle for the

	National Language territory character set (Must not be set during the installation of Oracle)
$NLS_LANG	Can be used with single version of Oracle for the National Language territory character set (Must not be set during the installation of Oracle)
$TNS_ADMIN	Must not be set during the installation of Oracle

Table 1.5: *Oracle Variables*

Handling Input and Output

Linux gives the administrator the ability to manage the input and output with shell commands. The output or input can be captured in a file or also by a command. Use the following characters to perform redirections:

<table>
<tr><th>Character</th><th>Explanation</th></tr>
<tr><td>|</td><td>The pipe character that enables redirection of the standard output of a program as standard input of another</td></tr>
<tr><td>></td><td>Redirection of standard output to a file (and overwrites the file if it already exists)</td></tr>
<tr><td><</td><td>Redirection that can use a file as standard input</td></tr>
<tr><td>>></td><td>Redirection that enables appending the standard output to a file</td></tr>
</table>

Table 1.6: *Characters and Explanations for Redirection*

The standard input and output redirection work as follows:

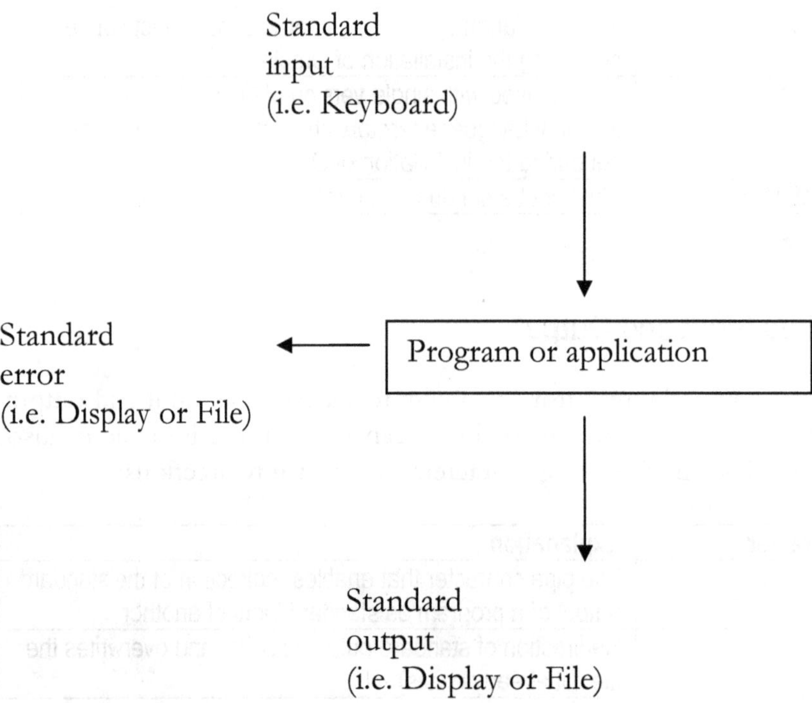

Figure 1.5: *Input and Output Redirection Chart*

Also use the *tee* command to write both to standard output and, at the same time, to a file. The results can be appended without overwriting the file by using the *–a* or *--append*. Used with *–h* or *–help*, help is given on the command. Here is an example of the *tee* command:

```
ps -efd | grep -i ora_ | tee List_of_all_oracle_background_process.txt |
grep -v grep
```

The command *xargs* enables the user to build and execute command lines from standard input. *xargs* reads items from the standard input, delimited by blanks, which can be protected with double or single quotes, a backslash, or newlines, and executes the command (default is */bin/echo*) one or more times with any initial arguments followed by items read from standard input.

Blank lines on the standard input are ignored. Here is an example of *xargs*:

```
ls | xargs -n 2 echo #
```

Sometimes files are not able to be deleted with *rm *.log*, as the list of files is too long, with this error - "rm: arg list too long". To solve that issue, use *xargs* with the following command:

```
ls | xargs -n 30 rm
```

 Exam Advice: Be capable of describing what the redirection commands are and also what commands can be use to perform the input/output redirection.

Bash Scripting

Bash scripting is a simple programming language that enables the developer to perform all the tasks that can be performed via the command line. After creating the script, change the permissions to make it executable with the command *chmod u+x <your script name>*. This will be explained with more details in Chapter 3, Linux Level 3. To insert comments in the script, start the line with the character #. All the text after the # character will not be interpreted. Always start the script with the following line as first line:

```
#!/bin/bash
```

It is possible to run all the Linux external commands in the scripts since nearly all the commands that can be typed at the command line can be used in a shell script. Here is a simple script to start the X11 programs with nohup in prefix of the commands and ampersand (&) at the ending of the commands. The *nohup* command enables the programs to still run even if the shell from which the commands were issued is closed. The & sets the command to be run in background.

```
#!/bin/bash
export BIN=/usr/bin/
nohup $BIN/xterm &
nohup $BIN/xeyes &
nohup $BIN/xclock &
exit 0
```

The script starts all the X11 applications and writes the result of the execution in a *nohup.out* file in the directory where the script is executed.

Bash Variables

Bash provides some special built-in variables which can be used in the scripts and get them as parameters. They always start with $ followed by either a number from 0 to 9 or a special character.

Characters	Explanation
$*	Expands to the positional parameters, starting from one. When the expansion occurs within double quotes, it expands to a single word with the value of each parameter separated by the first character of the IFS special variable.
$@	Expands to the positional parameters, starting from one. When the expansion occurs within double quotes, each parameter expands to a separate word.
$#	Expands to the number of positional parameters in decimal.
$?	Expands to the exit status of the most recently executed foreground pipeline.
$-	A hyphen expands to the current option flags as specified upon invocation, by the set built-in command, or those set by the shell itself (such as the -i).
$$	Expands to the process ID of the shell.
$!	Expands to the process ID of the most recently executed background (asynchronous) command.
$0	Expands to the name of the shell or shell script.
$n	Positional command line arguments
$_	The underscore variable is set at shell start-up and contains the absolute file name of the shell or script being executed as passed in the argument list. Subsequently, it expands to the last argument in the previous command, after expansion. It is also set to the full pathname of each command executed and placed in the environment exported to that command. When checking mail, this parameter holds the name of the mail file.

Table 1.7: *Bash Variable Characters and Explanations*

Example of a script using the built-in shell variables:

```
#!/bin/bash
# script name param_display.sh
# chmod u+x param_display.sh
export BIN=/bin/
$BIN/echo $1
$BIN/echo $2
$BIN/echo $3
$BIN/echo number of parameters $#
$BIN/echo show all parameters $*
$BIN/echo name of the script $0
exit 0
```

Execute the script and the following result should show up:

```
oracle@linux-mlpb:~/testos> ./param_display.sh one two three
one
two
three
number of parameters 3
show all parameters one two three
name of the script ./param_display.sh
```

Test conditions can also be used in Bash shell scripts. The conditions will need to be put inside brackets to use them:

```
[condition]
```

Tests conditions can be used on strings and file numbers. There can also be modified conditions in the scripts. Here is the exhaustive list of those conditions.

Test strings:

Value	Usage
s:	Not null
-z s:	Zero length
=:	Strings have the same value
<:	Less than
>:	Greater than
-n s:	Non Zero length

Test comparing numbers:

Value	Usage
-eq:	Equal
-gt:	Greater than
-ge:	Greater or equal
-lt:	Lower than
-le:	Lower or equal
-ne:	Is not equal to

Test on files:

Value	Usage
-d	Is a directory
-a	Does exists
-w	Can be written
-x	Can be executed

Modifying conditions:

Value	Usage
-o:	Or operator
-a:	And operator
!:	Not operator

Try these examples on the Linux:

```
test 3 -gt 4 && echo True || echo false

[ "abc" != "abc" ];echo $?

[ "abc" != "def" ];echo $?

set +o nounset
[ -o nounset ];echo $?
```

Conditional expressions can be used in the scripts for loops or list exits repeatedly as long as a condition is met; the case to take actions based on a list of conditions and if to test conditions and branch based on the results:

Syntax of *for*:

```
As loop: for
```

```
(initial expression; condition; statement)
                     do
                       commands
                     done
```

As list syntax:

```
for
NAME [in LIST];
do
commands;
done
```

Examples using *for*, as loop:

```
#!/bin/bash
# Conversion script for txt to doc files
LIST="$(ls *.txt)"
for
i in "$LIST"; do
     CHANGE_NAME =$(ls "$i" | sed -e 's/txt/doc/')
     cat beginfile > "$ CHANGE_NAME "
     cat "$i" | sed -e '1,25d' | tac | sed -e '1,21d'| tac >> "$CHANGE_NAME
"
     cat endfile >> "$CHANGE_NAME"
done
```

As list syntax:

```
#!/bin/bash
#generate your list file
ls *.txt > listing.txt
for i in `cat listing.txt `; do cp "$i" "$i".bak ; done
```

Syntax of *while*:

```
while condition
do
commands
done
```

Example using *while*:

```
#!/bin/bash
# Generates a log file with data every 2 minutes
while true; do
touch oracle_log`date +%s`.log
sleep 120
done
```

Syntax of *case*:

```
                    case value in
                          pattern1) commands ;;
                          pattern2) other commands ;;
                    esac
```

Example using *case*:

```
case "$1" in
    'start')
        # Start your Oracle databases:
        su - $USER -c "$ORACLE_HOME/bin/lsnrctl start"
        su - $USER -c $ORACLE_HOME/bin/dbstart
        ;;
    'stop')
        # Stop your Oracle databases:
        su - $USER -c $ORACLE_HOME/bin/dbshut
        su - $USER -c "$ORACLE_HOME/bin/lsnrctl stop"
        ;;
esac
```

Syntax of *if*:

```
                    if test-commands
                          then
                          command
                          else
                          command
                    fi
```

Examples using *if*:

```
#!/bin/bash
# delete file2 if file1 and file2 are identical
if cmp file1 file2
then echo idem file1 and file2 file deleted
rm file2
fi
```

```
#!/bin/bash
# finds out if the oracle account exists in your password file
if grep oracle /etc/passwd
then
echo "Oracle account exists"
else
echo "Oracle account does not exists"
fi
```

Try this example of a calculator that is a function:

```
function calculator ()
 {
   local x
   if [ $# -lt 1 ]; then
     echo "This function evaluates arithmetic for you if you give it some"
   elif (( $* )); then
     let x="$*"
     echo "$* = $x"
   else
     echo "$* = 0 or is not an arithmetic expression"
   fi
 }
```

Use the *type* command to describe the function:

```
oracle@linux-mlpb:~/scipts/ >type calculator
calculator is a function
calculator ()
{
    local x;
    if [ $# -lt 1 ]; then
        echo "This function evaluates arithmetic for you if you give it
some";
    else
        if (( $* )); then
            let x="$*";
            echo "$* = $x";
        else
            echo "$* = 0 or is not an arithmetic expression";
        fi;
    fi
}
```

> Exam Advice: Know what the bash built-in variables are and also the syntax of *for*, *while* and *case*.

/proc and Its Use

The */proc* is a virtual file system that contains files that show the status of the Linux operating system kernel. Most of the files have a size of 0 bytes, but they actually contain a large amount of data. The timestamps of these virtual files changes as the contents of the files are updated by the OS. The contents of the files can be seen with the classical command *cat*, thereby viewing the information of the CPU.

```
linux-mlpb:~ # cat /proc/cpuinfo

processor	: 0
vendor_id	: GenuineIntel
cpu family	: 6
model		: 9
model name	: Intel(R) Pentium(R) M processor 1700MHz
stepping	: 8
cpu MHz		: 1694.501
cache size	: 1024 KB
fdiv_bug	: no
hlt_bug		: no
f00f_bug	: no
coma_bug	: no
fpu		: yes
fpu_exception	: yes
cpuid level	: 2
wp		: yes
flags		: fpu vme de pse tsc msr mce cx8 apic sep mtrr pge mca
cmov pat clflush dts acpi mmx fxsr sse sse2 up pebs bts
bogomips	: 3408.43
clflush size	: 64
```

The following virtual files provide an indication, at the moment they are being viewed, about the system hardware:

- */proc/partitions*: Gives the size and name of partitions
- */proc/meminfo*: Memory statistics and segment sizes
- */proc/mounts*: List of the mount points
- */proc/uptime*: Uptime of the system
- */proc/interrupts*: List of interrupts on the system

There are also files that show system configuration information, like the files in the */proc/sys/* directory, about the network */proc/net* and also */proc/filesystems* about the file systems supported by the kernel.

The values of the virtual files can be changed by doing a redirection to the file to be changed, i.e. changing the value of the hostname:

```
echo oracle-srv1 > /proc/sys/kernel/hostname
```

To see the kernel values, use the *sysctl* command */sbin/sysctl.* It enables the administrator to configure kernel parameters at runtime.

🔔 Exam Advice: Be capable of explaining what is */proc directory*, the purpose and its files.

Linux and RPM

The Redhat Package Manager is a GPL open source packaging system that allows the performance of installation, un-installation, upgrades, verification and querying of the packages. Those are the five basic operations that can be performed; the user's package can also be built with RPM. Find the RPM package from diverse sources like Redhat's CD and DVD, https://rhn.redhat.com/, http://rpm.org/ and http://rpmfind.net/linux/RPM/. All the options from the RPM command can be found by doing *rpm --help* or *man rpm*. A description of the most frequently used commands is given in the next few lines.
RPM querying command:

```
rpm -q <your package name or part of it >
```

or:

```
rpm -qa | grep -i <your package name or part of it>
```

With the package make-3.81-103.1:

```
linux-mlpb:~ # rpm  -q make
make-3.81-103.1
```

or:

```
linux-mlpb:~ # rpm -qa | grep -i make
make-3.81-103.1
automake-1.10.1-25.1
```

RPM installation command:

```
rpm -ivh <your package name>
```

The option *i* is for installation, *v* is for verbose and *h* is for printing 50 hash marks as the package archive is unpacked.

RPM un-installation command:

```
rpm -e <your package name>
```

The option *e* stands for erase and removes the package given as an argument.

RPM upgrade command:

```
rpm -Uvh <your package name>
```

The option *U* is for upgrade, *v* is for verbose and *h* is for printing 50 hash marks as the package archive is unpacked. Note that the option *-U* allows for performing the upgrade by uninstalling the previous version and it does not remove any configuration files. This option must be used to upgrade the kernel as it cannot be removed.

RPM Verification command:

1. To verify which package contains the file name:

```
rpm -Vf < file name to verify >
```

2. To verify all installed packages on the system:

```
rpm -Va
```

3. To verify an installed package:

```
rpm -Vp <your package name>
```

In Chapter 6, Preparing Linux for Oracle, the necessary packages to be installed in order to perform a successful oracle installation will be covered.

> Exam Advice: Be capable of giving all the options for RPM and also the usage of each option as it might be a part of the exam.

Note: When using the *rpm* command, especially for the installation, upgrade and uninstallation, the DBA must be root.

Summary

This chapter gave an introduction of Linux along with its creation and history. It continued with the description of Linux kernels and their uses as well as the structure of Linux. Next, the collaboration of Linux and Oracle was covered in depth as well as the hardware that is supported by Oracle using Linux. The commands, programs, variables and other elements of Linux were also included. Then the chapter concluded with the commands in Linux via Redhat Package Manager.

Exercises

1. Write a Bash script that lists all the RPM packages and puts the result in a file.
2. Write a Bash script that starts xterm, xeyes and xclock using *nohup* and multitasking option *&*.

Q&A

Questions

1. Does Oracle support Linux that has a kernel that is tainted? Choose all that apply:

A. No support can be expected from Oracle when the kernel is tainted
B. Oracle supports all Linux kernels that are tainted
C. Oracle supports Linux kernels that are tainted with OCFS module
D. Oracle supports Linux kernels that are tainted with EMC powerpath module

2. In the Linux directory structure, what is the function of the */etc/inittab*?

A. The file is in charge of setting the user levels
B. Describes the user to be locked from the system
C. Describes the processes to be started or stopped

D. In this file, a description is given of all the files systems to be mounted

3. Does Oracle certify hardware?

A. No, Oracle lets the OS vendors certify the hardware platforms
B. Yes, Oracle supports all hardware related that can run Linux
C. No, Oracle does not certify hardware or software
D. Yes, Oracle supports all kind of hardware

4. What is the *lsmod* command used for?

A. To get a detailed list of all users logged on the system
B. To select the file system that will be used with Oracle
C. This command does not exist in Linux as it is a Windows command
D. To find out if the kernel is tainted or not

5. What are the two types of devices in Linux? Choose all that apply.

A. It can be a block device
B. It can be a raw device or character device
C. It can be long device
D. It can be redolog device

6. Bash Shell is originally based on what shell?

A. Korn Shell
B. C-shell
C. Bourne Shell
D. Z-shell

7. Set the following Linux commands with the correct description in the proper combination with the capital letter and lowercase letter that explains the purpose of this.

A. *cat*
B. *chown*
C. *killall*
D. *crontab*

a. Kill all processes by name
b. Display the contents of a file without page breaks
c. Schedule a command to run at a later time
d. Change owner of files and groups

8. How can a list be obtained of all the variables that are in the current Shell?

A. *echo $DISPLAY*
B. *echo $ALL*
C. *env*
D. *echo $TERM*

9. What is the correct result of the following Linux command?

```
ps -efd | grep -i ora_ | tee List_of_all_oracle_background_ps.txt | grep -v
grep
```

A.

```
oracle2    32371         1    0  21:04  ?           00:00:00  ora_pmon_orcl
oracle2    32373         1    0  21:04  ?           00:00:00  ora_vktm_orcl
oracle2    32377         1    0  21:04  ?           00:00:00  ora_diag_orcl
oracle2    32379         1    0  21:04  ?           00:00:00  ora_dbrm_orcl
oracle2    32381         1    0  21:04  ?           00:00:00  ora_psp0_orcl
oracle2    32385         1    0  21:04  ?           00:00:00  ora_dia0_orcl
oracle2    32387         1    0  21:04  ?           00:00:00  ora_mman_orcl
oracle2    32389         1    0  21:04  ?           00:00:00  ora_dbw0_orcl
oracle2    32391         1    0  21:04  ?           00:00:00  ora_lgwr_orcl
oracle2    32393         1    0  21:04  ?           00:00:00  ora_ckpt_orcl
oracle2    32395         1    0  21:04  ?           00:00:00  ora_smon_orcl
oracle2    32397         1    0  21:04  ?           00:00:00  ora_reco_orcl
oracle2    32399         1    0  21:04  ?           00:00:00  ora_mmon_orcl
oracle2    32401         1    0  21:04  ?           00:00:00  ora_mmnl_orcl
oracle2    32403         1    0  21:04  ?           00:00:00  ora_d000_orcl
oracle2    32405         1    0  21:04  ?           00:00:00  ora_s000_orcl
oracle2    32413         1    0  21:04  ?           00:00:00  ora_arc0_orcl
oracle2    32415         1    0  21:04  ?           00:00:00  ora_arc1_orcl
oracle2    32417         1    0  21:04  ?           00:00:00  ora_arc2_orcl
oracle2    32419         1    0  21:04  ?           00:00:00  ora_arc3_orcl
oracle2    32423         1    0  21:05  ?           00:00:00  ora_fbda_orcl
oracle2    32425         1    0  21:05  ?           00:00:00  ora_smco_orcl
oracle2    32427         1    0  21:05  ?           00:00:00  ora_w000_orcl
oracle2    32429         1    0  21:05  ?           00:00:00  ora_qmnc_orcl
oracle2    32431         1    0  21:05  ?           00:00:00  ora_q000_orcl
oracle2    32433         1    0  21:05  ?           00:00:00  ora_q001_orcl

And a file called tee is created
```

B.

```
oracle2       tty7                          2008-12-26    19:53    (:0)
oracle2       pts/0                       2008-12-26    19:08    (:0.0)
```

C.

```
oracle2    32371         1    0  21:04  ?           00:00:00  ora_pmon_orcl
oracle2    32373         1    0  21:04  ?           00:00:00  ora_vktm_orcl
oracle2    32377         1    0  21:04  ?           00:00:00  ora_diag_orcl
oracle2    32379         1    0  21:04  ?           00:00:00  ora_dbrm_orcl
oracle2    32381         1    0  21:04  ?           00:00:00  ora_psp0_orcl
oracle2    32385         1    0  21:04  ?           00:00:00  ora_dia0_orcl
oracle2    32387         1    0  21:04  ?           00:00:00  ora_mman_orcl
oracle2    32389         1    0  21:04  ?           00:00:00  ora_dbw0_orcl
oracle2    32391         1    0  21:04  ?           00:00:00  ora_lgwr_orcl
```

```
oracle2    32393     1   0  21:04  ?          00:00:00  ora_ckpt_orcl
oracle2    32395     1   0  21:04  ?          00:00:00  ora_smon_orcl
oracle2    32397     1   0  21:04  ?          00:00:00  ora_reco_orcl
oracle2    32399     1   0  21:04  ?          00:00:00  ora_mmon_orcl
oracle2    32401     1   0  21:04  ?          00:00:00  ora_mmnl_orcl
oracle2    32403     1   0  21:04  ?          00:00:00  ora_d000_orcl
oracle2    32405     1   0  21:04  ?          00:00:00  ora_s000_orcl
oracle2    32413     1   0  21:04  ?          00:00:00  ora_arc0_orcl
oracle2    32415     1   0  21:04  ?          00:00:00  ora_arc1_orcl
oracle2    32417     1   0  21:04  ?          00:00:00  ora_arc2_orcl
oracle2    32419     1   0  21:04  ?          00:00:00  ora_arc3_orcl
oracle2    32423     1   0  21:05  ?          00:00:00  ora_fbda_orcl
oracle2    32425     1   0  21:05  ?          00:00:00  ora_smco_orcl
oracle2    32427     1   0  21:05  ?          00:00:00  ora_w000_orcl
oracle2    32429     1   0  21:05  ?          00:00:00  ora_qmnc_orcl
oracle2    32431     1   0  21:05  ?          00:00:00  ora_q000_orcl
oracle2    32433     1   0  21:05  ?          00:00:00  ora_q001_orcl

And a file called List_of_all_oracle_background_ps.txt is created
```

D. `command not found`

10. What command shall be used to get a list of all packages installed on the system in a file called *list_pkg.txt* and on the display (one screen at a time)?

A. *rpm –qe | less*
B. *rpm –e < list_pkg.txt*
C. *rpm –qa | tee list_pkg.txt | less*
D. *rpm –Uvh | tee list_pkg.txt | cat*

11. Match the following command and options with the correct description.

A. *rpm –pppa test*
B. *rpm –Uvh test2.0.0-1.rpm*
C. *rpm –qa test*
D. *rpm –e test2.0.0-1.rpm*

a. Remove the package test2.0.0-1.rpm
b. This command returns an error
c. List all the packages containing the selected name test
d. Upgrade of the package test2.0.0-1.rpm while keeping the existing files

12. What is the following doing - *insmod?*

A. Inserts new modules in the rpm packages
B. Inserts a text string insmod into the file */proc/modules*
C. Inserts a value specified as argument in the */etc/oratab*
D. Inserts a module into the Linux kernel

Answers

1. C. Oracle supports Linux kernels that are tainted with the OCFS module and D. Oracle supports Linux kernels that are tainted with the EMC powerpath module are the correct answers.

HINT: The section on tainted kernels will help with this.

2. C. Describes the processes to be started or stopped.

HINT: Study the section on how Linux is structured again.

3. A. No, Oracle lets the OS vendors certify the hardware platforms.

HINT: Consult hardware support by Linux OS.

4. D. To find out if the kernel is tainted or not.

HINT: Read again the tainted kernel section.

5. A. It can be a block device and B. It can be a raw device or character device are the correct answers.

HINT: Devices in Linux should be read again.

6. C. Bourne Shell is correct.

HINT: Review the section *Bash Shell.*

7. A. cat / b. Display the contents of a file without page breaks; B. chown / d. Change owner of files and groups; C. killall / a. Kill all processes by name; D. crontab / c. Scheduling a command to run at a later time.

HINT: Refer to the section Commands and Programs in Linux.

8. C. env is the correct answer.

HINT: Commands and programs in Linux is the section to be reviewed.

9. The correct answer is C.

HINT: Study once again about commands and programs in Linux.

10. The answer that is correct is C. - *rpm –qa | tee list_pkg.txt | less*

HINT: Read again the section on Linux and RPM.

11. A. *rpm –pppa* : b. This command returns an error. B. *rpm –Uvh test2.0.0-1.rpm* : d. Upgrade of the package *test2.0.0-1.rpm* while keeping the existing files

C. *rpm –qa test* : c. List all the packages containing the selected name test D. *rpm –e test2.0.0-1.rpm* : a. Remove the package *test2.0.0-1.rpm*

HINT: The Linux and RPM section is valuable here.

12. D. Insert a module into the Linux Kernel is the only possibility with the command *insmod.*

HINT: The commands and programs section in Linux is helpful here also.

Solutions to Exercises

1. Write a Bash script that lists all the RPM packages and puts the result in a file.

```
#!/bin/bash
echo "List all the rpm packages installed"
/bin/rpm -qa | tee $HOME/list.txt
exit 0
```

Remember to change the permissions of the script in an executable version by using *chmod 744*.

2. Write a Bash script that starts xterm, xeyes and xclock using *nohup* and multitasking option *&*.

```
#!/bin/bash
# this script shall be executed in a xterm under X-Windows
# Control that your Display variable is set
if [ -n $DISPLAY ]
then
   echo DISPLAY is set to $DISPLAY
else
   echo set your DISPLAY and restart this script
   exit 1
fi
nohup  xterm&
nohup xeyes&
nohup xclock&
exit 0
```

Linux Level 2: File Permissions and Processes

CHAPTER

The chapter covers the following exam objectives:

1.3. Use common Linux commands
1.4. Write a simple bash shell script
3.1. Describe the Linux file system security

Users and Groups

Like most operating systems, in order to use Linux, a user account is needed. Once there is a user account, the DBA can log on and use the system. This is called a session. As has been shown before, Linux is a multi-user system, and not only can many users be logged on to the system simultaneously, but the same user can run multiple sessions and each session can run independently of every other session.

Linux uses the concept of groups to manage security and privileges for users, i.e. group members. Later it will be shown how file permissions are set for individual users, groups and everyone else. A Linux user must belong to at least one group.

When a user logs on or starts a new session, a number of things happen. Firstly, the username and password are authenticated. An initial default group is assigned which determines a set of privileges for the session. The kernel starts up a shell program where the programs can be run and navigation is enabled through the file system. By default, a location called the user's home directory is the starting point. A number of small hidden shell scripts are run which set some system and session variables and set up the remainder of the session environment.

Although the sequence above is typical, depending on how the session is started, the behavior can be different. The following sections will look into the files that Linux uses to administer users and groups in a little more detail. The files of interest are:

- */etc/passwd*
- */etc/shadow*
- */etc/group*
- */etc/skel/**

Users

Users under Linux typically have the following features:

- The user is protected with a password.
- The user is included in groups (GID Group Identifier numbers).
- The user has a home directory.
- The user has a default shell.
- The user has a user id (UID) number.

The information about the user is stored in a file called */etc/passwd*. This file stores basic user information such as username, UID, GID, encrypted password and the home directory. Sometimes a file called */etc/shadow* is used to store the encrypted passwords. If the */etc/shadow* file is used, then the */etc/passwd* file contains an asterisk (*) instead of an encrypted password.

The */etc/passwd* file has the following format:

```
<username>:<password>:<UID>:<GID>:<Comment>:<HOME directory>:<Default Shell>
```

Where:

username	The user name (up to 32 characters)
password	When it contains x, the */etc/shadow* is used to store the password
UID	The User Identifier, a unique number for the user
GID	The Group Identifier, a number which identifies a unique group and is the users' default group. This number corresponds to an entry in the */etc/group* file.
Comment	A free text field in which the username, phone number,

	etc. can be written. The *finger* command will print this information for a specific user.
HOME Directory	Identifies the initial home directory when the user logs in. It also sets the environment variable *$HOME* of the user.
Default Shell	Specifies the path to the default shell for the user. It also sets the *$SHELL* environment variable for the user session.

Table 2.1: *Breakdown of /etc/passwd File*

Example of */etc/passwd* entry:

```
oracle:x:1000:100:oracle admin account:/home/oracle:/bin/bash
```

So, in the above example, the user Oracle has an encrypted password stored in the */etc/shadow* file and the user is identified by UID 1000. The Oracle user is by default defined to be part of the group with GID=100. Note that the GID=100 identifies a group that is defined in the */etc/group* file. The */etc/group* file and group privileges will be explained later in this chapter. The Oracle user's home directory is set to */home/oracle*. This is the directory that the Oracle user will be directed to when logging in, *$HOME*, and it is not to be confused with the *$ORACLE_HOME* environment variable.

For completeness, the following is an example of a */etc/shadow* entry for the Oracle user defined above.

```
oracle:$2a$05$GlfVgRx6t2k0k8hZ30mim.embNYIyvwplFyOoWe2kYMzq9/N7L99O:14124:0:
99999:7:::
```

The format is:

- Username: Username of the login
- Password: The field contains the password that is encrypted
- Password change: A section concerning the date of the last password change (Days are starting since 1st January 1970, This date is related to the Linux/UNIX system calendar)
- Minimum days left: To change the password
- Maximum days left: To change the password

- Warning: Number of days left before the password is about to expire
- Deactivate: Number of days left before the password will be deactivated
- Expire: Number of days since 1st January 1970 when the account will be disabled, i.e. a date to specify when the login will no longer be in use

As stated earlier, there are a number of special hidden files which are run when the DBA logs in and these scripts set up the user's environment i.e. *.bash_profile*, *.bashrc*, *.bash_logout*, *dircolors*, *.vimrc* (a Linux file with a '.' prefix means that the file is a hidden file).

The directory */etc/skel* contains templates for these special files, and these can be copied to the user's home directory and then customized. Alternatively, the command *useradd* can be utilized with the *–m* and *–k* switches. This will create the user's home directory and copy a set of these templates to that directory. This and other user creation commands will be covered a little later, but first look at one more file called */etc/group*.

Groups

The information about the groups on the Linux system is stored in the file */etc/group* and references to the GID are also made in the file */etc/passwd.*

The */etc/group* file has the following format:

```
<group_name>:<passwd>:<GID>:<user_list>
```

Where:

- *<group_name>*: The name that is assigned to the group
- *<GID>*: The system-unique numerical ID assigned to the group
- *<user_list>*: A comma separated list of users that are allowed to be part of the group

The *<passwd>* is usually blank or contains x and is not often used anymore. It is considered antiquated to set passwords on the groups.

Here is an example of three common groups from the */etc/group* file:

- oinstall::500:oracle

- dba::501:oracle,tom,dick
- oper::502:oracle,tom,dick,harry

The Oracle user can belong to any of the oinstall, dba or oper groups. The users Tom and Dick can belong to either the dba or the oper group. If it is assumed that Tom's default group is the oper group, i.e. for Tom's entry in the */etc/passwd* file, there will be a GID value of 102. Then, when Tom logs in, he will be in the oper group. Since Tom is allowed to be part of the dba group also, he can change to that group by using the *newgrp* command.

The following example illustrates how to uses the *id* and *newgrp* commands to switch between groups.

```
tom@linux-mlpb:~> id
uid=501(tom) gid=502(oper) groups=501(dba),502(oper)
tom@linux-mlpb:~> newgrp dba
tom@linux-mlpb:~>
tom@linux-mlpb:~> id
uid=501(tom) gid=501(dba) groups=501(dba),502(oper)
```

Administering Users by Command

Administering users on Linux essentially involves administering the files */etc/passwd*, */etc/group*, */etc/shadow* and such. Editing these files by hand is possible, but there is a slight risk of corrupting them and furthermore, it is a rather tedious way of handling users. Instead, use the commands *useradd*, *usermod*, *userdel*, *groupadd*, *groupmod*, *groupdel* and *passwd.*

The *useradd*, *usermod*, and *userdel* commands are used to add, modify or delete entries in the */etc/passwd* file. Likewise, *groupadd*, *groupmod*, *groupdel* are used to add, modify or delete entries in the */etc/group* file. Additionally, *passwd* command is used to update the encrypted password in the */etc/shadow* file.

The following examples illustrate how these commands can be employed. As always, consult the *man* pages for help on the usage of the commands, or use the commands with the *--help* switch to get brief help information:

Actions	Command
New user creation	useradd [-D binddn] [-P path] [-c comment] [-d homedir] [-e expire] [-f inactive] [-G group,...] [-g gid] [-m [-k skeldir]] [-o] [-p password] [-u uid] [-r] [-s shell] [--service service] [--help] [--usage] [-v] [--preferred-uid uid] account
Example: Create a new user called ora10t (oracle 10g test) in the group dba and as other groups oinstall useradd -g oinstall -G dba -s/bin/bash -pmypasswd -d/home/ora10t -m ora10t	
Existing User modification	usermod [-D binddn] [-P path] [-g gid [-o]] [-p password] [--service service] [--help] [--usage] [-v] account
Example: Modify the ora10t user by swapping the primary group value and the other groups usermod –g oinstall –G dba ora10t	
User suppression	userdel [-D binddn] [-P path] [-r[-f]] [--service service] [--help] [-u] [-v] account
Example: Delete the user ora10t userdel -r ora10t	
Change user password	passwd [-f|-g|-s|-k[-q]] [name]
Example: Change the password of the user ora10t passwd ora10t Changing password for ora10t. New Password: Reenter New Password: Password changed.	

Actions	Command
New group creation	groupadd [-D binddn] [-P path] [-g gid [-o]] [-p password] [--preferred-gid gid] [-r] [--service service] [--help] [--usage] [-v] group
Example: Create a new group called dba with GID=504 groupadd -g 504 dba	
Existing group modification	groupmod [-D binddn] [-P path] [-g gid [-o]] [-p password] [-A user] [-R user] [--service service] [--help] [-v] [--usage] group
Example: Change the group name from dbo to dba	

groupmod –n dba dbo	
Group suppression	groupdel [-D binddn] [-P path] [--service service] [--help] [-u] [-v] group
Example: Delete a group called dba groupdel dba	

Table 2.2: *Commands Used in the /etc/passwd File*

Rules About the UID and GID

As described in the previous paragraphs, Linux uses numbers to identify the UID (User Identifier), and the GID (Group Identifier). A lot of Linux distributions use reserved numbers for the system administrator and other special users. For Redhat, any number beyond 500 can be used for ordinary users, but on Suse Linux, a number beyond 1000 must be used. Therefore, when Oracle accounts are created on a Linux server on Redhat, make sure that the value for the ID is higher than 500. The control can be performed with the *id* command:

```
oracle@linux-mlpb:~> id
uid=502(oracle) gid=504(oinstall)
groups=503(dba), 504(oinstall), 504(oper)
```

It is also possible to use the *grep* command on the */etc/group* file to find out what is the group of the DBA's user.

```
oracle@linux-mlpb:~> grep ^oper /etc/group
oper:x:50:
```

In Chapter 6, *Preparing Linux for Oracle*, the typical users and groups for Oracle under Linux will be described.

> Exam Advice: Be able to describe the files, restrictions and the methods to create, modify and delete users.

Who is the Boss?

With the root user, also called the super user account, all the system administration tasks can be performed. Typical system administration tasks are:

- Create, modify and suppress user accounts and groups
- Keep a record of all the system changes
- Be on duty for reboots and other system operational tasks
- Perform system backups
- Control and monitor diskspace, cpu load, memory usage, network connection, log files, et al
- Install, update and remove rpm packages and patches
- Control and allocate the different permissions in order to have a secure system
- Troubleshooting and tuning of the Linux systems

When logging in as the root account, be careful with the Linux delete command *rm* as this can have irreversible consequences for the system.

Who is Nobody User?

The opposite of the root user, who has all the power to perform system administration actions, is the nobody user. The nobody user has the least privileges in Linux. It uses the user UID 99 as a common value in Redhat. The nobody user, by default, belongs to the nobody group, also commonly set to group GID 99. As system administrator, the nobody user should be kept with only minimal privileges.

User nobody does not own files, is a member of a non-privileged group and has no specific abilities. The user is commonly used by daemon programs as they send signals to each other and perform *ptrace* and *strace* (Linux debugging system calls), so it can read and write to the memory of other processes. Linux standard base recommends that a specific account is created for each daemon process. Doing so makes the security monitoring much easier. Caveat: By default, Oracle uses the nobody user and nobody group to perform external jobs. This, however, is configurable.

How to Set Up a BASH Environment or Profile

As has been shown, when the DBA logs in or starts an interactive shell, there are a number of hidden script files that are executed and these scripts are used to set up the environment. If the default shell is bash, as specified in the */etc/passwd* file, then when the bash shell is started it executes, at first, the *file /etc/profile*. After that, it executes *$HOME/.bash_profile*, *$HOME/.bash_login* and at last, *$HOME/.profile*. This can be avoided by starting the bash shell with the switch *--noprofile*.

Here is an example of what the *$HOME/.profile* could contain for setting typical Oracle environment variables:

```
export ORACLE_BASE=/oracle/app
export ORACLE_HOME=/oracle/app/oracle/product/10.2.0/db_1
export ORACLE_SID=HUB
ORAENV_ASK=NO
export LD_LIBRARY_PATH=$ORACLE_HOME/lib32
export
CLASSPATH=$CLASSPATH:$ORACLE_HOME/JRE:$ORACLE_HOME/jlib:$ORACLE_HOME/rdbms/j
lib:$ORACLE_HOME/network/jlib
PATH=$PATH:$ORACLE_HOME/bin:/usr/sbin:/usr/bin:$HOME/bin:
```

In the example above, the variables *$ORACLE_BASE*, *$ORACLE_HOME*, *$ORACLE_SID* and other environment variables are set as soon as the shell is started. Notice the use of the *export* command. Normally, a variable can be assigned in the shell or in the scripts by using a simple assignment, e.g. *ORACLE_SID=HUB*. However, the scope of this assignment is only within the current shell or script. To make the assignment valid for all descendant shells and scripts called from the shell, use the *export* command, e.g. *export ORACLE_SID=HUB*.

When a script is called from the command line, the script will spawn a descendant shell (the one specified at the start of the script, e.g. */bin/bash*) and this shell will inherit any variables that were exported from the parent shell. However, any variables that are assigned, or even exported in the script, will not be available to the parent shell when the script has finished executing.

Sometimes it might be desired to set variables in the parent shell, but this should be done by calling a shell script. An example of this is the well-known *oraenv* script. To achieve this, run the script in the current shell rather than executing it in a spawned shell. This is called sourcing the script. This is equivalent to reading the commands in the sourced script file and running them directly in the current shell. To achieve this, use the dot-space syntax: a '.' followed by a space and then the file name (script) to be sourced:

```
/export/home/myuser >. oraenv
```

File Permissions

File Security and Administration

As Linux is a multi-user operating system, it is necessary to have security features on all files and also the possibility of access rights to owners and groups of owners. Files can be accessed in read mode (r), write mode (w) and executable mode (x). File permissions are defined for users, groups and others. Linux users are organized into groups for easier administration and access control. Every user belongs to at least one group. Others are all other users that are not in the users group. All this information is structure in a standard set of flags, called the file mode. The mode of a file can be seen by using the *ls* command with *–l* switch:

```
/export/home/myuser >ls -l test_export.sh
-rwxr--r--    1 myuser      users          89 Mar  2 18:20 test_export.sh
```

Here the mode of the file is *-rwxr--r--* which consists of 11 characters. In this example there are only 10 characters, but this is because the last character is blank, and therefore is not visible in the output.

The first character represents the file type. The next nine characters consist of three sets of three characters which represent the permissions for the file. The first three are for the file owner, the next three for the users in the specified user group, and the last three for all other users. The last one, the 11th character, is normally blank, which indicates that there are no extended permissions on the file. If, however, the 11th character is a '+' sign or a '@', this indicates that extended permissions, ACL, are in effect. For now, this chapter will concentrate on normal file permissions.

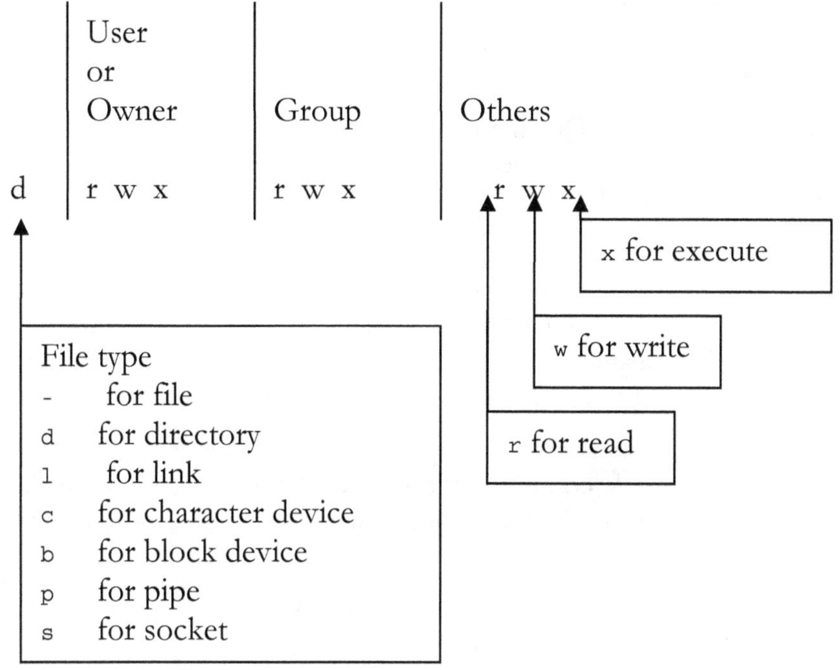

Figure 2.1: *Normal File Permissions*

As explained, the first character describes the file type. It can have the following values:

- - for an ordinary file: This can be a text file, a program, a graphics file, a database datafile, a compressed file, and such.
- *d* for directory: Directories are files just like the other Linux files, but the directories contain pointers based on the inodes of the files they contain.
- *I* nodes are index nodes that store all fundamental file information such as the file attributes and permissions. The inode value can be viewed with the Linux command *ls –i yourfilename.*
- *l* for symbolic links: These are special files that link to or reference another file or directory. The link is in the form of a relative or absolute path. This feature appears in the Berkley UNIX and is supported in the POSIX standard (Portable Operating System Interface).

- *c* for character device: Also called character special file. These files relate to hardware devices and provide the data to the hardware devices. The character devices are sequential and are located in */dev.*
- *b* for block device: This file relates to hardware devices and provides the data to the hardware devices. Block devices have typically large storage areas; for example, DVD-ROM or hard disks.
- *p* for named pipe: A named pipe makes it possible for Linux programs to communicate with each other, reading and writing through the named pipe in a FIFO (First In, First Out) manner. On some older Linux, a named pipe can be created with the *mknod* command. On the newer Linux releases, a named pipe can be created with the *mkfifo* command.
- *s* for sockets: The socket file type resembles a named pipe, but they are related to network communication. The files are analogous to TCP/IP sockets but they apply Linux permissions and protection to the inter-process networking.

All the other characters concern user permissions fields. There are three groups of three characters; the first is about the user, the second is concerning the user groups and the third is about all other users' privileges. The three characters can be:

- r = read: This is only found in the read field.
- w = write: This is only found in the write field.
- x = execute: This is only found in the execute field.
- s,S = set-uid: This is only found in the execute field.

If there is a "-" in a particular location, there is no permission. This may be found in any field whether read, write, or execute.

How to Change File Permissions

A file's permissions can be changed by using the change mode command *chmod.* The mode can be changed by changing the character flags (e.g. r, w, x, etc.) or by using an octal number. The octal format uses the digits 0 to 7 to set the permissions for each set: owner, group, others.

Each octal value translates to a 3-bit binary equivalent where each bit either sets or unsets the permission flags. The following table shows how the text values relate to the octal and binary representations:

Text Values	Octal Values	Binaries Equivalents	Description of the Privileges
---	0	000	No privileges set
--x	1	001	Execution bit is set
-w-	2	010	Write bit is set
-wx	3	011	Write and execution
r--	4	100	Read only access
r-x	5	101	Read and execution possible
rw-	6	110	Read and write possible
rwx	7	111	Read, write and execution possible

Table 2.3: *Relation of Text Values to Octal and Binary Representations*

So a very simple example would be *chmod 777*, which would give read, write and execute privileges to the owner, the group and all others. This would equate to a mode of *–rwxrwxrwx*.

Alternatively, the text format of the *chmod* command can be used where individual permissions can be set or cleared by specifying the symbolic flags (r, w, x, etc.) together with a (+) or (-) operator to set or remove the permission. The symbolic mode can be applied to a user (u), group (g), others (o) or all (a). The previous example could have been written as *chmod a+rwx*, which would have given read, write, and execute access to user, group and others, i.e. all.

Apart from changing permissions using the *chmod* command (change file mode bits), the DBA can also change the owner and file group associated with the file. This is done by using the *chown* (change file owner and group) command.

Examples:

After doing a *ls –l* on the oracle binary SQL*Plus, it is discovered that the following permissions are set:

```
-rwxr-x--x 1 oracle dba 10953 2008-09-02 14:15 sqlplus
```

The SQL*Plus program is owned by the Oracle user and the dba group. It can be seen that all users have permission to execute the SQL*Plus program. In this case, only the Oracle user, or users in the dba group, should have execute permissions on this file, so the execute permissions on the file can be removed using *chmod*. In order to change the permissions on the file, the administrator needs to be the owner (Oracle) or super user.

```
chmod o-x sqlplus
```

```
chmod 750 sqlplus
```

Another example is where the directory logs, belonging to the user ora10 and the group oinstall, must be changed to the user Oracle and the group dba. All files and subdirectories should also be changed to the same values. This can be done using the *chown* command with the switch *-R* for recursive:

```
chown -R oracle:dba logs
```

On the programs or files with the wrong permission, owned by other users or protected, *permission denied* will appear when trying to execute or access that file:

```
[oracle@sgr-23pibmsub01 ~]$ ls -al mypgm
-rw-r--r--  1 oracle dba 0 Mar 23 14:17 mypgm
-bash: ./mypgm: Permission denied
```

How to Create Links

To create a symbolic link for sharing the data between the two users oracle and ora10, use the Linux command *ln*. Observe that under Linux, there are two types of links: hard links and symbolic links. Hard links are only possible on files located on the same file system. When the files are located on different systems, symbolic links have to be used. See the following examples of links.

Hard link:

```
ln source_file.txt link_file.txt
```

Symbolic link:

```
ln -s /users/oracle/source_file.txt /u01/oracle/1020/docs/link_file.txt
```

Sticky Bits, Setuid and Setgid

Linux has three additional special permissions to the basic permissions described before:

- *Sticky bit* is used on directories to prevent users with write access on the files in the directory from deleting files that they do not own.
- *Setuid* or *SUID* is set in the owner execution field to allow normal users to execute an application by assuming the identity of the file owner.
- *Setgid* or *SGID* have the same purpose that *setuid* does, but is related to the group permissions.

The table below gives explanations and examples for each special permission:

Permission type	Explanation and Example
sticky bit	The user can see if the *sticky bit* is set by doing a *ls –al* on the files or directories and it will be known that the file has a *t* in the privileges instead of the execution bit *x*. If the directory has the *sticky bit* set, a file can be deleted only by the file owner, the directory owner, or by a privileged user. *-rwxrwxrwt execute* and *sticky bit* are set on this example. *-rwxrwxr-T*: Only the *sticky bit* is set and not execute. Can be set on the file or directory with the command *chmod*: *chmod +t your_file_name*. Example: drwxrwxrwt 18 root root 4096 2009-03-03 15:23 tmp Typical example where the public folder tmp includes files where all users have read and write access on all files. The *sticky bit* is set to avoid users from deleting other users' files.
Setuid	When it is set, the user gets an *s* or *S* instead of the *execution* bit x. An *s* means that both the *setuid* bit and the *execution* bit are set. An *S* means that only the *setuid* bit is set. *-rws------* : Both the *execution* and the *setuid* bit are set.

	-r-S------ : The *setuid* bit is set but not the *execution* bit *x*. Can be set on the file or directory with the command *chmod:chmod u+s your_file_name.* Example: -rwsr-xr-x 1 root root 29104 2008-12-08 10:14 /usr/bin/passwd Typical example where the *passwd* program can be executed by a normal user so that they can change their own password. Since the normal user will assume the SUID of root, they will be able to update the */etc/passwd* file even though this file is owned by root.
setgid	The purpose of the *setgid* is the same as *setuid* but it is on the group this time. *-rwxrws---* : *setgid* is set and the *execution* bit is set. *-rwxr-S---* : Only the *setgid* is set, but not the *execution* bit *x*. Can be set on the file or directory with the command *chmod*: *chmod g+s your_file_name*. Example: -rwxr-sr-x 1 root crontab 26928 2008-04-08 20:02 /usr/bin/crontab This example shows how normal users can run the *crontab* command with the effective group privileges of *crontab*.

Table 2.4: *Special Permissions Explanations and Examples*

The *chmod* command can also be used to set or unset with the following values as a prefix to the normal three numeric privileges:

Value	Explanation
0	setuid, setgid, sticky bits are unset
1	*sticky bit* is in place
2	*setgid* bit is in place
3	*setgid* and *sticky bits* are in place

4	*setuid* bit is in place
5	*setuid* and *sticky bits* are in place
6	*setuid* and *setgid* bits are on
7	setuid, setgid, sticky bits are activated

Table 2.5: *Values Using Chmod Command for Special Permissions*

The syntax will be, for example, to set the *uid*, *gid* and the *sticky bits*:

```
chmod 7750 sqlplus
```

What is umask?

umask is an abbreviation for user mask. It is a command and function used both in Linux and UNIX as it is available in POSIX environments. The purpose of *umask* is to set default permissions for new files and directories that are created. When a new file or directory is created, it gets some default permissions based on the *umask*. These can be changed later using *chmod.*

Since this relates to the file and directory permissions, it is quite important that the *umask* is set properly. The *umask* is an octal value which is set in the environment and the value can be examined by simply typing *umask*, without any parameters, at the command line. Like *chmod* command, it can also be represented by the symbolic value *umask –S*. The following example shows the same *umask* setting in octal and symbolic mode:

Note: Both the octal and the symbolic *umask* do not allow permissions to be executed to new created files in spite of *umask* having those values set. Only when a directory is created will the execute values be set.

```
linux-mlpb:~ #umask
0022
linux-mlpb:~ #umask -S
u=rwx,g=rx,o=rx
```

The *umask* works by subtracting the octal setting for *umask* from the mode 666 for files and 777 for directories. A common *umask* setting of 022 would mean that a new file created by the user would get mode 644. A new directory would get mode 755.

The *umask* can be tested by creating a file with the *touch* command or with text editor *vi*. Read Chapter 4 for more information about the Linux text editors.

```
linux-mlpb:~ # umask -S u=rwx,g=rwx,o=r
linux-mlpb:~ # touch umask_test
linux-mlpb:~ # ls -al umask_test
-rw-rw-r-- 1 oracle dba 0 2009-01-24 12:14 umask_test
```

Note that in symbolic format, the settings are complimentary, i.e. the setting that is not in the mask is cleared. In the example above, the *umask -S u=rwx, g=rwx, o=rw* is equivalent to an *umask* 002 in octal format.

A more secure *umask* value is 066, which will create a file with read and write permissions only (for a file, 600 or *rw-------* and for a directory, 700 or *rwx------*).

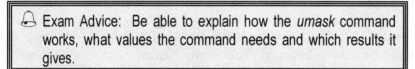

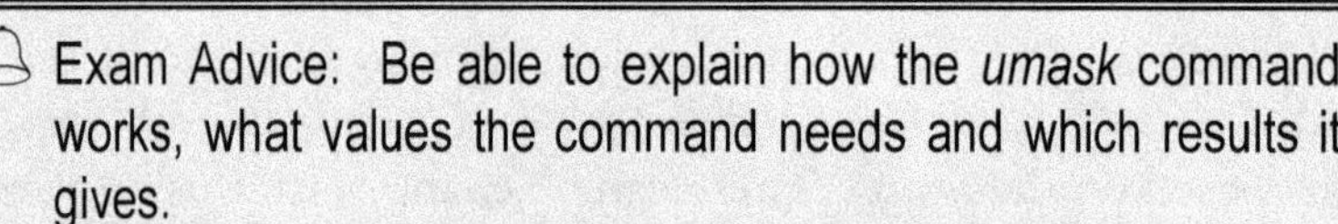

Exam Advice: Be able to explain how the *umask* command works, what values the command needs and which results it gives.

The *umask* value is set system wide in the */etc/profile* file but can be overridden by the user in their local file *$HOME/.bashrc*. This will override the values in */etc/profile* when the administrator logs in or starts a new bash shell. The Oracle Universal Installer controls that the *umask* value is set. For more information about the OUI, read Chapter 7, *Install Oracle under Linux*.

Processes

Linux and UNIX-like systems have two fundamental concepts: files and processes. A program (file) that is in execution is a process. A process uses a set of resources, such as open files and threads, and occupies address spaces and data segments. Since there is a limited set of resources, and there are many processes that may wish to use them, the user needs to be able to identify and manage these processes.

In order to perform easy process management, every process has a process descriptor associated with it. The process descriptor helps keep track of a process in memory. Linux provides a set of commands that can help manage processes. With these, the process state can be monitored, the PID (Process ID), PPID (Parent Process ID) and any child processes can be identified, any open files can be listed, who owns the process can be identified, how long the process has been executing can be seen, how much memory the process is consuming and so on.

Commands to Manage Processes

With the following commands in Table 2.6, the user will be able to manage their processes:

Command or Key Combination	Description and Example
ps	The *ps* command is used to list the current processes. The command used without any switches will show the processes that are running in the current session. Using different specific switches, information about system processes, other users' processes and so on can be obtained. By piping the results through *grep*, the information can be filtered. ps –efd | grep pmon oracle2 3189 1 0 20:07 ? 00:00:00 ora_pmon_orcl The *ps* command output can be formatted to give information on the user that owns the process (UID), the process identifier (PID), the Parent PID which started the process (PPID), the CPU utilization (C), the time the process was started (STIME), the terminal from where the process was started (TTY), how long the process was active (TIME) and the name of the program (CMD). ps –efd | head -3 UID PID PPID C STIME TTY TIME CMD root 1 0 0 20:03 ? 00:00:01 init [5] root 2 0 0 20:03 ? 00:00:00 [kthreadd]
your_program _name	This will start the program in the foreground. If the program name is entered on the command line, then the user will only get their command prompt back after the program has finished executing.
your_program _name &	If the & character is placed after the command, then the command executes in the background and the user will get the command prompt back immediately.
nohup your_program	By including the *nohup* command, which stands for no hangup, one ensures that the command will continue to run even after the shell is

&	closed.
Ctrl -z	While running a job in the foreground, the CTRL-Z key combination can be utilized to suspend the job and return to the bash prompt. Once there is a prompt, decide if the suspended job should continue running in the foreground, or if it should continue in the background. Use the *fg* and *bg* commands to decide whether the process continues in foreground or in background.
Ctrl -c	CTRL-C will interrupt the foreground process and return the user to the bash prompt. (SIGINT signal)
Ctrl -d	CTRL-D sends an exit signal to the application. If CTRL-D is sent in the shell, then the shell will be exited. If a CTRL-D is performed in SQL*Plus, it exits the program and the interactive bash prompt appears.
jobs	Lists all the jobs that are running in background and informs the user about the number and status of those jobs. Use the numbers as argument for the *fg* or *bg* commands to switch to the given process. jobs [1] Stopped ls [2] Stopped gimp [3] Stopped vi So *fg 3* will be executing the *vi* command in the foreground
kill	The *kill* command, as the name implies, is often used to kill or stop a process. In actual fact, *kill* does not always kill the process. In fact, it sends a signal to the process's signal handler, which traps the signal. The actual signal number that is sent to the process can be any of the signals defined on the system. The *–l* switch lists the available signals. kill -l 1) SIGHUP 2) SIGINT 3) SIGQUIT 4) SIGILL 5) SIGTRAP 6) SIGABRT 7) SIGBUS 8) SIGFPE 9) SIGKILL 10) SIGUSR1 11) SIGSEGV 12) SIGUSR2 13) SIGPIPE 14) SIGALRM 15) SIGTERM 16) SIGSTKFLT 17) SIGCHLD 18) SIGCONT 19) SIGSTOP 20) SIGTSTP 21) SIGTTIN 22) SIGTTOU 23) SIGURG 24) SIGXCPU 25) SIGXFSZ 26) SIGVTALRM 27) SIGPROF 28) SIGWINCH 29) SIGIO 30) SIGPWR 31) SIGSYS 34) SIGRTMIN 35) SIGRTMIN+1 36) SIGRTMIN+2 37) SIGRTMIN+3 38) SIGRTMIN+4

	39) SIGRTMIN+5 40) SIGRTMIN+6 41) SIGRTMIN+7 42) SIGRTMIN+8 43) SIGRTMIN+9 44) SIGRTMIN+10 45) SIGRTMIN+11 46) SIGRTMIN+12 47) SIGRTMIN+13 48) SIGRTMIN+14 49) SIGRTMIN+15 50) SIGRTMAX-14 51) SIGRTMAX-13 52) SIGRTMAX-12 53) SIGRTMAX-11 54) SIGRTMAX-10 55) SIGRTMAX-9 56) SIGRTMAX-8 57) SIGRTMAX-7 58) SIGRTMAX-6 59) SIGRTMAX-5 60) SIGRTMAX-4 61) SIGRTMAX-3 62) SIGRTMAX-2 63) SIGRTMAX-1 64) SIGRTMAX By default, *kill* sends the SIGTERM signal to a process. This may not always cause the process to stop, so the SIGKILL signal(9) is often used when a process really needs to be stopped. ps –efd | grep vi oracle 3450 3104 0 20:17 pts/0 00:00:00 vi 3450 is the PID, so use *kill* with -9 - that is the signal to kill. kill -9 3450
lsof	Provides a list of all the open files on the system including regular files, directories, special block or character files, libraries, and network files. If the results are piped through *grep*, search for files that are opened by a specific user (e.g. oracle). lsof | grep ora_ | head -2 oracle 3189 oracle 5w REG 8,17 12144 434229 /oracle/app/diag/rdbms/orcl/orcl/trace/orcl_ora_3181.trc oracle 3189 oracle 10w REG 8,17 236 434230 /oracle/app/diag/rdbms/orcl/orcl/trace/orcl_ora_3181.trm

Table 2.6: *Commands for Managing Processes*

Kernel Parameters

In Linux, it is possible to change the settings in the kernel so tuning can be performed on the memory, semaphores and network parameters. The changes can be made permanently by using the command */sbin/sysctl* and the file */etc/sysctl.conf*. The changes can also be made, temporarily, directly in the virtual device */proc/sys/*, i.e. in the directory kernel. In that case, the changes will be volatile or non-persistent. Oracle has recommendations that must be followed in the Linux production systems in order to have optimal performance and to get support. The following areas of the kernel can be changed:

- Semaphores
- Shared memory
- Network parameters

One other important area, shell limits, must also be set to appropriate values for the Oracle user. The shell limits determine things like the maximum number of open files for a user and also the number of processes. It is possible to set hard and soft limits for the shell. The intention of the limits is to avoid runaway situations where the user attempts to allocate many more resources than are available.

Introduction to Semaphores

Semaphores, invented originally by Edsger Dijkstra, are a means of controlling access to critical system resources by multiple processes or threads within a process. For example, when numerous Oracle processes require access to shared memory (SGA), then this access is controlled by means of semaphores.

If the semaphore is set, i.e. greater than zero, then the resource is available. If the semaphore is zero, then the resource is occupied, and the process must wait. This test and set mechanism is how a process gets access to a resource. In the simplest terms, semaphores are implemented as counters (variables) in the kernel, which are only accessible through system calls, e.g. *semop*, *semget*, and *semctl*. The process tests the value of the semaphore and if the semaphore is greater than zero, it can now gain access to the resource, but first it reduces the semaphore counter by 1 to indicate to others that it has occupied the resource.

When it is finished using the resource, the process increments the counter to indicate that the resource is now available. This mechanism, though, cannot protect against resource deadlocks, which could happen in the case where one process is occupying a resource and this process crashes before releasing the resource again.

As has just been mentioned, Oracle uses semaphores in order to control the access to shared memory (SGA). In principle, every Oracle process must be able to access the SGA, so there needs to be one semaphore for every Oracle process. Normally, an application allocates a semaphore set consisting of multiple semaphores rather than a single semaphore at a time.

So when an Oracle instance starts up, it allocates a semaphore set consisting of as many semaphores as there are processes as specified in the *init.ora processes* parameter. If the instance cannot allocate enough semaphores, then the Oracle instance will not start. Therefore, it is important that the kernel is set up so that it can allocate enough semaphores to handle all Oracle instances on the system.

Checking Semaphore Values

The kernel parameters that control the semaphore limits are specified on the system in the */proc/sys/kernel/sem* file. If this file is catted, the values for the parameters *semmsl*, *semmns*, *semopm* and *semmni* will be seen in that order.

```
cat /proc/sys/kernel/sem
```

```
250     32000   100     128
```

Where, in the example above:

- *semmsl*: 250, parameter set the maximum number of semaphores per set (array)
- *semmns*: 32000, parameter specifies the total number of semaphores on the Linux system
- *semopm*: 100, parameter indicates the maximum number of operations per semop calls, i.e. how many semaphores can be initialized with the same semop call
- *semmni*: 128, parameter sets the maximum number of semaphores sets

Alternatively, this information can be obtained using the *ipcs –ls* (InterProcess Communication status), which displays the information in a more user-friendly format:

```
linux-mlpb:~ # ipcs -ls

------ Semaphore Limits --------
max number of arrays = 128
max semaphores per array = 250
max semaphores system wide = 32000
max ops per semop call = 100
semaphore max value = 32767

linux-mlpb:~ #
```

The semaphore max value, 32767 in this example, is obsolete and is not used by Oracle.

The examples above show the current values of the running system. The persistent values of the system can be checked, meaning the values that will be set when the system reboots, by querying the *sysctl.conf* file.

```
linux-mlpb:~ # /sbin/sysctl -a | grep sem

kernel.sem = 250    32000   100     128
```

When the Linux server is prepared to host Oracle, the semaphore values will probably have to be changed depending on how many Oracle database instances will be running.

Metalink has the following document to control the semaphores values - Doc ID: 226209 Subject: *Linux: How to Check Current Shared Memory, Semaphore Values.* The next section will show which semaphore values Oracle recommends and how to change them.

Modifying Parameters for the Semaphores

Oracle recommends using the following values for the semaphore parameters.

- *semmsl*: 250 or the highest value of the *processes* Oracle initialization parameter and add 10 to the highest value.

- *semmns*: 32000 or the sum of all the *processes* Oracle initialization parameters of all the Oracle instances, add the largest value twice and also 10 for each database.
- *semopm*: 100 is the minimum value.
- *semmni*: 128 is the minimum value.

The kernel changes shall be performed with the root account. The values of the semaphores can be changed temporarily up to the next reboot by doing this:

```
linux-mlpb:~ # cd /proc/sys/kernel

linux-mlpb:/proc/sys/kernel # echo 250 32000 100 128 > sem
```

In the case where the values of the semaphores need to be kept after a system reboot, set the value in the file */etc/sysctl.conf*. Edit the line containing *kernel.sem* with the new values and then make changes active by doing */sbin/sysctl -p /etc/sysctl.conf*. This will apply the changes permanently. The values can be used for both 32-bit and 64-bit Linux versions.

Shared Memory Parameters

Oracle uses shared memory for the SGA (System Global Area) and the PGA (Program Global Area) as these areas need to be visible to all the database sessions. The kernel imposes restrictions on the shared memory segments, such as the maximum size and allocation number of segments.

The following shared memory parameters must be configured while preparing the Linux system to host an Oracle instance:

- *shmall*: Maximum amount of shared memory (in pages) that might be in use at any time on the system
- *shmmax*: Limits the size of each shared memory segment on the Linux system
- *shmmni*: Handles the maximum number of systemwide shared memory segments
- *shmseg*: Sets the maximum number of segments that one process possibly will attach

Again, these settings can be controlled by either using the *ipcs* command, by querying the */proc/sys/kernel/* virtual devices, or by querying the */etc/sysctl.conf* file as follows:

```
linux-mlpb:~ # ipcs -lm

------ Shared Memory Limits --------
max number of segments = 4096
max seg size (kbytes) = 67108864
max total shared memory (kbytes) = 17179869184
min seg size (bytes) = 1
linux-mlpb:~ #
```

The command *ipcs* provides information about the status of the inter-process communication facilities. With the option *–m*, the value shared memory segments can be displayed. It will give the following result:

```
oracle@orion ~]$ ipcs -m

------ Shared Memory Segments ------
key shmid   owner   perms   bytes    nattch
0xa3f82e08  800     oracle  640      938754048      2
```

The column description of the output is as follows:

- Key: Related to the hexadecimal or, more often, octal key used to identify a message queue, shared memory segments or a semaphore set.
- Shmid: The Shared Memory Identifier
- Owner: The owner of the Shared Memory
- Perms: Concerns the permissions related to that Shared Memory. The value is in octal.
- Bytes: The size allocated to that Shared Memory
- Nattach: The number of processes attached to the SHM. This value can increase when the number of sessions is increasing.
- The option *–q* shows only the message queues and *–s* only the semaphores.

Checking the files *in /proc/sys/kernel/*:

- linux-mlpb:~ # cat /proc/sys/kernel/shmall 4294967296
- linux-mlpb:~ # cat /proc/sys/kernel/shmmax 68719476736

- linux-mlpb:~ # cat /proc/sys/kernel/shmmni 4096
- linux-mlpb:~ #

Or querying the */etc/sysctl.conf* settings:

```
linux-mlpb:~ # /sbin/sysctl -a | grep shm
```

The *shmmax* parameter concerns the maximum size of each shared memory segment; the value of this parameter must be equal to or higher than the largest SGA on the Linux system. The parameter should not be too high as this will result in allocation failures. The value that Oracle recommends is 2 GB, but this depends on the configuration and size of the SGA.

For the *shmall* parameter, be sure that the value is correctly set on the system; otherwise, there will be out-of-memory messages on the system. Oracle recommends that on systems with 4 GB RAM to have a *shmall* of 2097152. The following formula can help find the correct value for the parameter.

```
 (Physical RAM Memory * 9) / Pagesize= SHMALL
```

Concerning the formula, be aware that at least 90% of the physical RAM shall be allocated and that the pagesize on Redhat Linux is 4KB (4096). The pagesize can be obtained using the *getconf* utility.

```
linux-mlpb:~ # getconf PAGESIZE
4096
linux-mlpb:~ #
```

Kernel Memory Parameter	**Non persistent file in */proc***	**Oracle recommendations**	**Minimum Values**
SHMMNI	*/proc/sys/kernel/shmmni*	4096	4096
SHMMAX	*/proc/sys/kernel/shmmax*	2147483648 (but depends on the largest SGA values)	Half the size of physical RAM memory (in bytes)
SHMALL	*/proc/sys/kernel/shmall*	2097152 (use the formula to find the values)	2097152

Table 2.7: *Kernel Memory Parameters*

Commands Used For Changing Values

Examine the actual values of the system shared memory by looking in the files *shmall*, *shmmax* and *shmmni* in the */proc* virtual device in */proc/sys/kernel.*

It is possible to change the values directly, until the next restart of the server, by simply changing these files:

```
linux-mlpb:~ # cd /proc/sys/kernel
linux-mlpb:/proc/sys/kernel # echo 2097152 > shmall
```

The given command can be performed on all the shared memory parameters. After the changes have been performed and the results have been tested on the database, it will be important to make the change persistent for the next reboot. In Redhat, edit the values in the */etc/sysctl.conf* and then make them permanent using the */sbin/sysctl* command. Alternatively, the */sbin/sysctl* command can be used with *–w* switch to make the changes directly.

```
/sbin/sysctl -w kernel.shmall = 2097152
```

Exam Advice: Be certain that knowledge on the semaphores and its tools is sufficient before taking the exam.

Network Parameters

The following network values must be set to enable IP port ranges to be allocated to Oracle Net with the parameter *ip_local_port_range*. The TCP/IP window parameters will need to be set for the read (rmem) size and write (wmem) size for the TCP/IP packets.

Kernel Network Parameters	Non-persistent File in */proc*	Oracle Recommendations
ip_local_port_range	*/proc/sys/net/ipv4/ip_local_port_range*	Minimum:1024 Maximum: 65000
rmem_default	*/proc/sys/net/core/rmem_default*	1048576
rmem_max	*/proc/sys/net/core/rmem_max*	1048576
wmem_default	*/proc/sys/net/core/wmem_default*	262144
wmem_max	*/proc/sys/net/core/wmem_max*	262144

Table 2.8: *Network Parameters for ip_local_port_range*

As with semaphores and shared memory parameters, it is possible to change the values in a non-persistent or persistent way. The non- persistent values can found this time in */proc/sys/net/core*. The persistent values can be changed by using the command below or by editing the file */etc/sysctl.conf* and executing the command *sbin/sysctl –p* to reload the new persistent values:

```
/sbin/sysctl -w net.core.rmem_default=1048576
```

File Handler Parameters

The kernel parameter *file-max*, also called *fs.file-max*, limits the maximum number of files that the Linux kernel can allocate. Oracle's background processes are continuously opening datafiles, redologs, archivelogs and log files such as the alertlog and trace files. The Linux default value is set to 65536 and this is also the value that Oracle recommends.

Kernel Network Parameters	Non persistent file in */proc*	Oracle recommendations (also Linux default value)
file-max	*/proc/sys/fs/file-max*	65536

Table 2.9: *File-max Kernel Network Parameters*

The value of the file handler can also be changed with the same method as the other kernel parameters. In the virtual devices, the non-persistent values are located in */proc/sys/fs/file-max*. It is possible to edit values in the file */proc/sys/fs/file-max* or by applying this command:

```
/sbin/sysctl -w fs.file-max=65536
```

Note that the values changed with the command */sbin/sysctl* will be applied immediately to the non-persistent and persistent values, but the command *sbin/sysctl –p* must be executed to reload the new persistent values.

Shell Limits Kernel Session

In Linux, it is possible to set limits for all users in the shell. The maximum number of files to be opened, the maximum number of processes that a user can have and the amount and type of memory and more can be limited. A user can query the current shell limit values by using the built-in command *ulimit* with the *–a* switch.

```
linux-mlpb:~ # ulimit -a
core file size          (blocks, -c) 0
data seg size           (kbytes, -d) unlimited
scheduling priority             (-e) 0
file size               (blocks, -f) unlimited
pending signals                 (-i) 71679
max locked memory       (kbytes, -l) 32
max memory size         (kbytes, -m) unlimited
open files                      (-n) 4096
pipe size            (512 bytes, -p) 8
POSIX message queues     (bytes, -q) 819200
real-time priority              (-r) 0
stack size              (kbytes, -s) 10240
cpu time               (seconds, -t) unlimited
max user processes              (-u) 2047
virtual memory          (kbytes, -v) unlimited
file locks                      (-x) unlimited
linux-mlpb:~ #
```

The Oracle user under Linux is particularly interested in two limits: the *nofile* and the *nproc* limits. The *nofile* limits the maximum number of files that the user can open at the same time. For Oracle, it means that the values shall be high enough to open *redologs* files, logs files, datafiles and also the parameter file. The *nproc* limits the number of processes that can be open at the same time. For an Oracle database, it means that the values shall be high enough to be able to start the background processes and all the database sessions. Oracle recommends that the values be set in the */etc/security/limits.conf* file.

Limits name in the file /etc/security/limits.conf	Description	Hard limit recommended by Oracle to be set in the file /etc/security/limits.conf
noproc	Maximum number of processes for specified user	65536
nofile	Maximum number of files for specified user	16384

Table 2.10: */etc/security/limits.conf File*

It is important to control and eventually increase the values of the system shell limits in the file */etc/security/limits.conf* with the following settings:

```
oracle              soft    nproc   2047
oracle              hard    nproc   16384
oracle              soft    nofile  4096
oracle              hard    nofile  65536
```

Concerning the shell limits, in the example above it is shown that there are soft and hard limits. Soft limits are values that the user gets when they initially log in to the shell, whereas the hard limits set the maximum value that can never be exceeded by the user. The current limits can be changed by using the *ulimit* command with the appropriate switch and limit value. Be aware that the *ulimit* switches are different in the Bourne and Bash shells when compared to the Korn shell.

Therefore, the following lines could be added to the */etc/profile* to override the soft limits that were specified in the */etc/security/limits.conf* file.

```
if [ $USER = "oracle" ]; then
        if [ $SHELL = "/bin/ksh" ]; then
              ulimit -p 16384
              ulimit -n 65536
        else
              ulimit -u 16384 -n 65536
        fi
fi
```

Notice that the changes will be effective after a new shell session is made and the Oracle instance is restarted in that shell.

Finally, Oracle recommends that the following lines are included in the file */etc/pam.d/login*:

```
session    required    /lib/security/pam_limits.so
session    required    pam_limits.so
```

> Exam Advice: Know how to set the kernel parameter as persistent and non-persistent, to give a definition of the parameters and how to set up the limits in the shell.

PAM stands for Pluggable Authentication Modules and provides a means of authenticating users as they log in. The configurations files for PAM are stored in */etc/pam.d/*. The file being worked here, */etc/pam.d/login*, concerns login services. The lines that were added above to the *etc/pam.d/login configuration* file actually cause PAM to read the settings in the */etc/security/limits.conf* file, and thereby set up the shell limits.

In case there are higher values than in the previously given parameters for the semaphores, shell limits and kernel values, do not change the values to the recommendation as this could have incidences on the system and the running applications.

Summary

This chapter covered users and groups of Linux operating systems. Users under Linux are examined in detail including a description of all their features as well as kinds of users. Next to be reviewed were file permissions and an explanation on types of files and file components. Finally, processes, which are files or programs that are in process, and various parameters in Linux were evaluated along with an introduction to semaphores.

Exercises

1. Create the groups and the Oracle user with the following settings:

- User: oracle
- Password: oracle
- Default group: oinstall
- Member of groups: dba, oper

2. Display the kernel settings of the Linux server. Change these values according to Oracle recommendations and make the changes persistent.
3. Display the shell limits of the Linux server and change them if necessary with the root account to the values recommended by Oracle.

Q&A

Questions

1. Lenny is a junior DBA and system administrator who needs to create an Oracle account on one's Linux server. Which of the following statements is true? Choose all that apply:

A. Since Oracle is an administrator account, it must have a user ID lower than 500.
B. He must use a user ID higher than 500 as the values under 500 reserved for Linux system accounts.
C. To create the Oracle user under Linux, he must use the command *create user.*
D. To create the Oracle user under Linux, he must use the command *useradd.*

2. What can the user *root* perform on a Linux system? Choose all that apply:

A. Perform system backups
B. Install Oracle software with the user *root*
C. Create, modify and suppress user's account and groups
D. Control and monitor diskspace, cpu load, memory usage, network connections, log files

3. Jack needs to change the values of the *umask* set on the Linux server to make the access secure so that only the file owners can read and write their own files. Look at the following values and chose the correct *umask*:

A. 022
B. 002

C. 066
D. 006

4. What are the two files that store the information about user accounts and passwords? Choose two answers that apply:

A. */etc/group*
B. */etc/hosts*
C. */etc/passwd*
D. */etc/shadow*

5. Henry, as junior Linux system administrator, needs to create a symbolic link from the source *users/oracle/source_file.txt* to the file *u01/oracle/1020/docs/link_file.txt*. Which command should he use?

A. *rm –fr /users/oracle/source_file.txt /u01/oracle/1020/docs/ link_file.txt*
B. *link -s /users/oracle/source_file.txt /u01/oracle/1020/docs/ link_file.txt*
C. *ln -s /users/oracle/source_file.txt /u01/oracle/1020/docs/ link_file.txt*
D. *ls /users/oracle/source_file.txt /u01/oracle/1020/docs/link_file.txt*

6. Where are the Linux system non-persistent files located?

A. */opt/var/*
B. */etc/*
C. */possessors*
D. */proc*

7. Choose the correct combination for the shared memory parameter and definition:

A. Parameter handles the maximum number of system wide shared memory segments
B. Parameter limits the size of each shared memory segment on the Linux system
C. Parameter limits the maximum amount of shared memory that might be in use at any time on the system
D. Parameter sets the maximum number of segments that one process may possibly attach

a. *shmseg*
b. *shmall*
c. *shmmax*
d. *shmmni*

8. What are the commands and the correct location for the persistent kernel parameters?

A. */etc/sysctl.conf*
B. */etc/systemctl.conf*
C. */sbin/sysctl*
D. */sbin/systemctl*

9. What is the correct value for the kernel parameter that handles the maximum number of files that the Linux kernel can handle?

A. *files.max* = 4096
B. *fs.file-max* = 65533
C. *fs.file-max* = 4096
D. *fs.file-max* = 65536

10. Which files must be updated to change the shell limits of the Oracle user? Choose two answers that apply:

A. */etc/pam.d/login*
B. */etc/sec/limits.conf*
C. */etc/pamela.d/login*
D. /etc/security/limits.conf

Answers

1. Lenny should be informed that B. He must use a user ID higher than 500 as the values under are reserved for Linux system accounts and D. To create the Oracle user under Linux, he must use the command useradd.

HINT: Review the section about the users and groups and particularly the rules about the UID and GID.

2. The correct answers are: A. Perform system backups, C. Create, modify and suppress user accounts and groups and D. Check and monitor diskspace, cpu load, memory usage, network connection, log files.

HINT: Study the section "Who is the Boss"?

3. Jack needs to change the values of the *umask* to C. 066 as this will result in each file creation being 600 or *rw-------*.

HINT: Review the section "*What is umask*"?

4. The two files that store the information about the user accounts and passwords are C. */etc/passwd* and D. */etc/shadow*.

HINT: Refer to the section concerning users and groups.

5. Henry should use the command C to create the link, C. ln -s /users/oracle/source_file.txt /u01/oracle/1020/docs/link_file.txt.

HINT: Read again the section "How to Create Links".

6. The Linux system's non-persistent files are located in D. */proc*.

HINT: The section on kernel parameters will help with this.

7. The correct combination for the shared memory parameter and definition is: A. Parameter handles the maximum number of systemwide shared memory segments / d. *shmmni*; B. Parameter limits the size of each shared memory segments on the Linux system / c. *shmmax*; C. Parameter limits the maximum amount of shared memory that might be in use at any time on the system / b. *shmall*; D. Parameter set the maximum number of segments that one process possibly will attach / a. *shmseg*

HINT: "Shared Memory Parameters" is the section to be reviewed.

8. The command and the correct location for the persistent kernel parameters are A. */etc/sysctl.conf*, and C. */sbin/sysctl*.

HINT: Again, review "Shared Memory Parameters".

9. The correct value for the kernel parameter that handles the maximum number of files is D. *fs.file-max* = 65536.

HINT: The section on file handler parameters is valuable here.

10. The files that must be updated to change the shell limits of the Oracle user are A. */etc/pam.d/login* and D. */etc/security/limits.conf*.

HINT: The section on shell limits kernel session is helpful.

Solutions to Exercises

1. Create the groups and the Oracle user with the following settings:

- User: oracle
- Password: oracle
- Default group: oinstall

- Member of groups: dba, oper

  The user root performs the following commands:

```
/usr/sbin/groupadd oinstall
/usr/sbin/groupadd dba
/usr/sbin/groupadd oper
/usr/sbin/useradd -g oinstall -G dba,oper oracle
```

2. Display the kernel settings of the Linux server. Change these values according to Oracle recommendations and make the changes persistent.

   As the user root, perform the following commands. Edit the file */etc/sysctl.conf* with the following values:

```
kernel.shmall = 2097152
kernel.shmmax = 2147483648
kernel.shmmni = 4096
kernel.sem = 250 32000 100 128
fs.file-max = 65536
net.ipv4.ip_local_port_range = 1024 65000
net.core.rmem_default = 1048576
net.core.rmem_max = 1048576
net.core.wmem_default = 262144
net.core.wmem_max = 262144
```

After that, restart the system or use the command *sbin/sysctl –p* to reload the new persistent values.

3. Display the shell limits of the Linux server and change them if necessary with the root account to the values recommended by Oracle.

   As the user root, perform the following commands. Edit the file */etc/security/limits.conf* with those values:

```
oracle              soft    nproc   2047
oracle              hard    nproc   16384
oracle              soft    nofile  1024
oracle              hard    nofile  65536
```

   After that, edit the file */etc/pam.d/login* with the values:

```
session    required     /lib/security/pam_limits.so
session    required     pam_limits.so
```

   When both files have been edited with root, edit the following file */etc/profile* with those values:

```
if [ $USER = "oracle" ]; then
        if [ $SHELL = "/bin/ksh" ]; then
              ulimit -p 16384
              ulimit -n 65536
        else
              ulimit -u 16384 -n 65536
        fi
fi
```

Linux Level 3: File Systems and Structures

CHAPTER

The chapter covers the following exam objectives:

1.3. Use common Linux commands
1.4. Write a simple bash shell script

File Systems

Linux supports many different types of file systems: ext2, ext3, FAT, NTFS, and ISO9660, to name but a few. Seen from the user's perspective, there is no real difference between the regular files on the underlying file systems. If the user issues a read function to retrieve a block from the file system, then there is no need to know the internal implementations of the underlying file system.

Instead, the read function (API) is implemented through a layer in the kernel, which interfaces with the underlying file system. This layer, which provides the API, is called the Virtual File System (VFS). Any file system which Linux supports must register with VFS and provide the underlying file system operations that can be accessed through VFS. The underlying file systems are either implemented directly in the kernel, as a loadable kernel module, or in user space, e.g. FUSE. The supported file systems in the Linux distribution can be seen by examining the file */proc/filesystems*. Every file system which has registered with VFS will be listed in this file.

In Chapter 8, *Managing Storage*, more details on file system features and types will be reviewed as well as what is mandatory for Oracle to work with in a file system.

Superblocks

Every file system has a structure called a superblock, which is used to store information about the file system type, the features that the file system supports, the size of the file system and other useful metadata. Without this information, accessing files on the file system would be impossible. If the superblock is lost or corrupted, then potentially there would be data loss. To counter this, the file system usually maintains multiple redundant copies of the superblocks. The contents of an *ext2/ext3* file system superblock can be examined by using the *dumpe2fs* command. The *–h* switch displays the superblock information in readable format.

```
root@linux-mlpb:~# dumpe2fs -h /dev/sda1
```

```
dumpe2fs 1.40.8 (13-Mar-2008)
Filesystem volume name:   <none>
Last mounted on:          <not available>
Filesystem UUID:          b6250886-c2ee-456a-8a15-126342b65a1d
Filesystem magic number:  0xEF53
Filesystem revision #:    1 (dynamic)
Filesystem features:      has_journal ext_attr resize_inode dir_index
filetype needs_recovery sparse_super large_file
Filesystem flags:         signed_directory_hash
Default mount options:    (none)
Filesystem state:         clean
Errors behavior:          Continue
Filesystem OS type:       Linux
Inode count:              9584640
Block count:              38321041
Reserved block count:     1916052
Free blocks:              36892006
Free inodes:              9377513
First block:              0
Block size:               4096
Fragment size:            4096
Reserved GDT blocks:      1014
Blocks per group:         32768
Fragments per group:      32768
Inodes per group:         8192
Inode blocks per group:   256
Filesystem created:       Thu May 22 15:57:25 2008
Last mount time:          Wed Feb  4 10:15:59 2009
Last write time:          Wed Feb  4 10:15:59 2009
Mount count:              13
Maximum mount count:      31
Last checked:             Tue Aug 19 23:40:50 2008
Check interval:           15552000 (6 months)
Next check after:         Sun Feb 15 22:40:50 2009
Reserved blocks uid:      0 (user root)
Reserved blocks gid:      0 (group root)
First inode:              11
Inode size:               128
Journal inode:            8
First orphan inode:       2000849
Default directory hash:   tea
Directory Hash Seed:      4df07f77-8d1d-41f3-8ecb-d9f773d60466
Journal backup:           inode blocks
Journal size:             128M
```

```
root@linux-mlpb:~#
```

To see the location of the superblocks, use the *dumpe2fs* command without any switches and filter for superblocks with *grep*.

```
root@linux-mlpb:~# dumpe2fs /dev/sda1| grep -i superblock

dumpe2fs 1.40.8 (13-Mar-2008)
  Primary superblock at 0, Group descriptors at 1-10
  Backup superblock at 32768, Group descriptors at 32769-32778
  Backup superblock at 98304, Group descriptors at 98305-98314
  Backup superblock at 163840, Group descriptors at 163841-163850
  Backup superblock at 229376, Group descriptors at 229377-229386
  Backup superblock at 294912, Group descriptors at 294913-294922
  Backup superblock at 819200, Group descriptors at 819201-819210
  Backup superblock at 884736, Group descriptors at 884737-884746
  Backup superblock at 1605632, Group descriptors at 1605633-1605642
  Backup superblock at 2654208, Group descriptors at 2654209-2654218
  Backup superblock at 4096000, Group descriptors at 4096001-4096010
  Backup superblock at 7962624, Group descriptors at 7962625-7962634
  Backup superblock at 11239424, Group descriptors at 11239425-11239434
  Backup superblock at 20480000, Group descriptors at 20480001-20480010
  Backup superblock at 23887872, Group descriptors at 23887873-23887882
root@linux-mlpb:~#
```

Here is shown the primary superblock and multiple redundant copies. From the two listings above, there are a few interesting things to notice. First, the block size of the file system is 4096 bytes. Second, 10 blocks are used as block group descriptors, which are structures that contain more metadata about the file system including where on the device the inode table is located. More about the inode table in the next section.

Third, the device is divided into block groups by the file system, and at each block group boundary, the superblock is duplicated. Block groups are used by file systems to help reduce fragmentation of the file system.

Inodes

On Linux, as well as on UNIX, there is a data structure called an inode, which the file system uses to store fundamental information about a file. So if the system needs to read a block from a file, it must first discover the inode number. The inode number is used to look up the inode table and retrieve the inode structure.

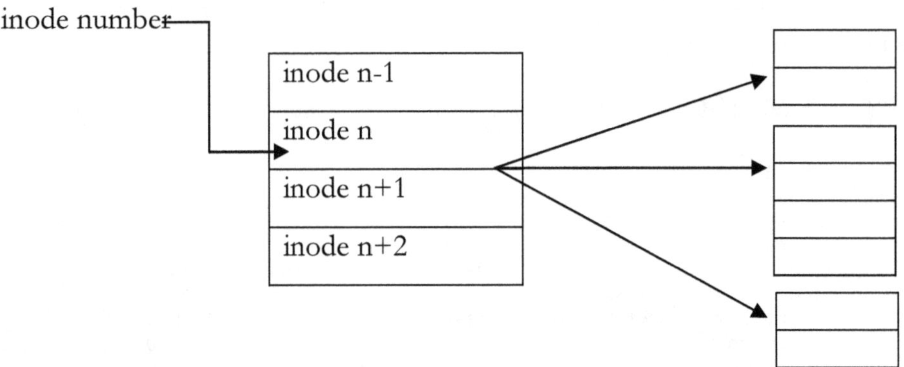

Figure 3.1: *Diagram of Inode Table*

Inodes contain the following information for Linux files:

- Permissions (mode)
- Owner
- Group
- Size of the file
- Time stamps of latest access, change and modification
- Type of the file (binary, directory, text, and such)
- Count of the number of hard links referencing the file
- Pointers to the disk blocks that store the file's contents

However, inodes do not store the name of the file. So how does the DBA convert between a file name and an inode number and vice versa?

The answer is partly from the information in the superblock, and partly in the fact that directories in Linux are actually just files that contain an array of inode numbers and filenames for files within the directory. If the superblock listing from the previous *dumpe2fs –h /dev/sda1* command is examined, it will be evident that the superblock contains the value of the first inode: 11 in this example. This means that the inode number 11 in the inode table points to the root of the file system: "/". The data contents of the "/" directory will contain inode numbers and filenames for the files and directories in the root directory. By this method, the directory hierarchy can be traversed until the inode number is found for the file that the DBA is looking for.

Now reading a block from a file, e.g. */home/export/tom/work/project1.txt*, would require starting at the root inode to access the *root* directory, then looking up the *home* directory inode to access the *home* directory, then looking up the export inode number to access the *export* directory, and so on, until eventually the inode for *project1.txt* is found. Obviously, this is not very efficient, so Linux uses two structures, called the inode cache and the directory cache, which are stored in memory and accessed by the VFS to quickly lookup files and directories.

Finally, be aware that as a user, the inode number of a file can easily be found by simply using the command *ls –i.*

```
oracle@linux-mlpb:~/Desktop> ls -i file.txt
86674 file.txt
```

Alternatively, the *stat* system call, implemented through VFS, will also provide this information and more.

```
oracle@linux-mlpb:~/Desktop> stat file.txt

File: `file.txt'
  Size: 6804         Blocks: 24         IO Block: 4096   regular file
Device: 803h/2051d  Inode: 86479       Links: 1
Access: (0644/-rw-r--r--)  Uid: ( 1000/ oracle2)   Gid: (  100/   users)
Access: 2009-02-15 13:57:45.000000000 +0100
Modify: 2009-02-15 13:57:45.000000000 +0100
Change: 2009-02-15 13:57:45.000000000 +0100
```

It is possible to use the inode number in the case where a file was created with special characters and cannot be deleted with a *find* command. See the example below.

```
oracle@linux-mlpb:~/Desktop> touch "\+Blue \-+-+9\eyes"
oracle@linux-mlpb:~/Desktop> ls -i *
86950 \+Blue \-+-+9\eyes
oracle@linux-mlpb:~/Desktop> find . -inum 86950  -exec rm -i {} \;
rm: remove regular empty file `./\\+Blue \\-+-+9\\eyes'? Y
oracle@linux-mlpb:~/Desktop> ls -al *
```

Journalized File Systems

Modern file systems like JFS (IBM Journalized File System) and ext3 use a circular log, also called a journal, to keep track of all changes applied before they are committed to the file system. Activities that are kept in the journal are updates that are intended to be performed but have not yet been committed to the file system.

Imagine that the system crashes while a directory is being deleted. The journal recorded that the intention was to delete this directory, but it was only partially deleted before the crash occurred. Maybe the directory entry was removed, but the inode entry was never marked as free. When the system recovers, it can read the journal and continue to perform the delete of the directory as intended, thereby maintaining data integrity, i.e. consistency.

Journaling is analogous to the redo log in Oracle, but there are also many differences. From the previous superblock example, it can be seen that in this case, the journal is located at inode number 8, and the journal size is 128 MB.

Handling File Systems

When file systems are considered, often storage on physical block devices, i.e. hard disks, CDROM, DVD, SAN, and more come to mind, but a file system can also be a virtual file system, which is not connected to a physical device. The obvious one that springs to mind is *procfs*, which provides access to memory structures within the kernel. The user accesses this through the virtual directory */proc* and through *procfs*, even though they might not be aware of this. However, as system administrator, the user will probably be mostly concerned with physical device storage and how this storage is organized and structured.

One very useful command is *fdisk* (fixed disk command), which allows the administrator to create, display and delete partitions, or subdivisions, of a physical disk. On each partition there can be separate file systems. A partition can be a physical primary partition or a logical partition. A logical partition is a subdivision of a primary partition. The *fdisk* utility enables the DBA to also change the partition type and to specify whether the partition is logical or physical.

Linux has a naming convention to identify devices connected to the different interfaces like IDE, SCSI or SATA, and such. For devices that are connected to an IDE interface, Linux will identify them as */dev/hd[a-h]* where *a* is the first device, *b* is the second and so on. For the devices connected on a SCSI or SATA controller, it will be */dev/sd[a-p]*. Therefore, the first IDE disk will have the name */dev/hda* and for the second, it will be */dev/hdb.*

So assuming there is one disk on a SCSI or SATA interface, this disk will be identified as */dev/sda.* This disk could then be partitioned as */dev/sda1, /dev/sda2,* and so on, where each partition on the disk is given a number so the partition can be easily identified.

Now primary partitions are identified on the disk by the numbers 1-4. Logical partitions are identified by numbers greater than 5. As has already been mentioned, an extended partition is really just a primary partition that can be subdivided into logical partitions. The following example using *fdisk –l* to list the disk partitions of */dev/sda* might illustrate the point.

```
root@linux-mlpb:~# fdisk -l /dev/sda
Disk /dev/sda: 160.0 GB, 160041885696 bytes
255 heads, 63 sectors/track, 19457 cylinders
Units = cylinders of 16065 * 512 = 8225280 bytes
Disk identifier: 0x302e3120

   Device Boot      Start         End      Blocks   Id  System
/dev/sda1   *           1       19083   153284166   83  Linux
/dev/sda2           19084       19457     3004155    5  Extended
/dev/sda5           19084       19457     3004123+  82  Linux swap / Solaris

root@linux-mlpb:~#
```

In the example above, partition 1 is a Linux primary partition, partition 2 is an extended (primary) partition, which is further subdivided into the first logical partition, i.e. partition 5, which is a Linux Swap partition.

In the example above, notice the partition types: Linux, Extended, Linux swap. In fact, *fdisk* supports many different partition types (systems).

```
 0  Empty           1e  Hidden W95 FAT1 80  Old Minix       be  Solaris boot
 1  FAT12           24  NEC DOS         81  Minix / old Lin bf  Solaris
 2  XENIX root      39  Plan 9          82  Linux swap / So c1  DRDOS/sec (FAT-
 3  XENIX usr       3c  PartitionMagic  83  Linux           c4  DRDOS/sec (FAT-
 4  FAT16 <32M      40  Venix 80286     84  OS/2 hidden C:  c6  DRDOS/sec (FAT-
 5  Extended        41  PPC PReP Boot   85  Linux extended  c7  Syrinx
 6  FAT16           42  SFS             86  NTFS volume set da  Non-FS data
 7  HPFS/NTFS       4d  QNX4.x          87  NTFS volume set db  CP/M / CTOS / .
 8  AIX             4e  QNX4.x 2nd part 88  Linux plaintext de  Dell Utility
 9  AIX bootable    4f  QNX4.x 3rd part 8e  Linux LVM       df  BootIt
 a  OS/2 Boot Manag 50  OnTrack DM      93  Amoeba          e1  DOS access
```

```
 b  W95 FAT32       51  OnTrack DM6 Aux 94  Amoeba BBT      e3  DOS R/O
 c  W95 FAT32 (LBA) 52  CP/M            9f  BSD/OS          e4  SpeedStor
 e  W95 FAT16 (LBA) 53  OnTrack DM6 Aux a0  IBM Thinkpad hi eb  BeOS fs
 f  W95 Ext'd (LBA) 54  OnTrackDM6      a5  FreeBSD         ee  EFI GPT
10  OPUS            55  EZ-Drive        a6  OpenBSD         ef  EFI (FAT-12/16/
11  Hidden FAT12    56  Golden Bow      a7  NeXTSTEP        f0  Linux/PA-RISC b
12  Compaq diagnost 5c  Priam Edisk     a8  Darwin UFS      f1  SpeedStor
14  Hidden FAT16 <3 61  SpeedStor       a9  NetBSD          f4  SpeedStor
16  Hidden FAT16    63  GNU HURD or Sys ab  Darwin boot     f2  DOS secondary
17  Hidden HPFS/NTF 64  Novell Netware  b7  BSDI fs         fd  Linux raid auto
18  AST SmartSleep  65  Novell Netware  b8  BSDI swap       fe  LANstep
1b  Hidden W95 FAT3 70  DiskSecure Mult bb  Boot Wizard hid ff  BBT
1c  Hidden W95 FAT3 75  PC/IX
```

The *fdisk* command can be called interactively from the Bash shell. It has a text-based interface that enables manipulation of the Linux partitions:

```
fdisk /dev/sda
```

The number of cylinders for this disk is set to 1044. There is nothing wrong with that, but this is larger than 1024 and could, in certain setups, cause problems with:

1. Software that runs at boot time, e.g. old versions of LILO
2. Booting and partitioning software from other OSs (e.g. DOS *fdisk, OS/2 fdisk)*

```
Command (m for help): m
Command action
```

```
   a   toggle a bootable flag
   b   edit bsd disklabel
   c   toggle the dos compatibility flag
   d   delete a partition
   l   list known partition types
   m   print this menu
   n   add a new partition
   o   create a new empty DOS partition table
   p   print the partition table
   q   quit without saving changes
   s   create a new empty Sun disklabel
   t   change a partition's system id
   u   change display/entry units
   v   verify the partition table
   w   write table to disk and exit
   x   extra functionality (experts only)
```

The *fdisk* command can also be used with specific switches like *–l* to output device characteristics and partitions with the cylinder information. The *–u* switch shows the same information presented in sectors, rather than cylinders.

```
fdisk -l  /dev/sda
```

```
Disk /dev/sda: 8589 MB, 8589934592 bytes
255 heads, 63 sectors/track, 1044 cylinders
Units = cylinders of 16065 * 512 = 8225280 bytes
Disk identifier: 0x0009fac0

   Device Boot      Start         End      Blocks   Id  System
/dev/sda1               1          64      514048+  82  Linux swap
/dev/sda2   *          65         717     5245222+  83  Linux
/dev/sda3             718        1044     2626627+  83  Linux
```

```
fdisk -l -u /dev/sda
```

```
Disk /dev/sda: 8589 MB, 8589934592 bytes
255 heads, 63 sectors/track, 1044 cylinders, total 16777216 sectors
Units = sectors of 1 * 512 = 512 bytes
Disk identifier: 0x0009fac0

Device Boot             Start         End      Blocks   Id  System
/dev/sda1                  63     1028159      514048+  82  Linux swap
/dev/sda2   *         1028160    11518604     5245222+  83  Linux
/dev/sda3            11518605    16771859     2626627+  83  Linux
```

It is also possible to see the SCSI driver's supported partitions in the file */proc/partitions*. Here is the following output from a RedHat server:

```
[oracle@orion ~]$ more /proc/partitions
major minor  #blocks  name
```

```
   8     0   16777216 sda
   8     1     522081 sda1
   8     2     522112 sda2
   8     3   15727635 sda3
   8    16   20971520 sdb
   8    17   20964793 sdb1
   8    32   20971520 sdc
   8    33   20964793 sdc1
   8    48   10485760 sdd
   8    49   10482381 sdd1
 253     0    2097152 dm-0
 253     1    2097152 dm-1
 253     2    2097152 dm-2
 253     3    2097152 dm-3
 253     4    4227072 dm-4
 253     5    2097152 dm-5
 253     6   20905984 dm-6
 253     7   10485760 dm-7
```

File System Creation

Once the partitions have been created, then most likely at least one of them should be used as a file system. To create a file system, format the partition and in Linux, this is done by using the *mkfs* (make file systems) command.

```
mkfs [ -V ] [ -t fstype ] [ fs-options ] filesys [ blocks ]
```

Here are the explanations of the columns of the *mkfs* command:

- -V: Generates verbose output of the *make* commands with details under the file system creation
- -t fstype: Used to specify the type of file system that should be created. By default it is ext2, but can be specified as ext3, msdos, reiser, jfs and many others types.
- fs-options: The *mkfs* utility actually calls other file system-specific utilities in order to create the file system. These file system-specific utilities can also accept additional options, *fs-options*. Consult the specific file system utility to know which options are supported, but most support the *–c* switch (to check the device of bad blocks), *-v* switch (to get even more verbose output) and *–l filename* (to read the bad blocks from a file).

The *filesys* argument is the name of the partition that needs to be formatted, e.g. */dev/sda3*. The *blocks* argument is used to specify the file system size in the event that it cannot be auto-detected.

The following example creates an ext3 journaled file system on the */dev/sda3* partition, then checks and reports any corrupt blocks on the file system:

```
# mkfs -t ext3 /dev/sda3 -c
```

mount and *umount*

After the file system is created, mount the volume, meaning attach the volume to a path. It is also possible to mount other physical storage like CD-ROM, DVD, USB or floppy disks. The command *mount* allows the administrator to mount the volumes.

This example connects the root of the floppy disk to the path */mnt/floppy*. Then the user can switch to the mount point and list the floppy contents.

```
$ mount /dev/fd0 /mnt/floppy
$ cd /mnt/floppy
$ ls
Autorun.inf  Drivers  Manual
$
```

In this example, a CD-ROM drive is mounted as an ISO9660 file system by using the *–t* switch. Normally, the *–t* switch is not needed because *mount* is able to guess the file system type, or it can read type information from configuration files; in some cases, from the superblock.

```
# mount -t iso9660 /dev/cdrom /mnt/cdrom
```

Disconnecting, or unmounting, the volume is performed with the simple command *umount.*

```
# umount /mnt/cdrom
```

One very practical use of the *mount* command is to be able to examine the contents of an ISO image file by mounting the file through a loop device and then accessing the files through the mount point.

```
# mount -o loop disk1.iso /mnt/disk1
```

Note: A loop device is a pseudo-device which makes a file accessible as a block device.

The system can be forced to permanently mount a volume after each restart of the system by making changes in the file */etc/fstab.* When a Linux system reboots, it issues a *mount –a* (or *automount* in some distributions) as part of the reboot process. The *mount –a* instructs the system to mount all devices in the */etc/fstab* file automatically unless the device has the *noauto* flag.

```
Oracle@linux-mlpb:~/ > cat /etc/fstab

LABEL=/            /            ext3    defaults          1 1
tmpfs              /dev/shm     tmpfs   defaults          0 0
devpts             /dev/pts     devpts  gid=5,mode=620    0 0
sysfs              /sys         sysfs   defaults          0 0
proc               /proc        proc    defaults          0 0
/dev/sda1          /mnt/usb     vfat    noauto            0 0
LABEL=SWAP-hda2    swap         swap    defaults          0 0
```

So in the example above, all the volumes are automatically mounted at reboot except for the USB device on */dev/sda1*.

If mounting the USB device is desired, just issue *mount /dev/sda1* since *mount* will read the *fstab* file to discover the filesystem type (*vfat*) and the mount point (*/mnt/usb*).

Column 4 of the *fstab* file contains options for the *mount* command:

- *auto* and *noauto* specify whether the file system is mounted automatically at restart.
- *ro* and *rw* specify if the file system is mounted read only or read-write.
- *exec* and *noexec* specify whether binaries can be executed or not.
- *sync* and *async* specify whether input and output operations are performed synchronously or asynchronously. The asynchronous method is advisable on Oracle physical files, but the synchronous option should be used for the Oracle binaries.
- *user* and *nouser* specify if someone is a normal user, and only *root* can mount the device.
- *defaults* option is equivalent to *rw, exec, auto, nouser, async.*

Column 5 is used for the *dump* options. When the backup command *dump* is used to backup the system, only file systems with a value of 1 will be backed up. File systems set to 0 will be skipped.

Column 6 is used by the *fsck* command. At reboot, the *fsck* is used to check consistency of the file systems. If the value is 0, then no check is performed. The root partition should always be set to 1, i.e. checked firsts, and other partitions should be set to 2.

Error Correction on File Systems

"File system check" or "file system consistency check" using the *fsck* command can help with correcting errors on the file systems. As was learned above, the */etc/fstab* entries determine how the file systems are checked during reboot, but this command can also be used after a reboot. However, it is necessary to unmount the partition before consistency checks can be performed. If the "/" root file system needs to be checked, then boot on a Linux CD-ROM in single user mode and perform the *fsck* operation. This is because the root file system cannot be unmounted while the system is running.

On a non-root partition, */dev/sdb2* mounted on */u02/oradata*, the *fsck* command might be run using the following options:

```
umount /u02/oradata
fsck -t ext3 /dev/sdb2
```

It is good to note that large partitions that are controlled with *fsck* at the system boot time will take much longer than smaller partitions. When journalized file systems like ext3 are being used, this process can be reduced significantly.

Swap

Random access memory (RAM) in Linux is divided into chunks of memory known as pages. Memory pages are used to hold process code, data files and constants, as well as variables allocated by the process or stack. Process code, also called text, data files and constants, are all associated with a file on the hard disk; i.e. they are either a copy of information that is already stored in a file or alternatively, if they have been modified in memory, they can be flushed back into a file and then easily retrieved. However, variables like memory allocated by a process are not backed up by a file and are known as anonymous memory pages. So memory is divided, roughly speaking, into file-backed chunks and anonymous chunks.

Additionally, chunks in memory are considered clean if the version in memory is exactly the same as the file version on the disk. They are considered dirty if the version in memory has been modified. In order for the chunk to be marked clean again, it first needs to be flushed to disk.

When a process needs to allocate memory, the kernel will try to allocate from free memory, but failing that it will attempt to allocate memory by discarding clean chunks since there is a reliable copy of these on disk. If no suitable clean chunks are available, then it must use dirty chunks by first flushing them to disk, or making them clean, and then discarding them. Nevertheless, the kernel tries to avoid this situation because disk I/O is much slower than memory access.

Anonymous pages, which are not associated with a file on the disk, can also be swapped out of memory to an area called the swap area. This area is usually set up as a special partition on the hard disk, which is formatted as a swap partition where the kernel can quickly dump, or retrieve, chunks of anonymous memory. Without this swap area, the physical memory would become cluttered with anonymous memory that could not be flushed to disk.

Therefore, it is very important that the Linux system has sufficient swap area defined, especially for programs that allocate large amounts of memory.

Use the *fdisk –l* command to see if any partition has been formatted as a swap partition, or alternatively, use *swapon –s* to display current swap usage.

```
# swapon -s
Filename                                Type            Size    Used
Priority
/dev/sda5                               partition       3004112 39864   -1
#
```

> Exam Advice: Be able to describe the basics of a file system configuration file in */etc/fstab*, the files used by Linux; also the files located in the virtual device */proc* and the *fsck* command purposes and advantages.

Startup Sequences for Linux

Linux servers built on x86 architectures usually start up this way: after the server is powered up, it starts to initialize the Bios (Basic Input Output System) which is a Read Only Memory chip that contains all the hardware definitions of the motherboard. The BIOS searches through the list of bootable devices looking for a specially formatted block called the master boot record (MBR) and reads it. Once the BIOS reads the MBR into memory, control is passed to the MBR. The MBR is then in charge of either loading the remainder of the operating system, or loading another program, called a bootloader, which is then responsible for continuing the startup process.

There are two common bootloaders used by Linux: LILO (Linux Loader) and GRUB (Grand Unified Bootloader). LILO accesses configuration information directly in the MBR and uses this to load the system, whereas GRUB uses the MBR to do some initializations before accessing the remainder of the grub configuration from the disk.

Both LILO and GRUB allow the user to install multiple operating systems on the server and provides a choice of which one to load when booting. Once the

Linux kernel is loaded, it will start the *init* process and load the binaries in */sbin*. The *initialization* process, or *init* process, has a PID (Process ID) value of one (1), as it is the first process started. The *init* process completes the remainder of the startup and shutdown operations by reading the definitions in the file */etc/inittab* which determine what actions to take at each run level. Run levels, also called *init* modes, are explained in the next section.

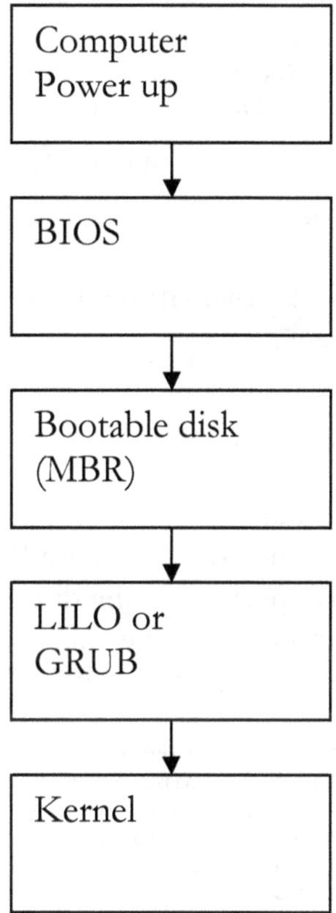

Figure 3.2: *Init Process Diagram*

init Modes

When Linux starts, it goes through a number of initialization modes, also called run levels, so that it can start up services and applications in the correct order. Unless instructed otherwise by the bootloader (LILO or GRUB), the *init* process will read the */etc/inittab* file to determine the default run level, usually 3 or 5. The *inittab* file will usually contain an entry like this:

```
#
# inittab       This file describes how the INIT process should set up
#               the system in a certain run-level.
#
# Author:       Miquel van Smoorenburg, <miquels@drinkel.nl.mugnet.org>
#               Modified for RHS Linux by Marc Ewing and Donnie Barnes
#

# Default runlevel. The runlevels used by RHS are:
#   0 - halt (Do NOT set initdefault to this)
#   1 - Single user mode
#   2 - Multiuser, without NFS (The same as 3, if you do not have
networking)
#   3 - Full multiuser mode
#   4 - unused
#   5 - X11
#   6 - reboot (Do NOT set initdefault to this)
#
id:3:initdefault:

# System initialization.
si::sysinit:/etc/rc.d/rc.sysinit
```

So in this example, the system will boot up to run level 3 (multi-user mode). On Red Hat Linux, the default run levels are 0-6, and the processes that are started by the run level are specified in the directory */etc/rc.d/rcX.d* where X is the run level. A symbolic link shall be made between the script located in */etc/rc.d/init.d/* and the directory */etc/rc.d/rcX.d* (X is the run level).

```
- /etc/rc.d/rc0.d # run level 0 : turn your computer off.
- /etc/rc.d/rc1.d # run level 1 : single user mode
- /etc/rc.d/rc2.d # run level 2 : multi user mode w/o NFS
- /etc/rc.d/rc3.d # run level 3 : multi user mode w/NFS
- /etc/rc.d/rc4.d # run level 4 : is for custom use
- /etc/rc.d/rc5.d # run level 5 : GUI X11-window mode
- /etc/rc.d/rc6.d # run level 6 : reboot your computer.
```

Note: The scripts in *\/etc/rc.d/rc.sysinit* are run during system initialization, i.e. before any scripts are run in the run level directories. This is defined in the *inittab* file with the entry *si::sysinit:/etc/rc.d/rc.sysinit*.

The run level directory contains the scripts used to stop and start the various applications. When a script starts the letter "S" (start), it will be used to start a service, but if it starts with the letter "K" (kill), it will be used to stop a service. By adding a number after the letter, the DBA can decide in what order a program will be started. As seen in this example of the */etc/rc3.d*, the *S10network* will be started before the *S12syslog*:

```
K02NetworkManager  K87auditd            S10network
S80collabnet_subversion
K05saslauthd       K88wpa_supplicant    S12syslog          S80sendmail
K05wdaemon         K89netplugd          S13irqbalance      S85gpm
K10dc_server       K89rdisc             S13portmap         S90crond
K10psacct          K90bluetooth         S14nfslock         S90xfs
K12dc_client       K91capi              S15mdmonitor       S95anacron
K20nfs             K94diskdump          S18rpcidmapd       S95atd
K24irda            K99readahead         S19rpcgssd         S97messagebus
K35smb             K99readahead_early   S19vmware-tools    S97rhnsd
K35winbind         S00microcode_ctl     S25netfs           S98cups-config-
daemon
K40smartd          S01sysstat           S26apmd            S98haldaemon
K50netdump         S02lvm2-monitor      S26lm_sensors      S99IBMSCMclient
K50tecad_logfile   S05kudzu             S28autofs          S99local
K73ypbind          S05openibd           S44acpid           S99tecad_logfile
K74ipmi            S06cpuspeed          S55cups            S99Tivoli_lcf1
K74nscd            S08iptables          S55sshd
K74ntpd            S09isdn              S56rawdevices
K85mdmpd           S09pcmcia            S56xinetd
```

The start and stop files present in the */etc/rc.d/rc<run-level>/* are actually links that point to the real startup files located in */etc/rc.d/init.d.*

```
ls -al /etc/rc.d/rc3.d/*network
lrwxrwxrwx  1 root root 17 Sep 19 16:14 /etc/rc.d/rc3.d/S10network ->
../init.d/network
```

During a system start, the *init* process calls the *init.d* scripts with a 'start' argument. During a shutdown, the *init* process calls the scripts with a 'stop' argument. See the following example of an Oracle start/stop script:

```
#!/bin/sh

ORA_HOME=/u01/app/oracle/product/10.2.0/db_1
ORA_OWNER=oracle

if [ ! -f $ORA_HOME/bin/dbstart ]
then
    echo "Oracle startup: Can't be started"
    exit
fi

case "$1" in
    'start')
        # Start the Oracle databases:
        su - $ORA_OWNER -c "$ORA_HOME/bin/dbstart $ORA_HOME"
        ;;
    'stop')
        # Stop the Oracle databases:
```

```
        su - $ORA_OWNER -c "$ORA_HOME/bin/dbshut $ORA_HOME"
        ;;
esac
```

With the root account, the *init* command can be used to change the run level from 1 to 5. The run level 0 will halt the system properly before shutting down the power, and run level 6 will reboot the system.

```
# change your run level from 5 to 3
init 3
```

> Exam Advice: Be able to describe the initialization, the role of the *inittab*, and explain the *init* levels and startup of a Linux system.

OS Patches

Depending on the Linux distribution that is being used, patches can be obtained to keep the system updated. It is recommended that Linux servers are kept updated on a regular basis. If Enterprise Linux, supported by the Unbreakable Linux Network (ULN), is being used, then patches can be received automatically from the website https://linux.oracle.com.

Summary

This chapter described various file systems and the structures associated with files such as superblocks and inodes. Also covered were details on how to handle file systems, how to swap RAM, and how to load the system during startup using Linux Loader (LILO) or Grand Unified Bootloader (GRUB). Finally, initialization modes, or run levels, were explained and the processes involved in startup.

Exercises

1. Create a new partition, make the file system and mount the partition.
2. Perform a *fsck* on one of the mount points. (not on */root*)

3. Change the initialization mode from 5, 3, 2 and up to 1 dynamically with the proper command.

Q&A

Questions

1. What are the benefits of using a journalized file system? Choose all that apply:

A. Decreases memory usage
B. Keeps the changes on the file system recorded before they are committed
C. Even if the system crashes, the journalized file system helps to maintain data integrity
D. Helps *fsck* run faster during the consistency checks

2. What command is used to create disk partitions?

A. *partitions*
B. f*ormatdisk*
C. *fdisk*
D. *desc_disk*

3. What is the command to build a file system?

A. *make*
B. *mkfs*
C. *makefile*
D. *mkofs*

4. Which file stores the different file system to be mounted? Choose all that apply:

A. */etc/hosts*
B. */etc/passwd*
C. */etc/mountlist*
D. */etc/fstab*

5. What commands allow the user to attach or disconnect from a file system on a specific location like */u02/oracle/product/*? Choose all that apply:

A. *bringfs*
B. *unmoun*t

C. *mount*
D. *umount*

6. What command will help perform a consistency check of the file system?

A. *ctl_fs*
B. *mkfs*
C. *fsck*
D. *iostat*

7. What is the value of the *init* PID (Process ID)?

A. 2
B. 3
C. 4
D. 1

8. Which of the following files provides the default value of the system's run level? Choose all that apply:

A. */etc/inittab*
B. */etc/rc.d/rc3.d*
C. */etc/rc.d/rc.sysinit*
D. */etc/rc0.d*

9. What are the prefixes on the scripts to perform start/stop of the application in the directories */etc/rc.d/rc3.d*? Choose all that apply:

A. S
B. X
C. K
D. Z

10. With what command can the run level be changed from 3 to 5 dynamically?

A. *init 3 5*
B. *initz 5*
C. *init 3*
D. *init 5*

Answers

1. The correct answers are: B. Keeps the changes on the file system recorded before they are committed; C. Even if the system crashes the journalized

file system helps to maintain data integrity; and D. Helps *fsck* to be faster during the consistency checks.

HINT: Review the section on journalized file systems.

2. Correct answer is C. *fdisk.*

HINT: The section "Handling File Systems" is useful for this question.

3. Correct answer is B. *mkfs.*

HINT: Refer to the section on file system creation.

4. Correct answer is D. */etc/fstab.*

HINT: The section on *mount* and *umount* will help answer this question.

5. C. *mount* and D. *umount* are the correct answers.

HINT: Once again, refer to the section on *mount* and *umount.*

6. C. *fsck* is the only correct answer.

HINT: Read the section "Error Correction on File Systems".

7. Only D. 1 is correct.

HINT: The section "Startup Sequences of Linux" has the answer.

8. A. */etc/inittab.*

HINT: Again, refer to "Startup Sequences of Linux" in this chapter.

9. A. S and C. K are the correct answers.

HINT: *Init* modes is where to read for this answer.

10. D. init 5 is the only correct answer.

HINT: The section on *init* modes will also help with this question.

Solutions for Exercises

1. Create a new partition, make the file system and mount the partition.

Since there may not be free space available on the system, an example of creating a 128MB primary partition is shown here where there is free space on a disk which currently has a root partition and a swap partition.

```
# fdisk /dev/hda
```

```
The number of cylinders for this disk is set to 9729.
```

There is nothing wrong with that, but this is larger than 1024 and could, in certain setups, cause problems with:

- Software that runs at boot time (e.g., old versions of LILO)
- Booting and partitioning software from other OSs, e.g., DOS *fdisk*, OS/2 *fdisk*

```
Command (m for help): p

Disk /dev/hda: 80.0 GB, 80026361856 bytes
255 heads, 63 sectors/track, 9729 cylinders
Units = cylinders of 16065 * 512 = 8225280 bytes

   Device Boot      Start         End      Blocks   Id  System
/dev/hda1   *           1        1912    15358108+  83  Linux
/dev/hda2            1913        2167     2048287+  82  Linux swap / Solaris

Command (m for help): n

Command action
   e   extended
   p   primary partition (1-4)
p
Partition number (1-4): 3
First cylinder (2168-9729, default 2168):
Using default value 2168
Last cylinder or +size or +sizeM or +sizeK (2168-9729, default 9729): +128M

Command (m for help): w

The partition table has been altered!

Calling ioctl() to re-read partition table.

WARNING: Re-reading the partition table failed with error 16: Device or
resource busy.
The kernel still uses the old table.
The new table will be used at the next reboot.
Syncing disks.

# fdisk -l /dev/hda

Disk /dev/hda: 80.0 GB, 80026361856 bytes
255 heads, 63 sectors/track, 9729 cylinders
Units = cylinders of 16065 * 512 = 8225280 bytes

   Device Boot      Start         End      Blocks   Id  System
/dev/hda1   *           1        1912    15358108+  83  Linux
/dev/hda2            1913        2167     2048287+  82  Linux swap / Solaris
/dev/hda3            2168        2184      136552+  83  Linux
#
```

The system must be rebooted before the kernel can use the new partition table.

```
# init 6
```

Once the system reboots, an ext3 file system can be created on the new partition.

```
# mkfs -t ext3 /dev/hda3
mke2fs 1.39 (29-May-2006)
Filesystem label=
OS type: Linux
Block size=1024 (log=0)
Fragment size=1024 (log=0)
34272 inodes, 136552 blocks
6827 blocks (5.00%) reserved for the super user
First data block=1
Maximum filesystem blocks=67371008
17 block groups
8192 blocks per group, 8192 fragments per group
2016 inodes per group
Superblock backups stored on blocks:
        8193, 24577, 40961, 57345, 73729

Writing inode tables: done
Creating journal (4096 blocks): done
Writing superblocks and filesystem accounting information: done

This filesystem will be automatically checked every 34 mounts or
180 days, whichever comes first.  Use tune2fs -c or -i to override.
```

Now the file system can be mounted so it can be used. First, create a mount point */mnt/tmp_part*, as in this example:

```
# cd /mnt
# mkdir tmp_part
```

Finally, mount the partition:

```
# mount /dev/hda3 /mnt/tmp_part
# df -h
Filesystem            Size  Used Avail Use% Mounted on
/dev/hda1              15G  4.6G  9.0G  34% /
tmpfs                 494M     0  494M   0% /dev/shm
/dev/hda3             130M  5.6M  117M   5% /mnt/tmp_part
```

2. Perform an *fsck* on one of the mount points. (not on / *root*)

Before using *fsck*, dismount the file system.

```
# umount /dev/hda3
#
```

Now a *fsck* can be performed on the partition.

```
# fsck /dev/hda3
fsck 1.39 (29-May-2006)
e2fsck 1.39 (29-May-2006)
/dev/hda3 is mounted.

WARNING!!!  Running e2fsck on a mounted filesystem may cause
SEVERE filesystem damage.

Do you really want to continue (y/n)? yes

/dev/hda3: recovering journal
/dev/hda3: clean, 11/34272 files, 9995/136552 blocks
#
```

3. Change the initialization mode from 5, 3, 2 and up to 1 dynamically with the proper command.

```
As root

init 5
init 3
init 2
```

Linux Measurements, Scheduling Tools and X Windows

CHAPTER

This chapter covers the following exam objectives:

7.2. Automate tasks using scheduling tools

8.3. Describe */proc/meminfo* contents

9. Using Linux Measurement Tools
9.1. Use Linux monitoring tools
9.2. Interpret memory measurements
9.3. Interpret I/O measurements

Linux Measurements Tools

Linux comes with a lot of measurement and performance analysis tools, both text-based and graphical, many of which have been ported or expanded from previous UNIX environments. In this chapter, some of these tools will be introduced and how they can be used for monitoring the system will be explored. Tuning topics will be shown later in Chapter 13 in the tuning performance section.

Start by looking at some memory measurement tools, especially the */proc/meminfo*, before going on to the system reporting tools and system log files, I/O measurement tools and other tools.

Memory Measurement Tools

/proc/meminfo

As already discovered in Chapter 3, Linux has the virtual file system *procfs* which provides non-persistent access to system and kernel information through the */proc* virtual device. One of the files, */proc/meminfo*, provides a snapshot about the state of the system memory and will be explained further.

If a DBA uses the command *cat* on the */proc/meminfo* file, they will see the values for the parameters.

```
[oracle@orion ~]$ cat /proc/meminfo

MemTotal:        254668 kB
MemFree:          19048 kB
Buffers:          34312 kB
Cached:           65524 kB
SwapCached:        5984 kB
Active:          148632 kB
Inactive:         44456 kB
HighTotal:            0 kB
HighFree:             0 kB
LowTotal:        254668 kB
LowFree:          19048 kB
SwapTotal:       522104 kB
SwapFree:        496776 kB
Dirty:              292 kB
Writeback:            0 kB
Mapped:          110060 kB
Slab:             36016 kB
CommitLimit:     649436 kB
Committed_AS:    580392 kB
PageTables:        2356 kB
VmallocTotal:    761848 kB
VmallocUsed:       3004 kB
VmallocChunk:    758644 kB
```

As also shown on the Redhat website, www.redhat.com, below are descriptions of the memory measurement tools offered:

- MemTotal is the total amount of usable physical RAM.
- MemFree is the amount of physical RAM that is currently unused on server.
- Buffers is the amount of physical RAM used by the file buffers.
- Cached is the amount of physical RAM used as page cache memory.
- Swapcached is the amount of swap used as cache memory. In the case where the memory is needed, it is not necessary to get it swapped out as it is already in the swapfile. This memory is reclaimable by the kernel.
- Active is the total amount of buffer or page cache memory in active use, meaning used recently. The kernel manages the system so that it always has enough inactive pages available.

- Inactive is the total amount of buffer or page cache memory not actively in use. This is also reclaimable by the kernel.
- HighTotal is the total amount of memory not mapped into the kernel memory space.
- HighFree is the total amount of free memory not mapped into the kernel memory space.
- LowTotal is the total amount of memory directly mapped into kernel space.
- LowFree is the amount of free memory directly mapped into kernel space.
- SwapTotal gives the total amount of swap available.
- SwapFree provides the total amount of free swap available. It should not be under 20% of the SwapTotal for long periods.
- Dirty shows the total amount of memory waiting to be written back to the disk. This value should be very low.
- Writeback lets the user know the total amount of memory actively being written back to the disk.
- Mapped is the total amount of memory which has been used to map devices, files, or libraries using the *mmap* command.
- Slab is total amount of memory used by the kernel to cache data structures for its own use.
- *Committed_as* gives information on the total amount of memory estimated to complete the workload. This value represents the worst case scenario value and it includes swap memory.
- PageTables reports the total amount of memory dedicated to the lowest page table level.
- VMallocTotal is the total amount of memory of allocated virtual address space.
- VMallocUsed shows the total amount of used virtual address space.
- VMallocChunk is the largest contiguous block of memory of available virtual address space.

The most important output values of the */proc/meminfo* to be familiar with are MemTotal, MemFree, Cached and SwapCached.

free

The utility *free* actually provides a subset of the information in */proc/meminfo* and is a useful way to get quick information on memory usage.

```
[oracle@orion ~]$ free

total Mem:         used         free      shared     buffers      cached
    254668       211148        43520           0       18976       81372

-/+ buffers/cache:       110800       143868
Swap:         522104         3868       518236
```

In the example above, there appears to be only 43520 KB of free physical memory, but it can also be seen that the used memory consists of 18976 KB of buffers and 81372 KB of cached memory. Since this memory is easily released by the kernel, if any program or application needs the space, they can have it. The next line of the output -/+ *buffers/cache:* shows the effective used and free values when the buffers and cached are taken into account.

CPU and Resource Usage: *top*

The utility *top* provides a lot of the things that are needed to monitor on the Linux server. It shows the load of the system, the memory and swap usage and the processes sorted by the one using the most CPU with all the information related to that process.

The normal output from *top* is divided into a summary section, a prompt section for supplying top options, a column header and a task information section.

```
top - 15:23:54 up 1 day,  2:03,  3 users,  load average: 0.03, 0.02, 0.00
Tasks:  93 total,   1 running,  92 sleeping,   0 stopped,   0 zombie
Cpu(s):  0.0% us,  5.0% sy,  0.0% ni, 95.0% id,  0.0% wa,  0.0% hi,  0.0% si
Mem:    254668k total,   209768k used,    44900k free,    23184k buffers
Swap:   522104k total,     3792k used,   518312k free,    76460k cached

  PID USER       PR  NI  VIRT  RES  SHR S %CPU %MEM    TIME+  COMMAND
14525 oracle     16   0  2800  992  764 R  4.8  0.4   0:04.01 top
    1 root       16   0  3028  544  468 S  0.0  0.2   0:01.17 init
    2 root       RT   0     0    0    0 S  0.0  0.0   0:00.00 migration/0
    3 root       34  19     0    0    0 S  0.0  0.0   0:00.12 ksoftirqd/0
    4 root        5 -10     0    0    0 S  0.0  0.0   0:00.62 events/0
```

The summary section shows memory usage statistics that are similar to the ones that can be seen using *free* and */proc/meminfo*. The CPU summary information also has useful information that tells how CPU resources, as a percentage, are being used for user processes (*us*), kernel processes (*sy*) and disk iowait (*wa*).

In interactive mode, the following options are available that can be shown by typing *h* in the prompt section while *top* is running.

- Z,B Global: 'Z' change color mappings; 'B' disable/enable bold
- l,t,m Toggle Summaries: 'l' load avg; 't' task/cpu stats; 'm' mem info
- 1,I Toggle SMP view: '1' single/separate states; 'I' Irix/Solaris mode
- f,o Fields/Columns: 'f' add or remove; 'o' change display order
- F or O: Select sort field
- <,> Move sort field: '<' next col left; '>' next col right
- R,H Toggle: 'R' normal/reverse sort; 'H' show threads
- c,i,S Toggle: 'c' cmd name/line; 'i' idle tasks; 'S' cumulative time
- x,y Toggle highlights: 'x' sort field; 'y' running tasks
- z,b Toggle: 'z' color/mono; 'b' bold/reverse (only if 'x' or 'y')
- u: Show specific user only
- n or #: Set maximum tasks displayed
- k,r: Manipulate tasks: 'k' kill; 'r' renice
- d or s: Set update interval
- W: Write configuration file
- q: Quit

It is also possible to use *top* in batch mode, e.g. *top –b >$HOME/top.list*, which could be used for redirecting output to another program or a file. In batch mode, it is not possible to send input to the top utility as can be done in interactive mode.

Virtual Memory Statistics*: vmstat*

To monitor and get statistics about the memory usage, use *vmstat*. It reports information on CPU activity, memory, paging, I/O and processes. The utility requires only two arguments: *<delay>* for the interval between statistics reports and <*count*>, the number of sample statistics produced. In this example, there is a five-second interval with only two samples:

```
[oracle@orion ~]$ vmstat 5 2

procs -----------memory---------- ---swap-- -----io---- --system-- ----cpu----
 r  b   swpd   free   buff  cache   si   so    bi    bo   in    cs us sy id wa
 0  0   3788  41308  26256  77292    0    0    50    47  167   124  1  3 96  0
 0  0   3788  41308  26272  77276    0    0     0    22 1010    77  0  0 99  0
```

The first report always shows the average values since the last boot, and subsequent reports show the values after each delay period. The information provided by *vmstat* is similar to that seen in *top*, *free*, */proc/meminfo* and other utilities.

System Reporting Tools

Linux has a very useful tool called SAR (System Activity Reporter) which collects statistics on CPU usage, I/O activity and memory information at regular intervals. These snapshots of the system are saved in special files on the files system, usually in the directory */var/log/sa.* In this directory there are 31 files, named *sa[1-31]*, where each number represents a day in the month, and each of these data files contains a single day's statistics.

To examine the contents of these files, use the *sar* command.

```
sar [-flags] [t] [n]
```

If *sar* is typed at the shell prompt without any parameters, then it will display the CPU statistics for the current day. If the interval *t* and count *n* arguments are used, then it will write statistics to the standard output every *t* seconds and *n* times.

```
$ sar 10 5

Linux  pc007751  2.6.24-23-generic  #1 SMP Mon Jan 26 00:13:11 UTC 2009
i686  04/17/2009

12:19:59  cpu %usr %nice   %sys %irq %softirq    %wait %idle          _cpu_
12:20:08  all    0     0      0    0        0        0   100
12:20:18  all    0     0      0    0        0        0   100
12:20:28  all    0     0      0    0        0        0   100
12:20:38  all    0     0      0    0        0        0   100
12:20:48  all    0     0      0    0        0        0   100
$
```

The example above displays five samples of CPU statistics, or default, every 10 seconds. Use *[-flags]* to define what output *sar* shall produce and where it shall be written. It can include statistics about CPU usage, memory usage, I/O, interrupts, network load, and system processes. The following *sar* command provides information about the system CPU stats that were collected on the 13th of the month using the *–f* flag and the corresponding *sar* data file:

```
$ sar -u -f /var/log/sa/sa13

Linux 2.6.9-78.0.17.ELsmp (orion)       03/13/2009

12:00:01 AM       CPU     %user     %nice   %system   %iowait     %idle
12:10:01 AM       all      0.53      0.01      2.46      0.49     96.50
12:20:01 AM       all      0.48      0.01      1.94      0.99     96.58
Average:          all      0.51      0.01      2.20      0.74     96.54
```

Other flags can be used like *–p* for paging statistics, *-d* for disk statistics, and *-r* for memory statistics to get other reports from SAR. The flags can also be combined.

```
$ sar -p -d -f /var/log/sa/sa13

Linux  pc007751  2.6.24-23-generic  #1 SMP Mon Jan 26 00:13:11 UTC 2009  i686  04/13/2009

00:00:01  device           read/s rdKb/s   write/s wrKb/s        rdwr/s _disk_
00:10:01  disk008-000        0.00   0.00      2.31  37.24          2.31
00:20:01  disk008-000        0.00   0.00      2.18  36.86          2.18
00:30:01  disk008-000        0.00   0.00      2.20  36.88          2.20
00:40:01  disk008-000        0.00   0.00      2.28  37.58          2.28
   :
   :
   :
23:40:01  disk008-000        0.00   0.00      2.39  37.69          2.39
23:50:01  disk008-000        0.00   0.00      2.04  37.10          2.04

00:00:01   pagein/s pageout/s     swapin/s swapout/s         fork/s       _page_
00:10:01       0.00     37.25         0.00      0.00           1.44
00:20:01       0.00     36.86         0.00      0.00           1.34
00:30:01       0.00     36.88         0.00      0.00           1.35
   :
   :
   :
23:40:01       0.00     37.69         0.00      0.00           1.39
23:50:01       0.00     37.11         0.00      0.00           1.39
```

There are a lot of useful ways to use SAR to examine kernel statistics and the man pages should be read to see how the flags can be combined. The synopsis below shows a typical SAR implementation on Linux/UNIX, but this may be different in the DBA's own distribution.

```
sar [-a] [-A] [-b] [-c] [-d] [-g] [-k] [-m] [-p] [-q] [-r] [-u] [-v] [-w] [-
y ] [ -o filename ] [ t ] [ n ]
sar [-a] [-A] [-b] [-c] [-d] [-g] [-k] [-m] [-p] [-q] [-r] [-u] [-v] [-w] [-
y ] [ -e time ] [ -f filename ] [-i sec ] [ -s time ]
```

System Log Files: */var/log/messages*

Linux maintains a log file, */var/log/messages,* which it uses to store information about boot messages at system startup, I/O errors, networking, and other general system errors. When some system troubleshooting is performed, it will probably be the first place to look as it contains most system messages. Since the *messages log* file can grow quite large, the system rotates these files so that the current file is called *messages* and previous files are numbered sequentially where the oldest file has the highest sequential number. This enables the DBA to go back in time and analyze previous issues.

```
$ ls -al /var/log/messages*

-rw-r--r--  1 root root  85607 Mar 23 21:24 messages
-rw-r--r--  1 root root 347876 Mar 22 03:40 messages.1
-rw-r--r--  1 root root 312438 Mar 15 01:00 messages.2
-rw-r--r--  1 root root  47194 Mar  8 04:02 messages.3
-rw-r--r--  1 root root 128674 Mar  1 04:02 messages.4
```

The log rotation of the *messages* files is configured with the file */etc/logrotate.conf.* An entry for the *messages* file in the *logrotate config*file might look like this:

```
/var/log/messages {
    rotate 4
    weekly
    postrotate
        /usr/bin/killall -HUP syslogd
    endscript
}
```

The system logger daemon *syslogd* is responsible for logging system and kernel messages in the *messages* file and other log files usually located in */var/log* directory. The configuration file */etc/syslogd.conf* is read by the *syslogd* process to determine which messages are directed to which log files. It is a good idea to look at the *syslogd.conf* file to determine what important logging information is being stored in which log files.

Bootup Messages*: dmesg*

As has been learned before, the */proc* virtual file system is used to provide important kernel information. In fact, *syslogd* uses information in the files */proc/kmsg* to retrieve kernel information and log it in various log files. When the system reboots, kernel messages will be written to the file */proc/kmsg* and this information can be retrieved by using the *dmesg* utility. The command *dmesg* examines this file and presents kernel messages that are related to the actual boot up.

```
[oracle@orion]$ dmesg

Linux version 2.6.9-78.0.17.ELsmp (mockbuild@hs20-bc1-5.build.redhat.com)
(gcc version 3.4.6 20060404 (Red Hat 3.4.6-10)) #1 SMP Thu Mar 5 04:52:17
EST 2009
BIOS-provided physical RAM map:
 BIOS-e820: 0000000000000000 - 000000000009f800 (usable)
 BIOS-e820: 000000000009f800 - 00000000000a0000 (reserved)
 BIOS-e820: 00000000000ca000 - 00000000000cc000 (reserved)
 BIOS-e820: 00000000000dc000 - 0000000000100000 (reserved)
```

Input/Output Measurement Tools: *iostat*

The command *iostat* is a useful tool that produces statistics about disk activity, queues and hotspots for partitions, devices and I/O information. It can help to identify and tune performance issues related to disk I/O that could affect the database or system. The *iostat* command produces not only device statistics, but also NFS statistics and CPU utilization statistics similar to *vmstat.*

The syntax of *iostat* is:

```
iostat <-flags> <intervals> <count>
```

The *<-flags>* are numerous, but the most interesting are *–x,* which displays extended statistics, and *–p [{ device | all }]* which provides statistics on all partitions on a named device, e.g. */dev/sd*, or all the partitions. The *<intervals>* and *<count>* are used exactly in *vmstat* and *sar.*

The following example shows how to get statistics on the partitioned device */dev/sda* from the time of the last system boot.

```
[oracle@orion ~]$ iostat -p sda

Linux 2.6.9-78.0.17.ELsmp (sgr-23pibmsub01)     03/23/2009

avg-cpu:  %user   %nice    %sys %iowait   %idle
           0.88    0.05    2.84    0.29   95.94

Device:            tps   Blk_read/s   Blk_wrtn/s   Blk_read   Blk_wrtn
sda               1.71        21.64        20.90    2605956    2516134
sda3             22.15         0.04         3.03       4885     364279
sda2              0.31         0.03         0.01       4144       1412
sda1              0.02         0.00         0.01        562        843
```

As with *vmstat*, the first report shows the collected statistics since the last system boot, and subsequent reports show statistics within the specified interval.

Network Measurement and Reporting Tools: ***netstat***

Linux uses the tool *netstat* to monitor and measure network activity and connections, interface statistics, routing tables, and socket connections. The generic net statistics can be displayed on the server with the following command:

```
$ netstat
```

Different types of statistics can be displayed by using various flags with the *netstat* command. The following example shows network connections, both source and destination IP addresses and ports in numerical format.

```
$ netstat -an
```

Use the *–r* flag to print the routing tables on the server:

```
$ netstat -rn
```

If the user needs to know how many active connections are performed on the listener, i.e. say the port 1521, perform the following command:

```
$ netstat -an |grep :1521 |wc -l
```

X Windows GUI Measurement Tools

X Windows, also known as X or X11, is a common Windows system available on UNIX/Linux systems. Many of the monitoring tools common in Linux have an X equivalent which presents results in a graphical user interface, making interpretation of these results much easier. The following sections look at two common X Windows measurement tools, but there are many others.

xosview

The utility *xosview* is an X Window tool used to monitor system activity on the CPU, memory, network and disk. The package can be downloaded for Enterprise Linux at http://xosview.sourceforge.net/.

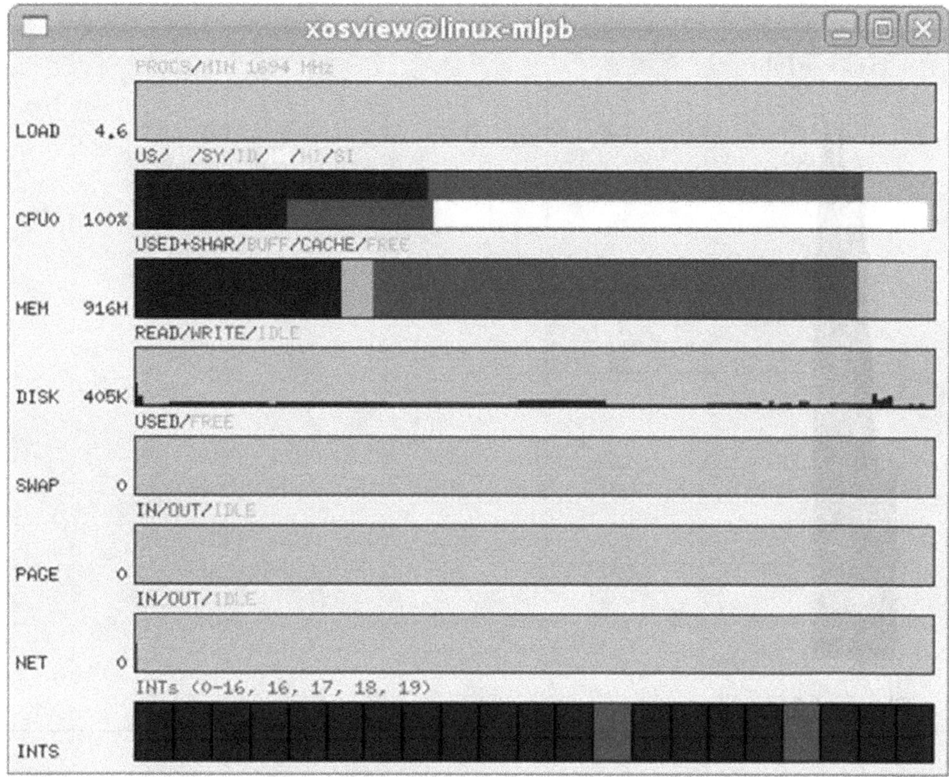

Figure 4.1: *Xosview Screen*

xload

The *xload* graphical utility is a system load average for X Windows that show histograms about the system performances. The tool can be started under X11 in an xterm shell window by typing *xload.*

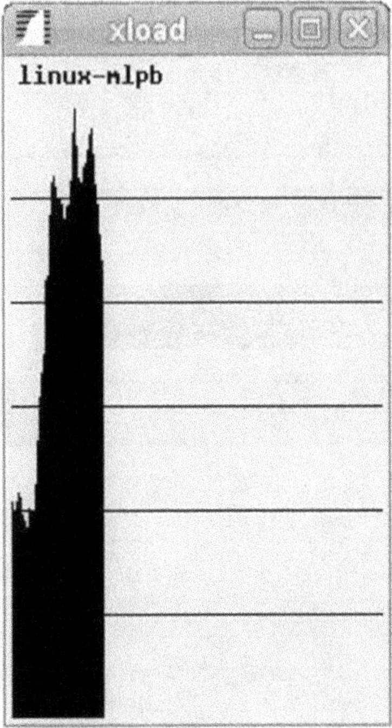

Figure 4.2: *xload Screen*

> Exam Advice: Be able to use the measurement and performance analysis tools and know what options are available for the various tools.

Note: Be aware that running X11 applications can, in themselves, be quite demanding on the system resources. Therefore, text-based tools will probably give a better view of the system performance.

Scheduling Tools

Linux has a number of scheduling tools which can be used to perform automated actions at regular intervals or at a particular date and time. Typically, things like backups would be scheduled to be run daily at a time when there is little system activity. Scripts that collect statistics are often scheduled to run at frequent short intervals. Clean up scripts that remove old log files from application directories might be scheduled to run weekly or monthly.

The OS commands or tools that can be used to schedule are:

- *at* and *batch*
- *cron*, *crontab* and *anacron*
- task scheduler

The next sections give a brief introduction to the scheduling tools along with examples of how to configure and start or stop them.

at and *batch*

The *at* and *batch* commands can be used to execute a one-time task at a specific point in time. A dedicated daemon called *atd* executes the *at* and *batch* commands. The *batch* command will only be executed when the load of the Linux system is below 0.8. Before using that command, it can be controlled if it is installed on the Linux system *rpm -q at.*

To create a scheduled job using *at*, the easiest way is to type *at <timestamp>* at the command prompt.

```
# at 23:10
warning: commands will be executed using /bin/sh
at>
```

Once the *at>* prompt is visible, type in the commands that will be run by *at* and finish with *<EOT>*, which is CTRL-D.

```
at> night_script.sh
at> <EOT>
```

```
job 5 at 2009-04-20 23:10
```

Now list this scheduled job in the *at* queue using the *atq* command. If this is done as root, all pending jobs for all users on the system will be seen.

```
#atq
```

```
4       2009-04-20 18:30 a root
5       2009-04-20 23:10 a root
```

If the particular details of a scheduled job need to be displayed, then use the *at –c* command with the job number. This will give a lengthy output, which not only shows the commands that are included in the job, but also the UID and GID of the user running the job as well as all the environment variables that are in effect for the job.

The following output has been shortened for readability:

```
# at -c 5
#!/bin/sh
# atrun uid=0 gid=0
# mail  oracle2 0
umask 22
LESSKEY=/etc/lesskey.bin; export LESSKEY
NNTPSERVER=news; export NNTPSERVER
:
:
:
:
mc=\(\)\ {\ \ .\ /usr/share/mc/bin/mc-wrapper.sh"
"}; export mc
cd /root || {
      echo 'Execution directory inaccessible' >&2
      exit 1
}

night_script.sh
#
```

If the decision is made to delete a job from the *at* queue, simply use the *atrm* command with the corresponding job number.

```
# atrm 5
```

It is possible to restrict the access to the *at* and *batch* commands with the files */etc/at.allow* and */etc/at.deny*. Write the name of the user in the *at.allow* or *at.deny* file depending on the expected result. When the *at.allow* and *at.deny* files are modified, it is not necessary to restart the *atd* service. The root user is always able to execute both commands regardless of the entries in these files. If the *at.allow* file is present on the system, it must contain the list of users who are allowed to execute *at* or *batch*, and the *at.deny* file is ignored. When the *at.allow* file is not present on the system, everyone is allowed to use the *at* and *batch* commands except those listed in the *at.deny* file.

The *atd* daemon can be started, stopped and tested using the service command */sbin/service*.

```
# service atd start|stop|status
```

cron, crontab

The *cron* process is also used to schedule tasks on the system, but unlike *at*, which schedules a one-off task, *cron* and *crontab* are used to schedule recurring tasks. The *cron* daemon is responsible for executing the *cron* scripts according to the schedule that is specified in a file called the *crontab*. Each user is responsible for maintaining their own personal *crontab*, and the system administrator is responsible for maintaining the system *crontab*. The Linux system must be running when a task is scheduled, otherwise the task will not be executed.

Start, Stop, Test

As with *atd*, the status of the *crond* daemon can be started, stopped or tested using the */sbin/service* commands.

```
# service crond start|stop|status
```

With the *at* command, it is possible to restrict the access to the *cron* command with the files */etc/cron.allow* and */etc/cron.deny*. These work in exactly the same way as the *at.allow* and *at.deny* files.

The main configuration file for *cron* is */etc/crontab* and it might contain the following lines:

```
# more /etc/crontab
```

```
SHELL=/bin/bash
PATH=/usr/bin:/usr/sbin:/sbin:/bin:/usr/lib/news/bin
MAILTO=root
#
# check scripts in cron.hourly, cron.daily, cron.weekly, and cron.monthly
#
01 * * * * root run-parts /etc/cron.hourly
02 4 * * * root run-parts /etc/cron.daily
22 4 * * 0 root run-parts /etc/cron.weekly
42 4 1 * * root run-parts /etc/cron.monthly
```

The first lines are dedicated to the variables that will be used in the environment when the *cron* is executing the different scheduled tasks. Use the *mailto* option to send email related to the tasks executed. Next to be defined is the schedule of the commands to be run. The format of the *crontab* entries are:

- *min*: Minute, integer 0-59
- *hour*: Hour, integer from 0-23
- *day*: Day of the month, integer from 1-31 (must be a valid date in the given month)
- *month*: The month in the year, integer from 1-12 or a short month name such as jan, feb, and such
- *dow*: Integer 0 to 7 (0 or 7 means Sunday) or a short day name such as sun, mon, and such
- *user*: The user under which the command will be run, e.g. root
- *command*: The command that shall be executed, it can be a script or a series of commands

An asterisk * in any field means all allowed values. Multiple values for a field can be specified as comma separated lists of values, or ranges, i.e. 1,2,9-12 in the hour field means hours is equivalent to 1,2,9,10,11,12. Also use a / to specify that the command should be executed by stepping through a range of values, e.g. */2 in the hour field would mean every second hour.

As previously mentioned, each user has his/her own *crontab*, which is configured in exactly the same way as the system *crontab*. There is however, no need to specify the shell environment variables as these are assumed to be the same as those in the */etc/passwd* file for that user. Also, it makes no sense to specify the user in the user's own *crontab*.

A final word of caution: do not edit the *crontab* by hand. Instead, use the *crontab –e* command which will open the *crontab* in the default editor and make the changes there. View the *crontab* by using the *crontab –l* command.

anacron

A task scheduler called *anacron* can be used to execute the daily, weekly, and monthly jobs usually run by *cron*, but the command does not require the system to be running constantly. In order to use the anacron service, the *anacron* RPM package must be installed. Use the rpm command *rpm -q anacron* to check that *anacron* is installed. Also use the */sbin/service* command to start, stop and test the *anacron* service.

The configuration file */etc/anacrontab* is used by *anacron* to schedule the tasks that must be run. The format of the file is as follows:

- period: Frequency to execute the tasks in days
- delay: Delay time in minutes
- job-identifier: An identifier that describes the task. It will be used by *anacron* as the name of the job on the timestamp file. The identifier can contain any non-blank characters apart from slashes.
- command: Command to be executed by the *anacron*

The *anacron* process controls whether or not the scheduled tasks have been executed. If the task has not been executed at the specified time, then *anacron* will try to execute the task again after a time specified by the delay field.

An example of the *anacrontab* file:

```
# /etc/anacrontab: configuration file for anacron

SHELL=/bin/bash
PATH=/usr/local/sbin:/usr/local/bin:/sbin:/bin:/usr/sbin:/usr/bin
# These entries are useful for a Red Hat Linux system.
2       4       cron.daily              run-parts /etc/cron.daily
5       12      cron.weekly             run-parts /etc/cron.weekly
26      11      cron.monthly            run-parts /etc/cron.monthly
```

The values *shell* and *path* are used to specify the environment variables, just as in *crontab*.

Task Scheduler

Linux has graphical scheduler tools which are really just front ends to the *cron* utility. The tools work under Gnome (Task Scheduler) or KDE (Kcron).

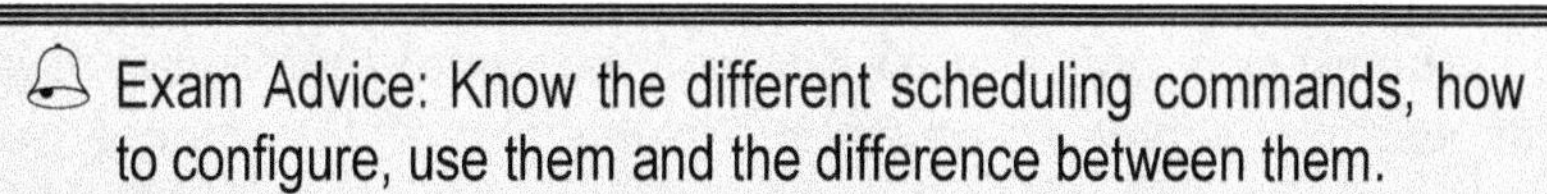

Exam Advice: Know the different scheduling commands, how to configure, use them and the difference between them.

Note: If a DBA needs to schedule daily tasks, they could also use the schedulers in Oracle Grid Controller or Oracle Enterprise Manager DB console.

X Windows

X Windows, also called X or X11, is a system that allows the administrator to run graphical applications on a graphical (bitmap) display and to manage input using keyboards and pointing control devices. Normally, when thinking of a graphical application, the application might be expected to be running locally on the same machine where there is an attached graphical display and a local keyboard and mouse. However, X Windows is designed from the start as a client-server model so that the applications, i.e. X clients, could use a network protocol to send output to a remote X server like the display and accept input from a remote X server such as the keyboard or mouse.

The X Windows server actually runs as an application on top of the kernel and manages connections from X clients, which can be local clients on the actual machine or clients that are running on a remote machine.

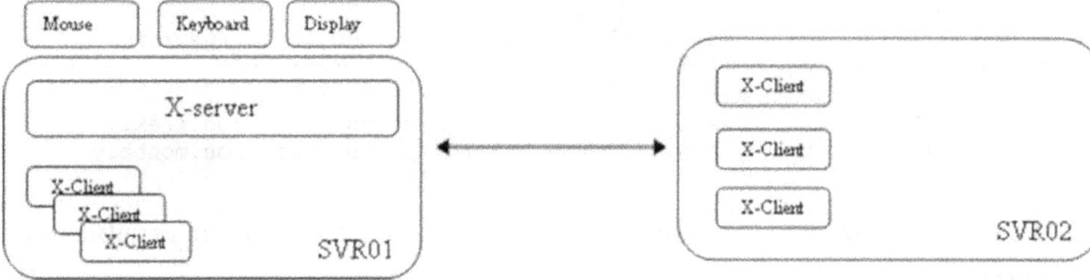

Figure 4.3: *X Windows Server Diagram*

In this example, SVR01 is running an X server, and so X client applications can be run locally on this machine. However, if SVR01 connects to SVR02, it is possible to run X client applications on SVR02 which can receive their input from the keyboard and mouse of SVR01 and the use of the display of SVR01. The client and the server communicate using the X11 protocol over the network.

Note: in this example it has been assumed that SVR01 is a Linux system, but in actual fact it could be any operating system that the X Windows server is able to run. On a Microsoft windows platform there are numerous commercial X Windows servers available like Exceed or Hummingbird and on Linux, XFree86® is a freely redistributable open-source implementation X Windows system.

If an example where SVR01 is running Linux is used and the user wishes is to run a graphical application on the local machine, then have the X11 server installed and running on the machine. Normally, when Linux is installed on the SVR01 platform, it will also be installed with an X11 server as well. During the installation, the install program identifies the video graphics card, display, keyboard, mouse and such, then completes the installation and configuration of the X11 server without too much difficulty. In the event that the installation program does not recognize all of the peripherals, there will be the need to complete the X11 configuration after installation.

Depending on which version of X11 has been installed, the configuration files may be located in different places and have different functionalities. For example, the Xorg – X11R7 X server usually places its configuration files in */etc/X11/xorg.conf*, whereas the XFree86 has its configuration files in */etc/X11/XF86Config*. Typically, these files have entries describing peripheral devices, keyboard layout, display, video chipsets, and more.

The following is an example of the sections present in the file */etc/X11/XF86Config*:

- Files	File pathnames
- ServerFlags	Server flags
- Module	Dynamic module loading
- InputDevice	description of Input device
- Device	description of Graphics device
- VideoAdaptor	description of Video adaptor
- Monitor	description of Monitor
- Modes	descriptions of Video modes
- Screen	Configuration of Screen
- ServerLayout	Overall layout
- DRI	Direct Rendering Infrastructure-specific configuration
- Vendor	Configuration that is Vendor-specific

Table 4.1: *Sections for File /etc/X11/XF86Config*

Once X11 is installed, next to be done is to start the X server in order to use it. This can be done in a number of ways, but the following is the most common:

Once SRV01 boots up, the typical runlevel is set to runlevel 3, as specified in the */etc/initab*, which actually means a multi-user environment but without X11. From a command prompt, simply type *startx* and the script will start up a *xinit* script with some predefined options which starts up an X Windows environment, typically Gnome or KDE.

```
$ startx
```

Another way to start X server automatically is to change the run level to run level 5, which in most Linux distributions means a multi-user environment with X11.

```
# init 5
```

In either case, an X Windows graphical environment will be displayed and the X Windows environment is now ready to be used. From within the desktop, start terminal programs, shell sessions, and various other graphical tools all managed within the X Windows environment.

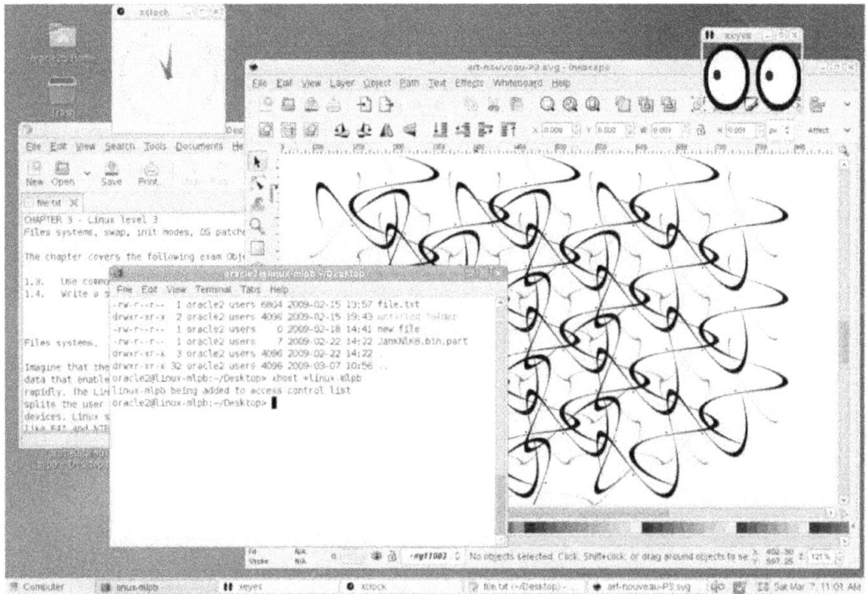

Figure 4.4: *Example of X Windows Environment*

To stop or immediately kill the X server, use the key combination Ctrl+Alt+Backspace, or as root, run the *init 3* command which returns the server to run level 3.

One important environment variable is the *$DISPLAY* environment setting. This can be used to control where to run the X11 applications. Typically, this is set to *localhost:0.0* which means the X server is located on the local machine (localhost) and uses the default display and keyboard (:0.0). This comes in handy if the user wants to run graphical applications from another server, say SVR02. Instead of physically going to SVR02, starting X, and running the applications locally on SVR02, make use of the X11 protocol instead and remote login to SVR02, but redirect the *$DISPLAY* back to SVR01. In other words, the clients on SVR02 use the X server on SVR01 and, subsequently, the display and keyboard located there.

Telnet into SVR02 from SVR01:

```
SVR01$ telnet svr02
```

Now set the *$DISPLAY* environment variable to point to SVR01.

```
SVR02$ echo $DISPLAY
localhost:0.0
SVR02$ export DISPLAY=svr01:0.0
SVR02$ echo $DISPLAY
svr01:0.0
```

Instead of the hostname, it is also possible to use the IP address of the server for *$DISPLAY*, thus bypassing hostname resolution. The parameter *:0.0* means the first display on the Linux server. It is possible to run multiple X Windows servers on a single computer; in that case, there will be :1.0 that will be the second X server session.

Now, if an xterm is run on SVR02, the xterm window will appear on the graphical display on SVR01.

```
SVR02$ xterm&
```

One final thing: X11 has a number of different methods to allow or deny which hosts or users can run clients on the X server. The simplest method is to allow all connections from a particular host. In this example, it would probably be best to allow connections from SVR02 to access the X server on SVR01. This is done by updating the *xhosts* configuration file. This can be accomplished simply by:

```
SVR01# xhost +SVR02
```

```
SVR02 being added to access control list
```

Summary

This chapter examined various Linux tools such as measurement tools, X Windows and scheduling tools. Examples of each were given with details and sample scripts. For instance, the memory measurement tool */proc/meminfo* gives a synopsis of the state of the system memory. X Windows is a Windows system used in Linux and UNIX that presents results in a graphical user interface for easier understanding. It is also described under graphical scheduler tools in detail with information given about X clients and X servers, whether they be local or remote.

The next chapter will cover the Linux Text Editor.

> 🔔 Exam Advice: Be able to describe what is X11, what is the configuration file, and how to configure and start/stop the X server.

Exercises

1. Use the measurement tools to collect some statistics on the Linux system.

2. Use the scheduling command to make a list of the processes that are running on the server and store the result in a file.

3. Get the Linux in the run level 3, start X Windows, authorize the server to connect, launch the X Windows application like *xclock*, *xload* and *xeyes*. When finished, stop the X server by using the correct key combination.

Q&A

Questions

1. Select the correct description for the names on the */proc/meminfo* (match the correct answers):

A. MemTotal
B. MemFree
C. Cached
D. SwapCached

a. Is about the amount of swap used as cache memory
b. Concerns the amount of physical RAM unused on server, in kilobytes
c. Is about total memory amount of physical RAM
d. Has to do with the amount of physical RAM used as cache memory

2. What does the utility *free* do? (choose the correct answer):

A. Gives the disk space that is free
B. This command does not exist in Linux
C. Gets the information about the free used physical and swap memory

D. Informs on the free buffers for the network

3. Match the following commands with the description:

A. *iostat*
B. *top*
C. *wmstat*
D. *netstat*
E. *xload*
F. *sar*
G. *xosview*

a. Perform reporting of the system activities related to memory, I/O and the CPU usage
b. Enable viewing in an X Window the system activities on the CPU, memory, network and disk
c. Print network connections, routing tables, interface statistics and multi-cast membership
d. Show histograms about the system performances
e. Statistics about the memory usage, CPU activity, memory, paging, I/O and processes
f. It shows the load of the system, the memory and swap usage and the processes sorted by the one using the most CPU with all the information related to that process
g. Network measurement and reporting tool

4. What is the purpose of the command *dmesg*?

A. It provides disk messages
B. It shows directory messages
C. It informs about the *$DISPLAY* messages
D. It displays information related to the system boot

5. What is the file */var/log/messages* collecting? (Choose all that apply):

A. Networking errors and general system errors
B. I/O errors
C. I/O and memory statistics
D. Information about the boot messages at system startup

6. Are the following options of *iostat* doing extended or a partition-wise statistics? (Choose all that apply)

A. *iostat –x 10 5*

B. *iostat –B 5 4*
C. *iostat –c 5 4*
D. *iostat –p sda 15 5*

7. What scheduling command can be used to execute regular tasks? Note that the system will always be running. (Choose all answers that apply)

A. anacron
B. Enterprise Manager DB console
C. crontab
D. at

8. How can a DBA make sure that the X Windows display is set? (Choose all that apply)

A. *env | grep –i display*
B. *printf $DISPLAY*
C. *echo $DISPLAY*
D. *echo display*

9. Which of the following configuration files is used by XFree86? (Choose the correct answer)

A. */etc/Xwindows/XF86Config*
B. */etc/X11/XF86Config*
C. */etc/X11/XF86set-up*
D. */etc/XF86Config*

10. How can X Windows be started in a bash shell as oracle or as root? (Choose all that apply)

A. *win*
B. *startx*
C. *xwing*
D. *init 5* (executed as root)

Answers

1. Correct combination is:

A. MemTotal / c. Is about total memory amount of physical RAM
B. MemFree / b. Concerns the amount of physical RAM unused on server, in kilobytes

C. Cached / d. Has to do with the amount of physical RAM used as cache memory
D. SwapCached / a. Is about the amount of swap used as cache memory

HINT: The section "Memory Measurement Tools: */proc/meminfo"* can be helpful with this question.

2. C. Get the information about the free used physical and swap memory is the only correct answer.

HINT: As stated above, the section on memory measurement tools and specifically */proc/meminfo* is useful for this.

3. The following are the correct matches:

A. *iostat* / d. Measurements on the I/O disk activities, queues and hotspots for partitions and devices
B. *top* / f. It shows the load of the system, the memory and swap usage and the processes sorted by the one using most CPU with all the information related to that process
C. *wmstat* / e. Statistics about the memory usage, CPU activity, memory, paging, I/O and processes
D. *netstat* /g. Network measurement and reporting tool
E. *xload* / d. Show histograms about the system performances
F. *sar* / a. Perform reporting of the system activities related to memory, I/O and the CPU usage
G. *xosview* b. Enable viewing in an X Window the system activities on the CPU, memory, network and disk

HINT: Refer to the whole section "Memory Management Tools".

4. The only correct answer is D. It displays information related to the system boot.

HINT: Read again the section "Bootup messages: *dmesg"*.

5. The correct answers are: A. Networking errors and general system errors; B. I/O errors and D. Information about the boot messages at the system startup.

HINT: The section "System Log files: */var/log/messages*" will help answer this question.

6. The correct answers are: A. *iostat –x 10 5* for the extended statistics and D. *iostat –p sda 15 5* for the partition statistics

HINT: The section "Input/Output Measurement Tools: *iostat*" can answer this.

7. The correct answers that apply are: B. Enterprise Manager DB console and C. crontab.

HINT: Refer to the section on scheduling tools.

8. To control that the X Windows display is properly set do either:

A. *env | grep –i display*
B. *printf $DISPLAY*
C. *echo $DISPLAY*

HINT: The section on X Windows has the answer to this question.

9. Only correct answer is: B. */etc/X11/XF86Config*

HINT: Again, refer to the section "X Windows".

10. B. *startx* and D. *init 5* (executed as root) are the only correct answers.

HINT: Lastly, the section on X Windows also will help with this question.

Solutions to the Exercises

1. Use the measurement tools to collect some statistics on the Linux system.

```
cat /proc/meminfo >$HOME/statistics.txt
free >>$HOME/statistics.txt
top -b >>$HOME/statistics.txt
vmstat 15 22 >>$HOME/statistics.txt
sar -u 2 4 >>$HOME/statistics.txt
dmesg >>$HOME/statistics.txt
```

2. Use the scheduling command to make a list of the processes that are running on the server and keep the result in a file.

```
linux-mlpb:~ # at 18:10
warning: commands will be executed using /bin/sh
at> ps -efd >$HOME/process_list.txt
at> <EOT>
job 4 at 2009-02-18 18:10
```

3. Get the Linux in the runlevel 3, start X Windows, authorize the server to connect, launch the X Windows application like xclock, xload and xeyes. When finished, stop the X server with the key combination.

```
su -
init 3
startx
# in a xterm X Windows
xclock &
xload &
xeyes &

# stop or immediately kill your X server
    Ctrl+Alt+Backspace
```

Linux Text Editor

CHAPTER 5

Introduction

This chapter about the text editor program vi is not an exam requirement, but it is important to have a basic knowledge of the tool as it will be necessary to edit text, scripts and PL/SQL files under Linux.

The text editor vi was originally written in C by Bill Joy in 1976 for a BSD UNIX. The name vi is an abbreviation for the command 'visual in ex' (Extended is a UNIX line editor). There are many different implementations of vi in Linux, but the most popular of them is vim (vi improved) and this is usually installed on most Linux distributions. This chapter will give the basics of vi.

Launch vi

To begin editing a file, start vi with the filename as follows:

```
[oracle@orion ~]$ vi my_text_file
```

If the file exists already, then it will be opened in vi and it can continue to be edited. If the file does not exist, then an empty file will be created:

```
~
~
~
~
"my_text_file" [New file]
```

The cursor is placed on the first line of the new file and empty lines are represented by the ~ character.

Modes with vi

The vi text editor has three modes to perform the various editing tasks: insert mode, command mode, and line mode.

- Insert mode: When in insert mode, whatever is typed in will be inserted in the file at the cursor position. To make vi enter insert mode, type one of the following characters:

Inserting Text	
A	Go to the end of the current line, and begin inserting text.
a	Begin entering text after the current cursor position.
I	Go to the beginning of the line and begin inserting text.
i	Begin inserting text at the current cursor position.
O	Insert a blank line before the current line and begin inserting text.
O	Insert a blank line after the current line and begin inserting text.

Table 5.1: *Characters for Entering Insert Mode*

Once the text has been entered, leave insert mode by pressing the escape (Esc) key. This will bring the user back to the default (initial) command mode.

- Command mode: When a file is opened with vi, the DBA will initially be in command mode. In this mode, the file can be navigated through, the cursor position can be moved, lines in the file can be cut and pasted, recent changes can be redone and undone, and more. The manipulation can be performed with short sequences of letters. Some of the most important ones are shown here, but there are many others.

Navigation Commands	
Left, Right, Up, Down arrow keys	Move the cursor to the left or right or up and down one line
h,l,k,j	Alternative method to move cursor left, right, up and down
B, $	Go to beginning, end of current line
CTRL-F, CTRL-B	Page down, Page up

CTRL-D, CTRL-U	Half-Page down, Half-Page up
Deleting, Cut and Paste Commands	
x	Delete a single character at the cursor position By using a number before the x command, a DBA can delete more than one character at a time. 10x deletes 10 characters.
dw, d$	Delete something… dw delete to end of word at cursor, d$ delete from cursor to end of line. Also use D Places deleted contents in buffer.
Dd	Delete the current line and store in the buffer By using a number before the dd command, several lines can be deleted, e.g.10dd delete 10 lines from the current position.
P	Paste the buffer contents before the cursor
p	Paste the buffer contents after the cursor
yy	Copy (yank) the current line into the buffer By using a number before the yy command, one can copy several lines, e.g. 10yy copies 10 lines from the current line position
yw, y$	Yank to end of current word, yank to end of line and place in buffer
Repeat and Undo	
U	Undo all changes on the current line
u	Undo the last change
.	Repeat the last command
r	Replace a single character at the cursor. The replaced character is not placed in the buffer.

Table 5.2: *Characters for Commands*

- Line mode: The line mode can be used to enter commands at the vi prompt and is often used to do search and replace actions or to set special vi attributes. The line mode is entered by typing colon (:). The cursor will be placed on the bottom of the screen with a prompt that starts with a colon.

Load, save quit	
:r name_of_your_file	load a file into vi
:w name_of_your_file	Save contents to file (if the file name is left out, then the contents are written to the current file that was opened).
:wq name_of_your_file :x name_of_your_file	Save contents to file and then quit. :x is equivalent to :wq
:q or :q!	:q Quit the current file and discard any changes. :q! force quit, i.e quit the file even if no changes have been made.
Searching	
/<pattern>	Search forward for <pattern> in the file from the cursor position and go to that position. The search can be repeated to the next occurrence using n and to the previous occurrence using N
?<pattern>	Search backwards for <pattern> in the file from the cursor position and go to that position. The search backwards can be repeated to the next occurrence using n and to the previous occurrence using N
Set Commands	
:set	Displays all the set options and the current values
:set all	Display all the set options available
:set showmode	Displays if you are in the insert mode
:set nu or :set number	Turn on the line numbers
set nonu or :set nonumber	Turn off the line numbers
Shell Commands	
:!<your command>	By using the *:!* command, the shell commands can be run from within vi, e.g. *:!pwd* will temporarily leave the vi screen and display the current directory. Once the command completes it returns to vi. ~ ~ :!pwd

	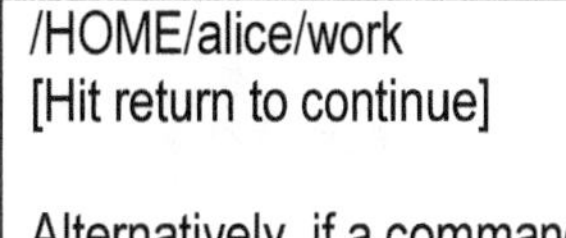 /HOME/alice/work [Hit return to continue] Alternatively, if a command is not specified, e.g. *:!* the user will simply get a normal shell where several commands can be done. Return to vi by exiting the shell. Note on some distributions, *:shell* instead of *:!* must be used.

Table 5.3: *Characters for Line Mode*

Finally, some very useful combinations of command mode and insert mode commands that will often be used are the *cw, cc, c$, C change* commands.

- *cw* deletes the remainder of the current word from the cursor position and places the user in insert mode. The text that is entered will replace the text that has been deleted. Press <ESC> when editing is finished.
- *cc* deletes the current line and switches to insert mode. The text that is entered will be inserted from the beginning of the line replacing the deleted text. Press <ESC> when finished with editing.
- *C, c$* deletes the text from the cursor to the end of the line and switches to insert mode. The text that is entered will replace the text that was deleted. Press <ESC> when editing is done.

Many other options are available to manipulate text using vi, and the above are really only the essentials. However, it should be enough to get started. As the DBA becomes more familiar with vi, consulting the manual pages (man vi) will be a tool for much more information.

Preparing Linux for Oracle

CHAPTER

This chapter covers the following exam objectives:

2. Preparing Linux for Oracle
2.1. Use the package manager to determine and update package support
2.2. Set up the operating system environment for Oracle database
2.3. Create the necessary groups and users for Oracle database

Oracle on Linux

Before installing Oracle on the Linux server, the user must ensure that a number of mandatory prerequisites are fulfilled. The first thing to check is that the OS release and architecture is compatible and certified with the version of Oracle software that is being installed. This can be checked by using Oracle Metalink (My Oracle Support) under the Certify section.

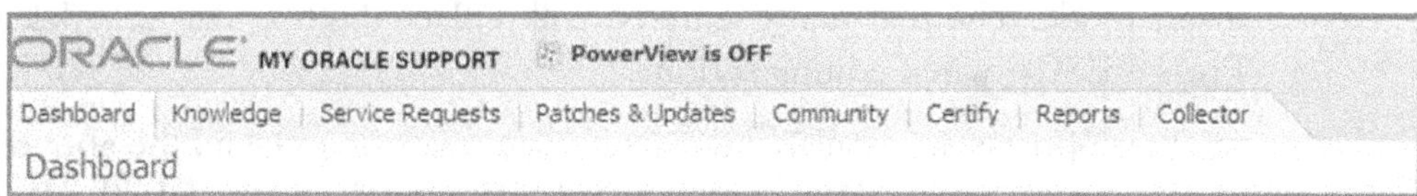

Figure 6.1: *My Oracle Support Screen Header*

Metalink – My Oracle Support

In Metalink, also called My Oracle Support, information can be looked up either by OS platform or by Oracle product. The following example shows the certification status for a Linux x86-64 bit platform running Red Hat Enterprise AS/ES 3 and Oracle Database Enterprise Edition 10gR2:

```
Certify - Additional Info Oracle Database - Enterprise Edition Version 10gR2
64-bit On Linux x86-64
```

```
Operating System: Linux x86-64 Version Red Hat Enterprise AS/ES 3
Oracle Database - Enterprise Edition Version 10gR2 64-bit
N/A Version N/A
Status: Certified
Product Version Note:

None available for this product.

Certification Note:

See MetaLink Note 742060.1 Release Schedule of Current Database Patch Sets
```

Note: before doing a new installation on a new OS and platform, it is highly recommended that Metalink (My Oracle Support) be consulted. The document ID # 169706.1 Oracle® Database on UNIX AIX®,HP-UX®,Linux®,Mac OS® X,Solaris®,Tru64 UNIX® Operating Systems Installation and Configuration Requirements Quick Reference (8.0.5 to 11.1) provide detailed information about the Oracle prerequisites installation.

Once it has been verified that the Oracle software can be installed on the platform, make sure that the system satisfies the remaining hardware and software requirements.

Hardware Requirements

To be able to install Oracle 10gR2 on a Linux server, the following minimum hardware requirements need to be fulfilled:

- A minimum of 1 GB RAM memory available
- At least 400 MB free space in */tmp*
- Up to 4 GB free space to install the Oracle binaries
- An additional 1.2 GB for the example database
- Sufficient swap space according to the following table:

Swap Space to be Configured	Physical RAM
2 * Physical RAM	Up to 512 MB
1.5 * Physical RAM	Between 1G and 2G
1 * Physical RAM	Between 2G and 8G
0.75 * Physical RAM	More than 8G

Table 6.1: *Minimum Hardware Requirements for Oracle 10gR2 Install*

Use something like the following script to help collect configuration information and control the prerequisites:

```
#!/bin/sh
echo Total Physical Memory  > $HOME/Oracle_pre_req.txt
grep MemTotal /proc/meminfo >> $HOME/Oracle_pre_req.txt

echo Total Swap >> $HOME/Oracle_pre_req.txt
grep SwapTotal /proc/meminfo >> $HOME/Oracle_pre_req.txt

echo >> $HOME/Oracle_pre_req.txt

echo free memory >> $HOME/Oracle_pre_req.txt
free >> $HOME/Oracle_pre_req.txt

echo >> $HOME/Oracle_pre_req.txt

echo disk free on /tmp >> $HOME/Oracle_pre_req.txt
df -B 1M /tmp | grep -v Filesystem | awk 'BEGIN {FS = " "} {if ($3 > 400)
{print "OK - " $3 "MB in /tmp"} else {print "NOK - only " $3 "MB in /tmp,
need at least 400 MB"} }'>> $HOME/Oracle_pre_req.txt

echo >> $HOME/Oracle_pre_req.txt

echo All the disk free space >> $HOME/Oracle_pre_req.txt
df -k >> $HOME/Oracle_pre_req.txt

echo >> $HOME/Oracle_pre_req.txt

echo Model of you linux server >> $HOME/Oracle_pre_req.txt
grep "model name" /proc/cpuinfo >> $HOME/Oracle_pre_req.txt
# For redhat releases you should by uncomment the next line
# more /etc/redhat-release >> $HOME/Oracle_pre_req.txt
```

> Exam Advice: Be able to describe all the prerequisites and the different requirements.

RPM Packages

The following RPM packages, or later versions, must be installed to perform a successful Oracle installation:

Red Hat Enterprise Linux 3.0:

- make-3.79.1-17
- compat-db 4.0.14-5.1
- control-center-2.2.0.1-13
- gcc-3.2.3-47
- gcc-c++-3.2.3-47
- gdb-6.1post-1.20040607.52
- glibc-2.3.2-95.30
- glibc-common-2.3.2-95.30
- glibc-devel-2.3.2-95.30
- glibc-devel-2.3.2-95.20 (32 bit)
- compat-db-4.0.14-5
- compat-gcc-7.3-2.96.128
- compat-gcc-c++-7.3-2.96.128
- compat-libstdc++-7.3-2.96.128
- compat-libstdc++-devel-7.3-2.96.128
- gnome-libs-1.4.1.2.90-34.2 (32 bit)
- libstdc++-3.2.3-47
- libstdc++-devel-3.2.3-47
- openmotif-2.2.3-3.RHEL3
- sysstat-5.0.5-5.rhel3
- setarch-1.3-1
- libaio-0.3.96-3
- libaio-devel-0.3.96-3

Red Hat Enterprise Linux 4.0:

- binutils-2.15.92.0.2-10.EL4
- compat-db-4.1.25-9
- control-center-2.8.0-12
- gcc-3.4.3-9.EL4
- gcc-c++-3.4.3-9.EL4
- glibc-2.3.4-2
- glibc-common-2.3.4-2
- gnome-libs-1.4.1.2.90-44.1
- libstdc++-3.4.3-9.EL4
- libstdc++-devel-3.4.3-9.EL4
- make-3.80-5
- pdksh-5.2.14-30
- sysstat-5.0.5-1
- xscreensaver-4.18-5.rhel4.2

SUSE Linux Enterprise Server 9:

- binutils-2.15.90.0.1.1-32.5
- gcc-3.3.3-43.24
- gcc-c++-3.3.3-43.24
- glibc-2.3.3-98.28
- gnome-libs-1.4.1.7-671.1
- libstdc++-3.3.3-43.24
- libstdc++-devel-3.3.3-43.24
- make-3.80-184.1
- pdksh-5.2.14-780.1
- sysstat-5.0.1-35.1

- xscreensaver-4.16-2.6

A script like the one below can help to control what RPM packages are installed on the Linux server:

```
#!/bin/sh
echo Linux RPM packages Installed
# Perform the update of the script regarding the script that you need
# use the list given in that section to perform the changes
#
rpm -q --qf '%{NAME}-%{VERSION}-%{RELEASE}  (%{ARCH})\n' \
binutils compat-db control-center gcc gcc-c++ glibc glibc-common gnome-libs
\
libstdc++ libstdc++-devel make pdksh sysstat xscreensaver libaio
```

> Exam Advice: Be proficient in knowing what the required RPM packages are and how to perform the installation and upgrade of the RPM packages.

Operating System Settings

It is preferable that one of the following operating systems is being used:

- Red Hat Enterprise Linux AS/ES 3.0 or 4.0 (Update 4 or later)
- SUSE Linux Enterprise Server 9.0 with SP2 or later

The kernels that should be used are:

- Red Hat Enterprise Linux AS/ES 3.0 : 2.4.21-27.EL
- Red Hat Enterprise Linux AS/ES 4.0 : 2.6.9-11.EL
- SUSE Linux Enterprise Server 9.0 : 2.6.5-7.201

The following script will help the administrator get the operating system values:

```
#!/bin/sh
echo Linux Version Installed > $HOME/Oracle_OS_pre_req.txt
cat /proc/version  >> $HOME/Oracle_OS_pre_req.txt
echo Kernel Version >> $HOME/Oracle_OS_pre_req.txt
uname -r >> $HOME/Oracle_OS_pre_req.txt
```

Linux Kernel Parameters

The Linux kernel parameters should be configured properly, not only for a successful Oracle installation, but also in preparation for a running database instance.

Minimum Kernel Value Recommended by Oracle	Command to Control the Actual Values
shmmax = 2147483648	cat /proc/sys/kernel/shmmax
shmall = 2097152	cat /proc/sys/kernel/shmmni
shmall = 2097152	cat /proc/sys/kernel/shmall
shmmin = 1	ipcs -lm |grep "min seg size"
shmseg = 10	hard coded in the kernel
semmsl = 250	cat /proc/sys/kernel/sem | awk '{print $1}'
semmns = 32000	cat /proc/sys/kernel/sem | awk '{print $2}'
semopm = 100	cat /proc/sys/kernel/sem | awk '{print $3}'
semmni = 128	cat /proc/sys/kernel/sem | awk '{print $4}'
file-max = 65536	cat /proc/sys/fs/file-max
ip_local_port_range = 1024 65000	cat /proc/sys/net/ipv4/ip_local_port_range

Table 6.2: *Kernel Values and Commands*

The following script will help in collecting and controlling the values of the kernel.

```
#!/bin/sh
echo Control you kernel settings >
$HOME/Oracle_OS_kernel_settings_pre_req.txt
echo shmmax value >> $HOME/Oracle_OS_kernel_settings_pre_req.txt
cat /proc/sys/kernel/shmmax >> $HOME/Oracle_OS_kernel_settings_pre_req.txt
echo shmmni >> $HOME/Oracle_OS_kernel_settings_pre_req.txt
cat /proc/sys/kernel/shmmni >> $HOME/Oracle_OS_kernel_settings_pre_req.txt
echo shmall >> $HOME/Oracle_OS_kernel_settings_pre_req.txt
cat /proc/sys/kernel/shmall >> $HOME/Oracle_OS_kernel_settings_pre_req.txt
echo min seg size >> $HOME/Oracle_OS_kernel_settings_pre_req.txt
ipcs -lm |grep "min seg size" >> $HOME/Oracle_OS_kernel_settings_pre_req.txt
echo semmsl >> $HOME/Oracle_OS_kernel_settings_pre_req.txt
cat /proc/sys/kernel/sem | awk '{print $1}'
>>$HOME/Oracle_OS_kernel_settings_pre_req.txt
echo semmns >> $HOME/Oracle_OS_kernel_settings_pre_req.txt
cat /proc/sys/kernel/sem | awk '{print $2}'
>>$HOME/Oracle_OS_kernel_settings_pre_req.txt
echo semopm >> $HOME/Oracle_OS_kernel_settings_pre_req.txt
```

```
cat /proc/sys/kernel/sem | awk '{print $3}'>>
$HOME/Oracle_OS_kernel_settings_pre_req.txt
echo semmni >> $HOME/Oracle_OS_kernel_settings_pre_req.txt
cat /proc/sys/kernel/sem | awk '{print $4}'>>
$HOME/Oracle_OS_kernel_settings_pre_req.txt
echo file-max >> $HOME/Oracle_OS_kernel_settings_pre_req.txt
cat /proc/sys/fs/file-max >> $HOME/Oracle_OS_kernel_settings_pre_req.txt
echo ip_local_port_range >> $HOME/Oracle_OS_kernel_settings_pre_req.txt
Note: It is not necessary to change the kernel values if these values are
higher than the recommended values.
cat /proc/sys/net/ipv4/ip_local_port_range>>
$HOME/Oracle_OS_kernel_settings_pre_req.txt
```

> Exam Advice: Be sure to know what values can be changed for the kernel settings and also review the descriptions of all the kernel parameters in Chapter 2 with an introduction to semaphores, shared memory parameters, network parameters and file handler parameters:.

Groups and User

Typical Groups for Oracle under Linux

Oracle requires the following groups to be installed to enable the installation of the software binaries and the allocation of all the Oracle physical files.

Linux Group Name	Group Name	Details
oinstall	Oracle inventory	The group oinstall owns the Oracle repository which is the catalogue (inventory) of all the Oracle software installed on the Linux server. During the first installation, the Oracle Universal Installer asks what user shall be the owner of the Oracle repository. Sometimes the dba group is chosen instead of the oinstall group. In case the oinstall group already exists, it should be the primary group for Oracle users.

dba	OSDBA	The first time Oracle is installed, a prompt will appear to specify the name of the OSDBA group. The OSDBA group is the group that has Oracle database administrator privileges, also called SYSDBA privileges. The most common name for that group is dba (Database Administrator). The oracle user must also belong to this group.
oper	OSOPER	The operator group, oper, is an optional group that has a limited set of Oracle database administrator privileges. Members of this group have SYSOPER privileges. These members are able to perform start and stop of the Oracle instance.

Table 6.3: *Group Names and Details for Oracle Under Linux*

Oracle Users

To perform the Oracle installation, the DBA must have at least the oracle user on the Linux server:

oracle

The user oracle must be created on the Linux system as it will be the owner of the Oracle binaries and will own all Oracle physical files. The oracle user should belong to the primary group oinstall and be a member of the other groups, dba, and optionally, oper.

During installation, the oracle user is configured with the correct environment variables *$ORACLE_HOME* and *$ORACLE_BASE,* which point to the Oracle binaries. It is possible to have multiple oracle users, i.e. oracle10, ora10 and such, which can be used for different installed versions. Alternatively, there can be just one oracle user that can change the *$ORACLE_HOME* and *$ORACLE_SID* with the *oraenv* script.

```
nobody
```

The nobody user is an unprivileged system user. Oracle uses this to execute external jobs. Oracle installs the external jobs executable *$ORACLE_HOME/bin/extjob* to be owned by the user nobody.

> Exam Advice: Be able to describe the different groups and users that are required to perform an Oracle installation. The DBA should also know how to verify both the groups and users created after the installation.

Download the Oracle Installation

It is possible to download the Oracle installation package from the Oracle OTN site on the following link:

http://www.oracle.com/technology/software/products/database/index.html

It is possible to download the patch sets, CPU patches and patches in the section Patches & Updates in Metalink, https://metalink.oracle.com/.

Note: It is recommended that X Windows is running, as the Oracle Universal Installer needs to have X11 to perform the installation. Otherwise, the installation will have to be performed in silent mode.

Additional Resources and Tools

On the Oracle support, the user can download a tool called RDA that can make Health Check and pre-installation checks. More information is available on the document ID# 250262.1 RDA 4 - Health Check / Validation Engine Guide on the My Oracle Support website.

If installing or using RDA is not desired, there is the pre-installation checks script that can be found on My Oracle Support, document ID# 334531.1 Pre-install checks for 10gR2 RDBMS (10.2.x) - Linux x86 Platforms. However, this tool is no longer supported. In Chapter 13, the RDA tool will covered in detail.

To get the result of the prerequisites controls with the RDA tool, execute the *rda.sh* command, option *–T*, and it will inform on the status of all the prerequisites of the Linux server. It is necessary to inform RDA what control should be performed by giving the release of the Oracle RDBMS. If results are obtained with the *failed* status, it will be necessary to fix them before performing the installation of Oracle.

```
[oracle@orion ~]$ $ORACLE_HOME/rda/rda.sh -T hcve
Processing HCVE tests ...
Available Pre-Installation Rule Sets:
   1. Oracle Database 10g R1 (10.1.0) PreInstall (Linux-x86)
   2. Oracle Database 10g R1 (10.1.0) PreInstall (Linux AMD64)
   3. Oracle Database 10g R1 (10.1.0) PreInstall (IA-64 Linux)
   4. Oracle Database 10g R2 (10.2.0) PreInstall (Linux AMD64)
   5. Oracle Database 10g R2 (10.2.0) PreInstall (IA-64 Linux)
   6. Oracle Database 10g R2 (10.2.0) PreInstall (Linux-x86)
   7. Oracle Database 11g R1 (11.1.0) PreInstall (Linux AMD64)
   8. Oracle Database 11g R1 (11.1.0) PreInstall (Linux-x86)
   9. Oracle Application Server 10g (9.0.4) PreInstall (Linux)
  10. Oracle Application Server 10g R2 (10.1.2) PreInstall (Linux)
  11. Oracle Application Server 10g R3 (10.1.3) PreInstall (Linux AMD64)
  12. Oracle Application Server 10g R3 (10.1.3) PreInstall (IA-64 Linux)
  13. Oracle Application Server 10g R3 (10.1.3) PreInstall (Linux-x86)
  14. Oracle Portal PreInstall (Generic)
Available Post-Installation Rule Sets:
  15. Oracle Portal PostInstall (generic)
  16. RAC 10G DB and OS Best Practices (Linux)
  17. Data Guard PostInstall (Generic)
Enter the HCVE rule set number
Hit 'Return' to accept the default (1)
> 6

Enter value for < Planned ORACLE_HOME location or if set >
Hit 'Return' to accept the default (/u01/oracle/product/10.2.0/db_1)
>


Test "Oracle Database 10g R2 (10.2.0) PreInstall (Linux-x86)" executed at
Mon Jun 15 20:02:45 2009
```

```
Test Results
~~~~~~~~~~~~

ID     NAME                 RESULT  VALUE
====== ==================== ======= ==================================
A00010 OS Certified?        PASSED  Adequate
A00020 User in /etc/passwd? PASSED  userOK
A00030 Group in /etc/group? PASSED  GroupOK
A00040 Input ORACLE_HOME    RECORD  /u01/oracle/product/10.2.0/db_1
A00050 ORACLE_HOME Valid?   PASSED  OHexists
A00060 O_H Permissions OK?  PASSED  CorrectPerms
A00070 Umask Set to 022?    PASSED  UmaskOK
A00080 LDLIBRARYPATH Unset? PASSED  UnSet
A00100 Other O_Hs in PATH?  FAILED  OratabEntryInPath
A00110 oraInventory Permiss PASSED  oraInventoryOK
A00120 /tmp Adequate?       PASSED  TempSpaceOK
A00130 Swap (in MB)         RECORD  2047
A00140 RAM (in MB)          FAILED  582
A00150 Swap OK?             FAILED  NA
A00160 Disk Space OK?       PASSED  DiskSpaceOK
```

```
A00170 Kernel Parameters OK FAILED  NA
A00180 Got ld,nm,ar,make?   PASSED  ld_nm_ar_make_found
A00190 ulimits OK?          FAILED  StackTooSmall NoFilesTooSmall Maxupro..>
A00200 EL4 RPMs OK?         PASSED  NotEnterprise
A00201 EL5 RPMs OK?         PASSED  NotEnterprise
A00204 RHEL3 RPMs OK?       PASSED  NotRHEL3
A00205 RHEL4 RPMs OK?       FAILED  [compat-libstdc++-296(i386)] not inst..>
A00206 RHEL5 RPMs OK?       PASSED  NotRHEL5
A00209 SUSE SLES9 RPMs OK?  PASSED  NotSuSE
A00210 SUSE SLES10 RPMs OK? PASSED  NotSuSE
A00213 Asianux1 RPMs OK?    PASSED  NotAsianux
A00214 Asianux2 RPMs OK?    PASSED  NotAsianux
A00215 Asianux3 RPMs OK?    PASSED  NotAsianux
A00218 Patch 3006854 Instal PASSED  NotRHEL3
A00219 ip_local_port_range  PASSED  ip_local_port_rangeOK
A00220 Tainted Kernel?      PASSED  NotVerifiable
A00230 Other OUI Up?        PASSED  NoOtherOUI
Result file: /home/oracle/output/RDA_HCVE_A200DB10R2_lnx_res.htm
[oracle@orion ~]$
```

Summary

Oracle Metalink, also known as My Oracle Support, was introduced in this chapter as a way to prepare for installing Oracle on a Linux server. My Oracle Support can be used to look up information either by OS platform or by Oracle product. Also shown were the hardware, packages and operating system settings needed for a successful installation.

Tables illustrating kernel parameters as well as users and groups under Linux were given for additional information. The next chapter will examine the steps needed to install Oracle binaries.

Exercises

1. Control the hardware and software prerequisites to install the Oracle software.
2. Create the groups and users necessary for the Oracle installation.

Q&A

Questions

1. Jack has a server with 512 MB memory, 300 MB free space on */tmp* and 4 GB free space to install the Oracle binaries. (Select the correct answers):

A. Installation can be performed on that server
B. More memory is needed, at least 1 GB is required
C. Diskspace on */tmp* is sufficient
D. The server does not have enough free diskspace on */tmp*

2. John has a server with 4 GB physical memory. He needs to configure his swap memory. What is the recommended size of the swap? (Select the correct answer):

A. 2 times the size of RAM
B. 0.75 times the size of RAM
C. 1.5 times the size of RAM
D. Equal to the size of RAM

3. On the server proxima, the RPM packages make and gcc are not installed. What should be done? (Choose the correct answer):

A. Neither package is needed to install Oracle
B. Install only the make package, as it is the only one needed
C. Install both the make and gcc package, as both are needed
D. Install only the gcc package as it is the only one needed

4. The server andromeda has higher values than the recommended kernel values. What should be done? (Choose the correct answer):

A. Reduce the kernel values that are higher than expected
B. Decrease only the *shmmax* to match the value of the user's SGA
C. Do not change the higher values
D. Reduce the value of the SGA to avoid issues

5. Which of the following groups is optional? (Select the correct answer):

A. dba
B. oinstall
C. oper
D. nobody

6. What is exactly the purpose of the oinstall group? (Select the correct answer):

A. It is an optional group
B. It owns the Oracle binaries
C. It is the Oracle repository owner
D. It is the group dedicated to operators (SYSOPER

privileges)

7. What mandatory groups should be allocated to the oracle user? (Choose all that apply):

A. dba
B. oper
C. oinstall
D. nobody

8. Where can Henry, as junior DBA, download the Oracle CPU patches?

A. It cannot be downloaded; Henry has to order a CD-ROM from Oracle
B. This can be done on Metalink
C. The CPU patch can be ordered on the OTN webpage
D. It can be downloaded on the OTN website

9. How can Tom ensure that he will get support and his installation is certified by Oracle?

A. By reading the OTN documentation
B. By reading the *Read_me.txt* file delivered with the Oracle installation
C. Oracle Universal Installer will register the product with Oracle for support
D. Connect to Metalink, also called My Oracle Support, to get the certification information

10. John has a Linux server that does not have X Windows installed. What can he do? (Choose all that apply):

A. Install and configure X Windows so he can use Oracle Universal Installer
B. Perform a silent install without using X Windows
C. X Windows is mandatory and must be installed, otherwise it is impossible to install Oracle
D. Install Windows XP instead of X Windows

Answers

The correct answers are:

1. B. More memory is needed, at least 1 GB is required and D. The server does not have enough free disk space on */tmp*.

HINT: Refer to the section "Hardware Requirements".

2. D. Equal to the size of RAM

HINT: Once again, refer to the section on hardware requirements.

3. C. Install both the make and gcc package as both are needed.

HINT: Check the section on RPM packages.

4. C. Do not change the higher values.

HINT: Consult the section "Linux Kernel Parameters" for information on this subject.

5. C. oper

HINT: "Typical groups for Oracle under Linux" is the section with the answer to this question.

6. C. It is the Oracle repository owner.

HINT: Again, the section "Typical Groups for Oracle under Linux" is helpful here.

7. A. dba, B. oper and C. oinstall.

HINT: Refer to the section on Oracle users.

8. B. This can be done on Metalink.

HINT: Consult the section "Download the Oracle Installation".

9. D. Connect to Metalink, also called My Oracle Support, to get the certification information.

HINT: Reread the section on Metalink for this answer.

10. A. Get X Windows installed and configured; and B. Perform a silent install, without using X Windows.

HINT: Like #8, the answer is found in the section "Download the Oracle Installation".

Solutions to Exercises

1. Control the hardware and software prerequisites to install the Oracle software.

Use the script:

```
#!/bin/sh
echo Total Physical Memory  > $HOME/Oracle_pre_req.txt
```

```
grep MemTotal /proc/meminfo >> $HOME/Oracle_pre_req.txt
echo Total Swap >> $HOME/Oracle_pre_req.txt
grep SwapTotal /proc/meminfo >> $HOME/Oracle_pre_req.txt
echo >> $HOME/Oracle_pre_req.txt
echo free memory >> $HOME/Oracle_pre_req.txt
free >> $HOME/Oracle_pre_req.txt
echo >> $HOME/Oracle_pre_req.txt
echo disk free on /tmp >> $HOME/Oracle_pre_req.txt
df -B 1M /tmp | grep -v Filesystem | awk 'BEGIN {FS = " "} {if ($3 > 400)
{print "OK - " $3 "MB in /tmp"} else {print "NOK - only " $3 "MB in /tmp,
need at least 400 MB"} }'>> $HOME/Oracle_pre_req.txt
echo >> $HOME/Oracle_pre_req.txt
echo All the disk free space >> $HOME/Oracle_pre_req.txt
df -k >> $HOME/Oracle_pre_req.txt
echo >> $HOME/Oracle_pre_req.txt
echo Model of you linux server >> $HOME/Oracle_pre_req.txt
grep "model name" /proc/cpuinfo >> $HOME/Oracle_pre_req.txt
# For redhat releases you should by uncomment the next line
# more /etc/redhat-release >> $HOME/Oracle_pre_req.txt
echo Linux RPM packages Installed
# Perform the update of the script regarding the script that you need
# use the list given in that section to perform the changes
#
rpm -q --qf '%{NAME}-%{VERSION}-%{RELEASE}  (%{ARCH})\n' \
binutils compat-db control-center gcc gcc-c++ glibc glibc-common gnome-libs
\
libstdc++ libstdc++-devel make pdksh sysstat xscreensaver libaio
#
echo Linux Version Installed > $HOME/Oracle_OS_pre_req.txt
cat /proc/version  >> $HOME/Oracle_OS_pre_req.txt
echo Kernel Version >> $HOME/Oracle_OS_pre_req.txt
uname -r >> $HOME/Oracle_OS_pre_req.txt
#
echo Control your kernel settings >
$HOME/Oracle_OS_kernel_settings_pre_req.txt
echo shmmax value >> $HOME/Oracle_OS_kernel_settings_pre_req.txt
cat /proc/sys/kernel/shmmax >> $HOME/Oracle_OS_kernel_settings_pre_req.txt
echo shmmni >> $HOME/Oracle_OS_kernel_settings_pre_req.txt
cat /proc/sys/kernel/shmmni >> $HOME/Oracle_OS_kernel_settings_pre_req.txt
echo shmall >> $HOME/Oracle_OS_kernel_settings_pre_req.txt
cat /proc/sys/kernel/shmall >> $HOME/Oracle_OS_kernel_settings_pre_req.txt
echo min seg size >> $HOME/Oracle_OS_kernel_settings_pre_req.txt
ipcs -lm |grep "min seg size" >> $HOME/Oracle_OS_kernel_settings_pre_req.txt
echo semmsl >> $HOME/Oracle_OS_kernel_settings_pre_req.txt
/proc/sys/kernel/sem | awk '{print $1}'
>>$HOME/Oracle_OS_kernel_settings_pre_req.txt
echo semmns >> $HOME/Oracle_OS_kernel_settings_pre_req.txt
cat /proc/sys/kernel/sem | awk '{print $2}'
>>$HOME/Oracle_OS_kernel_settings_pre_req.txt
echo semopm >> $HOME/Oracle_OS_kernel_settings_pre_req.txt
cat /proc/sys/kernel/sem | awk '{print $3}'>>
$HOME/Oracle_OS_kernel_settings_pre_req.txt
echo semmni >> $HOME/Oracle_OS_kernel_settings_pre_req.txt
cat /proc/sys/kernel/sem | awk '{print $4}'>>
$HOME/Oracle_OS_kernel_settings_pre_req.txt
echo file-max >> $HOME/Oracle_OS_kernel_settings_pre_req.txt
cat /proc/sys/fs/file-max >> $HOME/Oracle_OS_kernel_settings_pre_req.txt
echo ip_local_port_range >> $HOME/Oracle_OS_kernel_settings_pre_req.txt
```

```
cat /proc/sys/net/ipv4/ip_local_port_range>>
$HOME/Oracle_OS_kernel_settings_pre_req.txt
```

2. Create the groups and users necessary for the Oracle installation.

```
su - root
groupadd oinstall
groupadd dba
groupadd oper
useradd -c "Oracle software owner" -g oinstall -G dba,oper oracle
passwd oracle
```

Installing Oracle on Linux

CHAPTER 7

This chapter covers the following exam objectives:

3. Installing Oracle on Linux
3.2. Install multiple versions of Oracle Database software on the same server
3.3. Accommodate multiple Oracle homes on one database server

This chapter will describe all the operations to perform in order to have Oracle binaries installed on the Linux server. There is also added additional information that is not part of the exam objectives about the JAVA NCOMP, the OUI silent installation and the cloning of the Oracle binaries.

Oracle Account Settings

Before starting the installation of the Oracle binaries, confirm all the prerequisites given in Chapter 6 and also the following about the Oracle Linux account. Make sure that the Linux Oracle account has all the variables and *$PATH* is properly set as shown next in the DBA's profile file as this is important for performing the installation without any issues:

- The minimum values that must be present in the profile of the Oracle Linux user should be the *$PATH* values (*PATH=/usr/bin:/bin:/usr/X11R6/bin:/usr/local/bin*) and that the X Windows *$DISPLAY* is properly set and working. Therefore, the profile should at least contain the *$PATH* values and have *$DISPLAY* set in the environment.
- The *oraenv* script will add *$ORACLE_HOME* at the end of the *$PATH* variable. After the Oracle binaries are installed, the *$ORACLE_HOME* is a mandatory value that is present in the profile.

In options, the following variables can also be set in the profile as needed by Oracle or by the database administrators.

- *$ORACLE_BASE*: The root directory for the Oracle binaries and software
- *$ORACLE_SID*: The Oracle instance name of the user's database
- *$ORACLE_HOSTNAME*: If there are multiple network cards activated, this value of the Oracle hostname will need to be set.
- *$ORACLE_DOC*: Location of the Oracle documentation
- *$ORA_NLS10*: Character set files location
- *$LANG*: Language of the Linux system
- *$TMPDIR* or *$TMP*: In case the */tmp* is too small and cannot be changed, use the variable to set an alternative temporary location for the installation.
- *$AGENT_HOME*: The home of the Oracle Enterprise Manager agent home
- *$LD_LIBRARY_PATH*: The path that contains the C libraries. The other user libraries are set in *$PATH*, i.e. */usr/lib*.
- *$ORACLE_OWNER*: Used to define what the Oracle Linux user is
- $ORACLE_TERM: Used to set the X Windows terminal windows, typically if the value is *xterm*

Note: The profile files for the shells Bash can be: *.bash_profile*, *profile* and *.bashrc*. Bourne is *.profile*. C is *.login* and *.cshrc*. Korn is *.profile* and *.kshrc*.

 Exam Advice: Be familiar with all the variables that can be set and their purpose.

OFA (Optimal Flexible Architecture)

The Optimal Flexible Architecture (OFA) was introduced in Oracle 8 with the purpose of making the administration easier and optimizing the relationship between the system files and the database files. For administration purposes, it distributes the files across multiple mount points; as a result, it balances I/O and increases the reliability. Therefore, it makes it possible to have multiple Oracle releases installed on the same server and easily monitor the growth of both the binaries and the database physical files. OFA compliance requires at least two different mount points. The first mount point is dedicated to the Oracle binaries and software. The second mount point is reserved for the Oracle database physical files. The mount points are named with the given considerations:

- Name of the mount points */pm* or */pm/q/db*
- *p* value is a string.
- *m* value is a two- up to four-digit number as a unique identifier.
- *q* is a datafile stored, usually named *oradata* for the datafiles. *Db* concerns the database name.

With ASM, the mount point concerns for the Oracle physical files are suppressed.

The *$ORACLE_BASE* and *$ORACLE_HOME* should be complaint to the OFA architecture. *$ORACLE_BASE* is the root directory that is at a higher level than *$ORACLE_HOME* and is used to store datafiles, logs and administration files in the directories below. *$ORACLE_HOME* is the location of the Oracle binaries and some administration files such as *pfile*, *password file* and *spfile*.

```
ORACLE_BASE=/u02/app/oracle
ORACLE_HOME=$ORACLE_BASE/product/10.2.0/db_1
```

The *$ORACLE_BASE* shall be preferably created by *root* account, but must be owned by the oracle user and the inventory group (oinstall or dba depending on the one that will be chosen during the installation). After the $*ORACLE_BASE* directory has been created with the *root* account, the owner must be changed with the command *chown –R oracle:oinstall $ORACLE_BASE* so the OUI will be able to write in the directory. The $*ORACLE_HOME* is created by the Oracle Universal Installer.

Multiple Oracle Versions on the Same Server

It is possible to have multiple Oracle versions on the same server, but new $*ORACLE_HOME* values will have to be provided to install the new Oracle versions. OFA recommends the following given naming convention below and also takes into consideration that it is better to have separate trees for each release because when a release is no longer needed, it can be easily deleted.

- Name of the mount points */h/product/v*
- *h* value of the *$ORACLE_BASE*
- Product will be identified to say that this contains binaries.
- *v* value is the release of the Oracle binaries.

So as a result, for Oracle 9i it is */u01/app/oracle/product/9.2.0* and for Oracle 10g, */u02/app/oracle/product/10.2.0.* The values can be found in the file */etc/oratab.* It is stored as shown in the example below.

```
Example of the /etc/oratab content:
prd:/u01/app/oracle/product/9.2.0:Y
dev:/u03/app/oracle/product/10.2.0:Y
uat:/u04/app/oracle/product/10.2.0:Y
test:/u05/app/oracle/product/10.2.0:Y
educ:/u02/app/oracle/product/9.2.0:Y
```

With the script *oraenv*, the *$ORACLE_SID* can be changed and it is *$ORACLE_HOME* values in the user's shell environment where the script *oraenv* is located in */usr/local/bin.* It is possible to put the *oraenv* script in the profile, so it will perform every time a new shell session is opened by adding the variable *oraenv_ask=no.* It will not prompt the DBA for the *ORACLE_SID* as it set the script in non-interactive mode. In case it needs to be prompted for *ORACLE_SID* when a new shell is open, set the *oraenv_ask=.* This will set the *oraenv* in interactive mode. If the variable *oraenv_ask* is not set or has another value other than *no,* the user will be prompted for the *ORACLE_SID.* Korn, Bash and Bourne shells use the *oraenv* and the C-shell uses the *coraenv* script. The Oracle environment script *oraenv* calls another script *dbhome* that reads the *oracle_home* associated to the *oracle_sid* in the file */etc/oratab.*

```
Content of the file /etc/oratab
test:/u01/oracle/product/10.2.0/db_2:N
prd:/u01/oracle/product/10.2.0/db_1:N
uat:/u01/oracle/product/10.2.0/db_4:N
dev:/u01/oracle/product/10.2.0/db_3:N
```

With the *oraenv_ask=no* set:

```
[oracle@orion ~]$ export ORAENV_ASK=NO
[oracle@orion ~]$ . oraenv
[oracle@orion ~]$
```

Without the *oraenv_ask=not* set or a value that is blank:

```
[oracle@orion ~]$ export ORAENV_ASK=
[oracle@orion ~]$ . oraenv
ORACLE_HOME = [/home/oracle] ? test
[oracle@orion ~]$ env | grep ORACLE
ORACLE_SID=test
ORACLE_BASE=/u01/oracle
ORACLE_HOME=/u01/oracle/product/10.2.0/db_2
```

It is important to remember to always run the *oraenv* with "." as it will resource the script into the actual shell, so the syntax will be *./oraenv*. Otherwise, the command forks a new shell to execute the command, exits and return to the actual shell.

> Exam Advice: Be able to explain what OFA is doing and if it is possible to have multiple releases of Oracle binaries. The DBA's knowledge must also include the *oraenv* script and how it can be configured.

Download the Installation Files

With a view to install Oracle on the Linux server, the 10g Release 2 (10.2.0.1.0) Oracle installation packages from the Oracle Technical Network website will need to be obtained from this address: http://www.oracle.com/technology/software/products/database/index.html. The Companion CD 10g Release 2 is also needed to avoid NCOMP issues later with the Oracle installation. The patch set 10.2.0.4 can be downloaded from Metalink via https://metalink.oracle.com/ in the section "Patches & Updates". On the same site, interim or one-off patches can be found. More information about the patch set's availability can be seen on http://www.oracle.com/technology/software/products/database/index.html. Oracle also provides Critical Patch Updates that are updated regularly and must be installed on the Oracle binaries of the DBA. Visit the webpage http://www.oracle.com/technology/deploy/ security/alerts.htm to get more information about the next CPU patches available.

For x86 32-bits, get the following packages from the websites:

- 10201_database_linux32.zip (the Base Software)
- 10201_companion_linux32.zip (the Companion Software with NCOMP)
- p6810189_10204_Linux-x86.zip (patch set to update to 10.2.0.4)

For x86 64-bits, get the following packages from the websites:

- 10201_database_linux_x86_64.cpio.gz (the Base Software)
- 10201_companion_linux_x86_64.cpio.gz (the Companion Software with NCOMP)
- p6810189_10204_Linux-x86-64.zip (patch set to update to 10.2.0.4)

After the packages have been downloaded, it is highly recommended to make sure that the download has been performed without any issues by controlling the checksum of the files and the values given on the Oracle website. The commands *cksum* and *md5sum* will help to perform those checks.

```
[oracle@orion]$ md5sum  p6810189_10204_Linux-x86.zip
32add083c469004071819c263f0b4ce6  p6810189_10204_Linux-x86.zip
```

It is possible to create an installation CD-ROM that contains the Oracle installation packages. First, uncompress the installation package files with the commands *cpio* and *gunzip*, and be certain that there is enough free space to uncompress and unpack the installation files.

```
[oracle@orion]$ gunzip 10201_database_linux_x86_64.cpio.gz
[oracle@orion]$ cpio -idmv < 10201_database_linux_x86_64.cpio
Disk1/stage/Components/oracle.server/10.2.0.1.0/1
Disk1/stage/Components/oracle.server/10.2.0.1.0
Disk1/stage/Components/oracle.server
(...)
```

When all the installation packages are uncompressed and unpacked, carry out the creation of the ISO image.

```
[oracle@orion]$ mkisofs -r Disk1 | cdrecord -v dev=0,0,0 speed=20 -
```

The CD-ROM can be mounted on the Linux server by doing the following command, depending on if the device is identified as CD-ROM */dev/cdrom* or DVD-ROM */dev/dvdrom*:

```
[oracle@orion]$ mount -t iso9660 /dev/cdrom /mnt/cdrom
```

Note: In case */etc/fstab* already contains the definition to mount the CD-ROM or DVD-ROM device, a simple command like mount */mnt/cdrom* will be sufficient to get the installation CD-ROM mounted.

Installation

The Oracle binaries installation will be performed with the Oracle Linux user, and two commands will need to be run under the *root* account to finish the installation. With the Oracle Universal Installer, which is an Oracle installer base on Java and also called OUI, the installation of the binaries can be performed. The OUI tool is identical on all the platforms and for all the Oracle products. It is important that the *$DISPLAY* is properly set in X Windows when an installation with OUI is performed in interactive mode; otherwise, OUI will not be able to open the installation windows. If it is not possible to install under X Windows, perform a silent installation that does not require X Windows. This type of installation is explained later in this chapter.

```
[oracle@orion database]$ ./runInstaller
Starting Oracle Universal Installer...
Checking installer requirements...

Checking operating system version: must be redhat-3, SuSE-9, redhat-4,
UnitedLinux-1.0, asianux-1 or asianux-2
                                        Passed
All installer requirements met.
Preparing to launch Oracle Universal Installer from /tmp/OraInstall2009-03-
29_02-23-52PM. Please wait
```

If the DBA's operating system is newer or not present in the pre-requisites, it is possible to bypass the control by using the argument *ignoreSysPrereqs* on the *runInstaller.sh.*

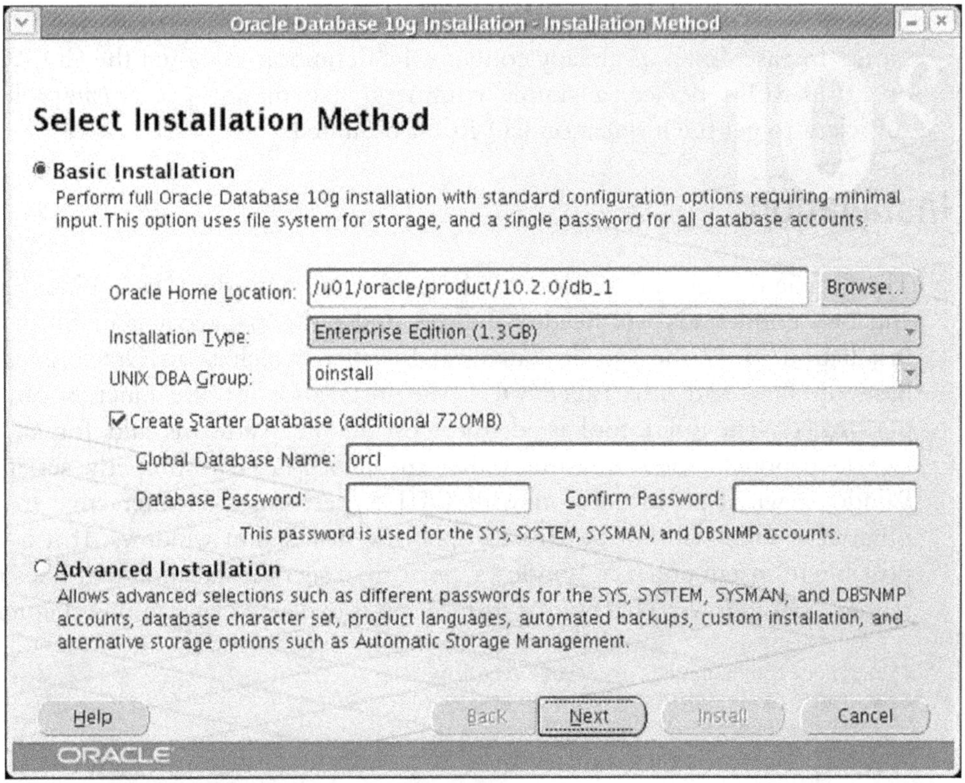

Oracle Database 10g Installation - Installation Method

Select Installation Method

◉ **Basic Installation**

Perform full Oracle Database 10g installation with standard configuration options requiring minimal input.This option uses file system for storage, and a single password for all database accounts.

Oracle Home Location: /u01/oracle/product/10.2.0/db_1 Browse...

Installation Type: Enterprise Edition (1.3GB)

UNIX DBA Group: oinstall

☑ Create Starter Database (additional 720MB)

Global Database Name: orcl

Database Password: Confirm Password:

This password is used for the SYS, SYSTEM, SYSMAN, and DBSNMP accounts.

○ **Advanced Installation**

Allows advanced selections such as different passwords for the SYS, SYSTEM, SYSMAN, and DBSNMP accounts, database character set, product languages, automated backups, custom installation, and alternative storage options such as Automatic Storage Management.

Help Back Next Install Cancel

ORACLE

Figure 7.1: *Choice of Installation Method Screen*

On the installation package for the 10g 10.2.0.1, there is now the possibility of performing a rapid installation of Oracle and creating a database. However, if specific components need to be installed, it is recommended to perform the installation with the advanced installation option.

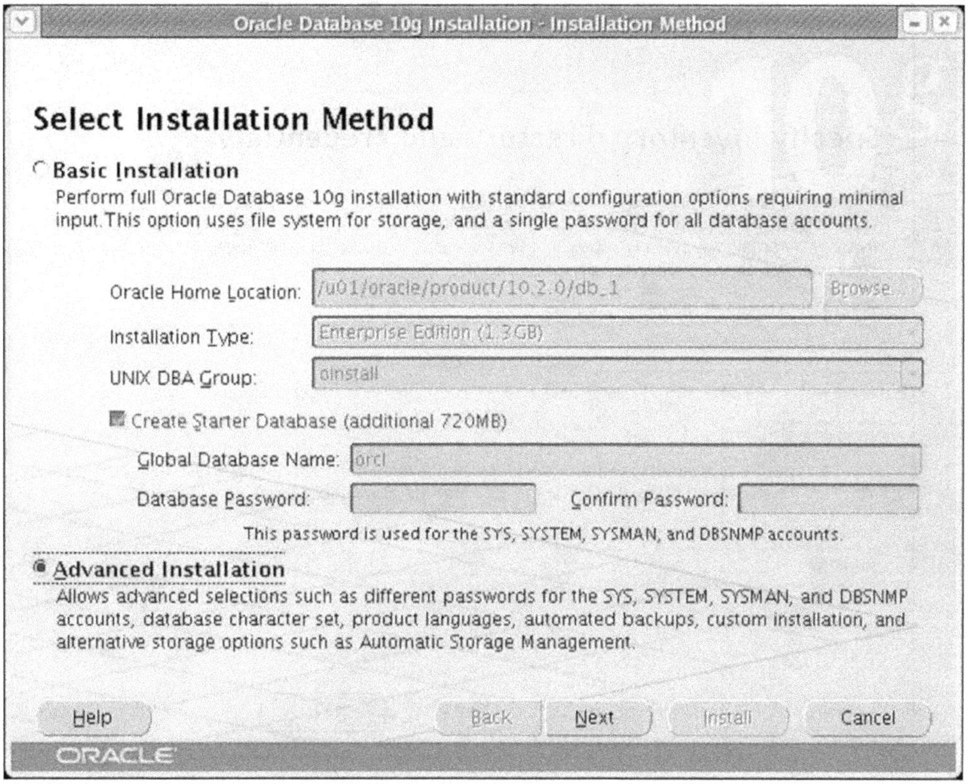

Oracle Database 10g Installation - Installation Method

Select Installation Method

Basic Installation

Perform full Oracle Database 10g installation with standard configuration options requiring minimal input. This option uses file system for storage, and a single password for all database accounts.

Oracle Home Location: /u01/oracle/product/10.2.0/db_1 Browse...

Installation Type: Enterprise Edition (1.3GB)

UNIX DBA Group: oinstall

Create Starter Database (additional 720MB)

Global Database Name: orcl

Database Password: Confirm Password:

This password is used for the SYS, SYSTEM, SYSMAN, and DBSNMP accounts.

Advanced Installation

Allows advanced selections such as different passwords for the SYS, SYSTEM, SYSMAN, and DBSNMP accounts, database character set, product languages, automated backups, custom installation, and alternative storage options such as Automatic Storage Management.

Help Back Next Install Cancel

ORACLE

Figure 7.2: *Advanced Installation Method Being Chosen*

The OUI needs a repository to store the information related to the different Oracle installations that are present on the server. The inventory also keeps the installation logs of all the installation performed on the server. The inventory location is set only on the first installation and it is recommended that the DBA takes a backup of the directory since it contains all the information on the Oracle installation.

If there is a previous release of Oracle installed on the server, there may already be an existing repository. In the inventory location window, the Linux group that will own the inventory must also be specified. The default value for the Oracle inventory is *$ORACLE_BASE/inventory*.

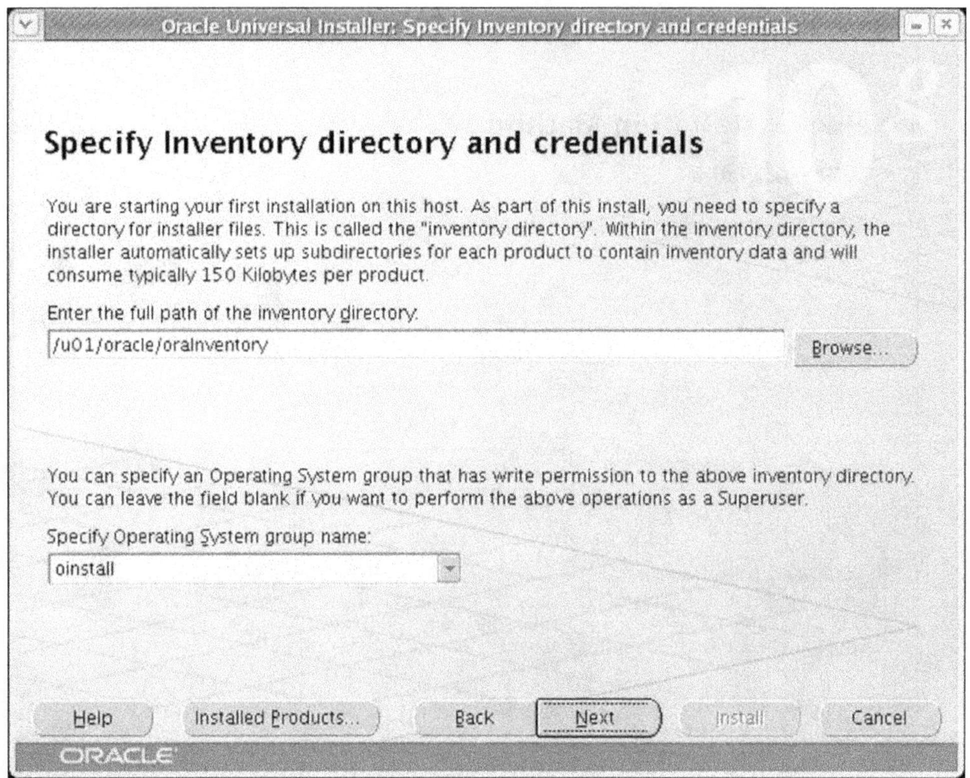

Figure 7.3: *Default Location of Oracle Inventory*

After the inventory is defined, it is possible to consult the logs files of the Oracle installation in that directory. Read the paragraph "Oracle Universal Installer Log Files" later in the chapter to get more details.

It is necessary to specify what type of Oracle installation needs to be performed. When Enterprise Manager is selected, it will install the products Partitioning, OLAP, Spatial and Advanced Security that are licensed products with a high cost, so be careful. It is recommended that the user has a discussion with their License manager in order to avoid high license cost on unused products. Therefore, always perform a custom installation to be certain what products will be installed.

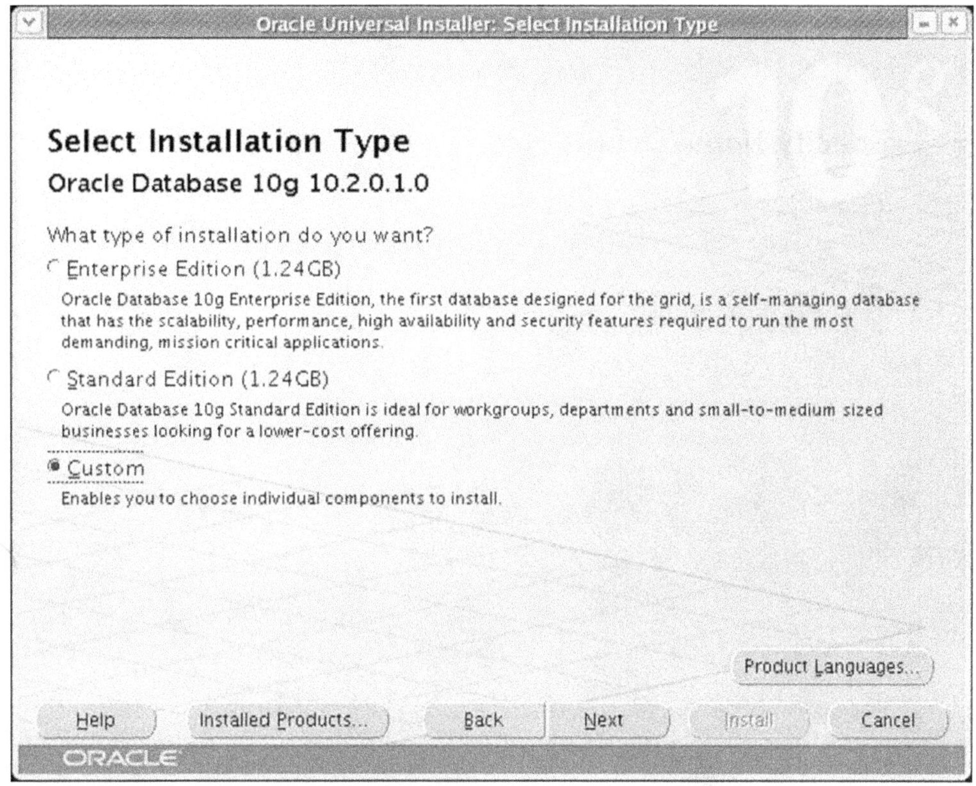

Figure 7.4: *Selecting Custom Installation*

After that, specify the name and location of the *$ORACLE_HOME* and ensure that the specified directory is empty; otherwise, an error message will be received from the OUI.

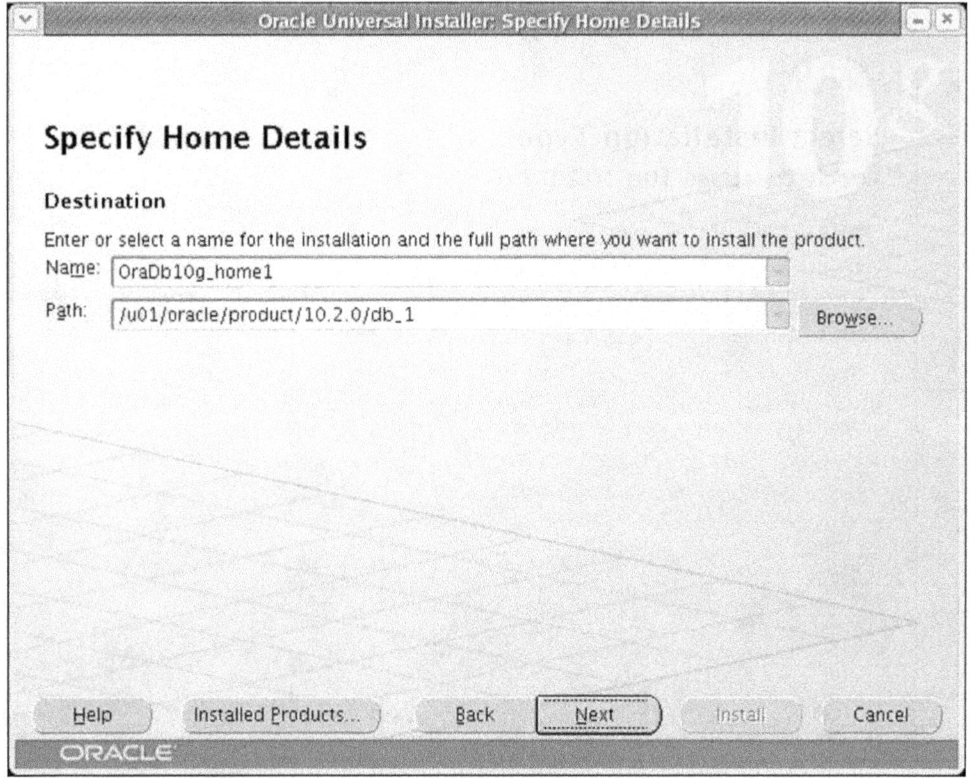

Figure 7.5: *Specifying Name and Location of $ORACLE_HOME*

In the product components, it is possible to select the option that needs to be installed for the Oracle binaries on the server.

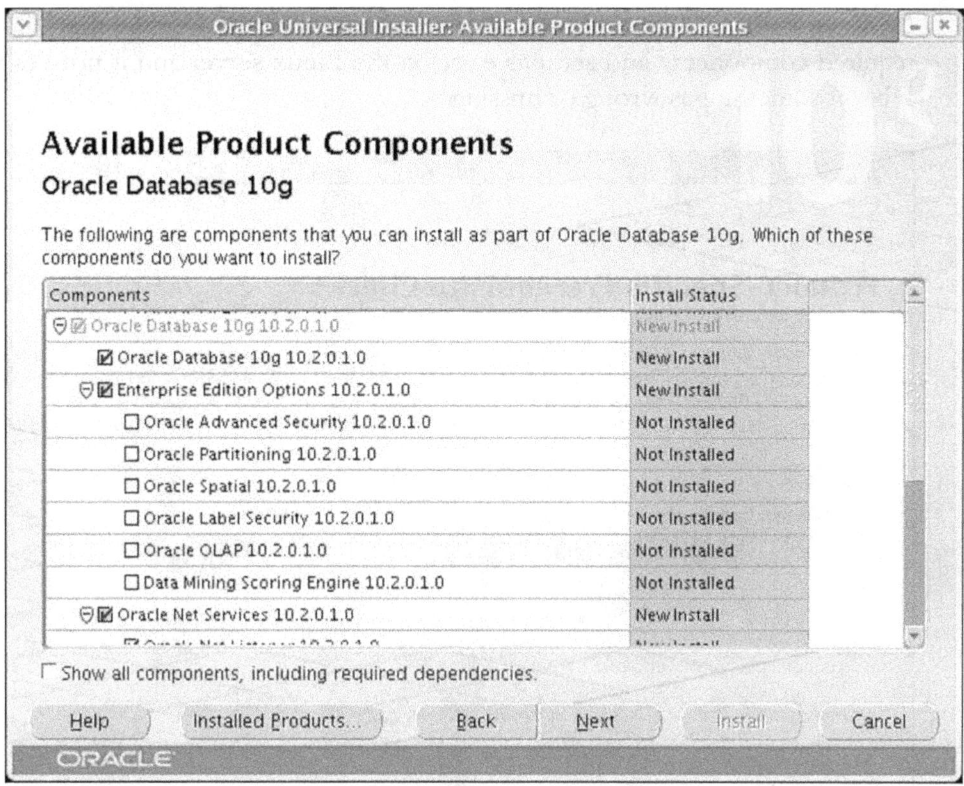

Figure 7.6: *Products Component List*

If the DBA tries to remove a component that is required by Oracle to be installed, the following error window will appear.

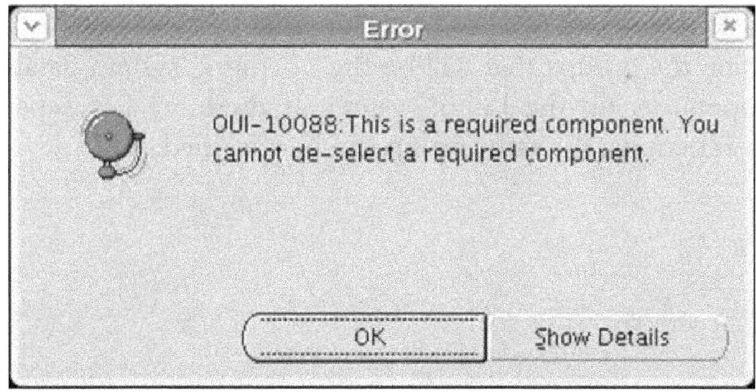

Figure 7.7: *Product Component Error Message*

OUI performs a verification of the prerequisites to be certain that all the required components and settings exist on the Linux server and it notifies the DBA if something is wrong or missing.

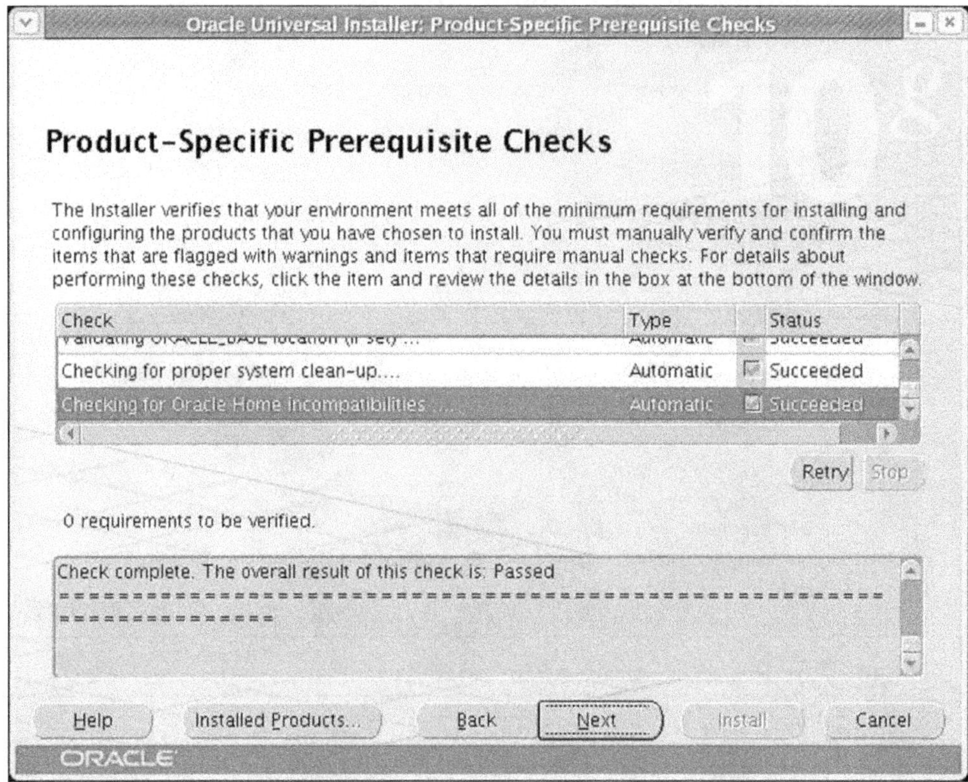

Figure 7.8: *Verifying Product-Specific Prerequisites*

It is necessary to define the groups that will be the operating system database administrators and operators on the Linux system. If there are not separate groups for those two functions, the same group can be specified.

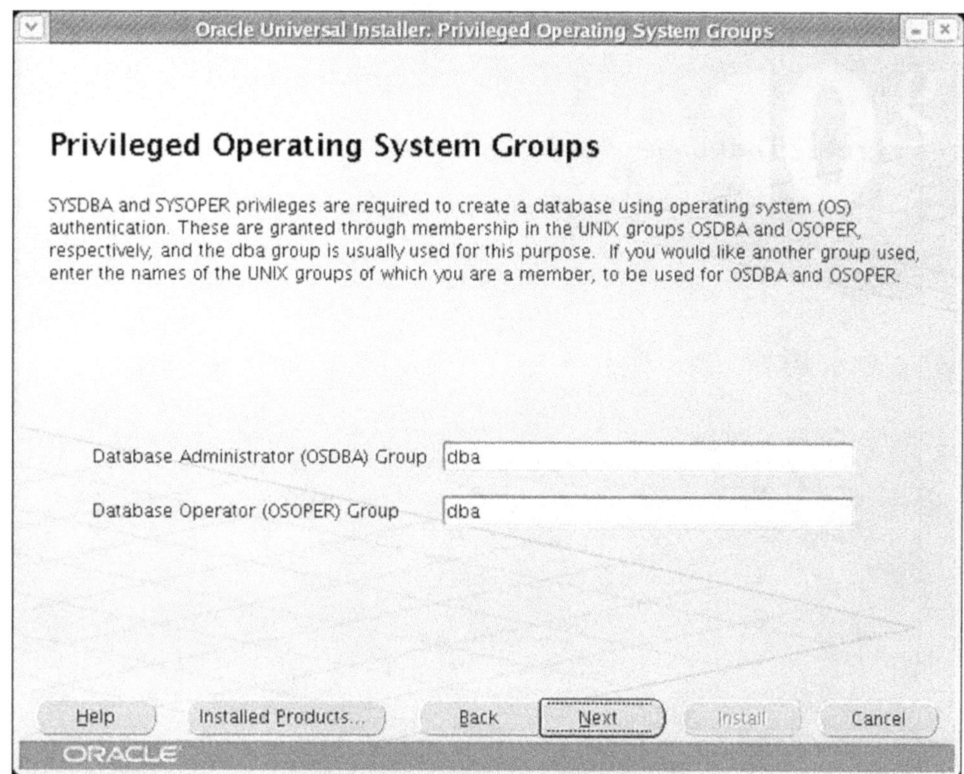

Oracle Universal Installer: Privileged Operating System Groups
Privileged Operating System Groups
SYSDBA and SYSOPER privileges are required to create a database using operating system (OS) authentication. These are granted through membership in the UNIX groups OSDBA and OSOPER, respectively, and the dba group is usually used for this purpose. If you would like another group used, enter the names of the UNIX groups of which you are a member, to be used for OSDBA and OSOPER.
Database Administrator (OSDBA) Group
dba
Database Operator (OSOPER) Group
dba
Help
Installed Products...
Back
Next
Install
Cancel
ORACLE

Figure 7.9: *Choosing Privileged Operating System Groups*

It is possible after the installation is successfully performed to create a database directly after, so OUI will start a *dbca* session to do that.

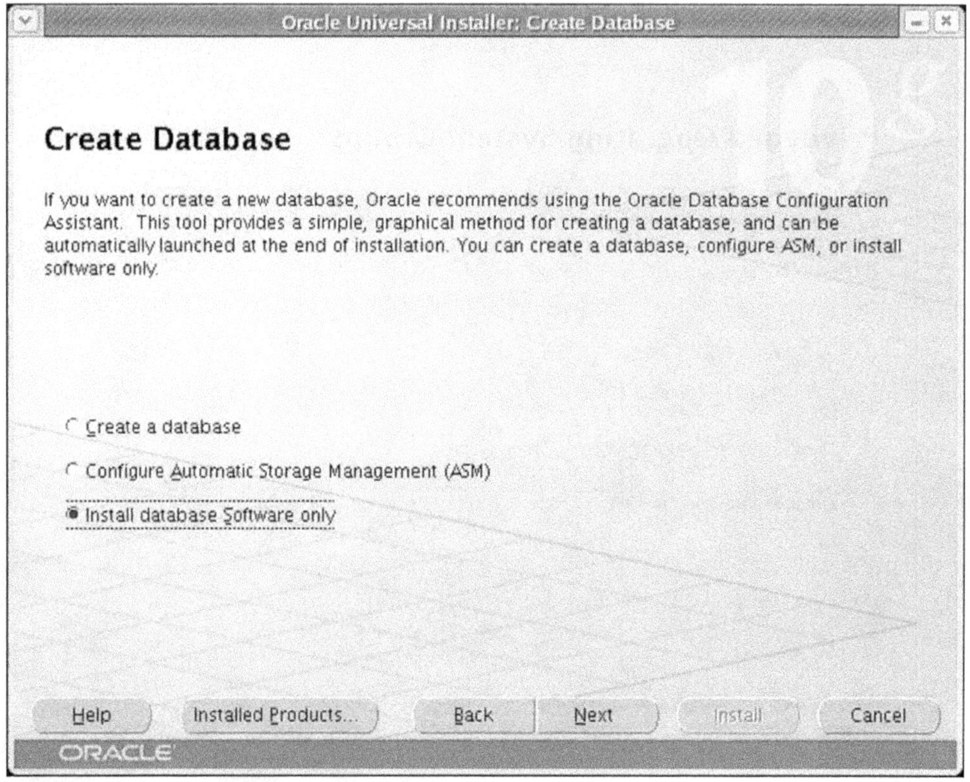

Figure 7.10: *Creating a Database*

On the next window, a summary of the entire list of components is produced by OUI so that what the components are that will be installed is controlled as well as where and with what options.

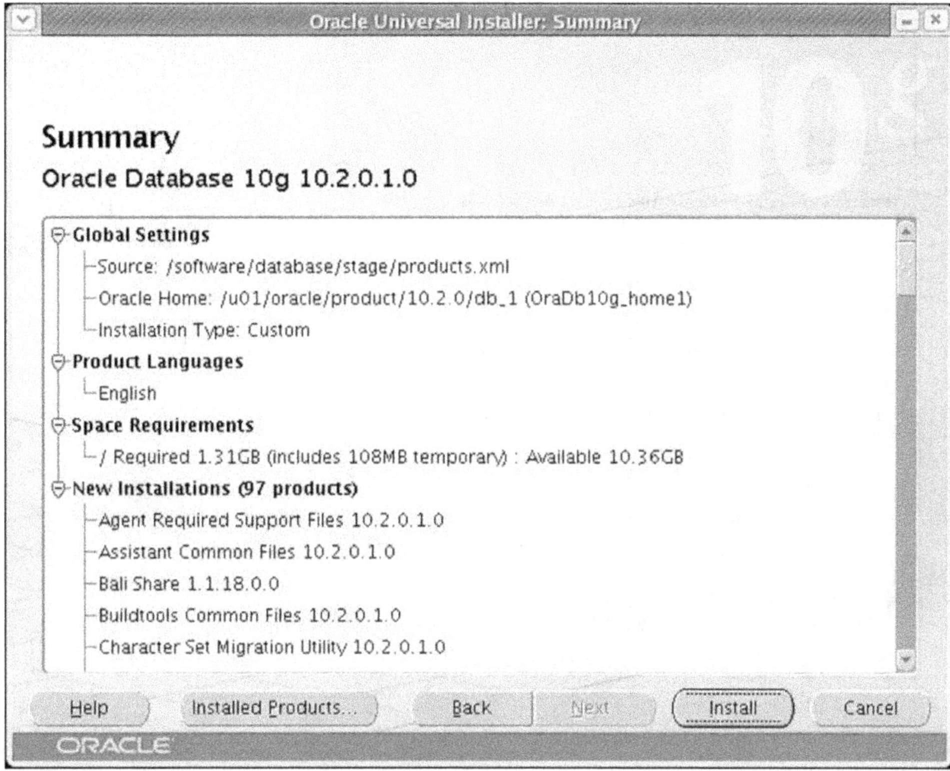

Figure 7.11: *Summary of Installed Components*

After the install button is clicked, there is a progress bar that shows the ongoing installation and the steps that are finished.

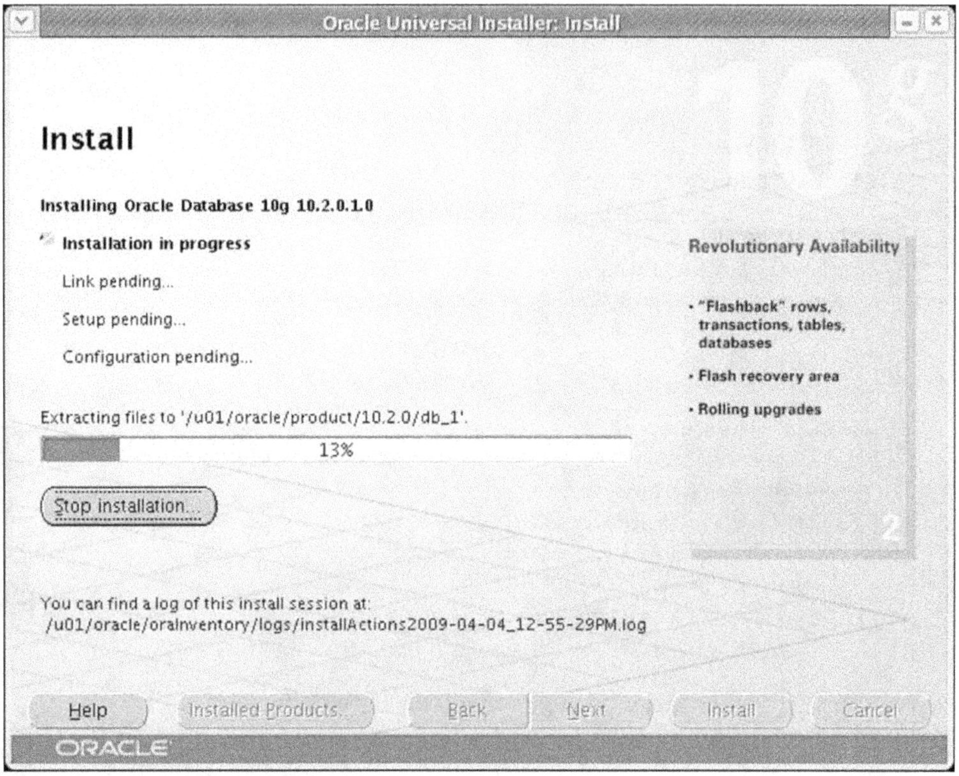

Figure 7.12: *Installation Progress Bar*

After the installation, linking, setup and configuration is finished, there will be the window shown next with instructions to execute two scripts as root in an xterm or shell window. The first is the script *oraInstRoot.sh* located in *$ORACLE_BASE* that is creating the file */etc/oraInst.loc*, which contains the location of the inventory and also the group name of the inventory owner. The file */etc/oraInst.loc* is quite important to remove or upgrade the Oracle software.

The second script *root.sh*, located in the *$ORACLE_HOME*, creates the */etc/oratab* file, sets up the *oraenv/coraenv* scripts and performs some links. Oracle strongly suggests that a copy be kept of the original *root.sh* scripts since sometimes information contained by this file is required.

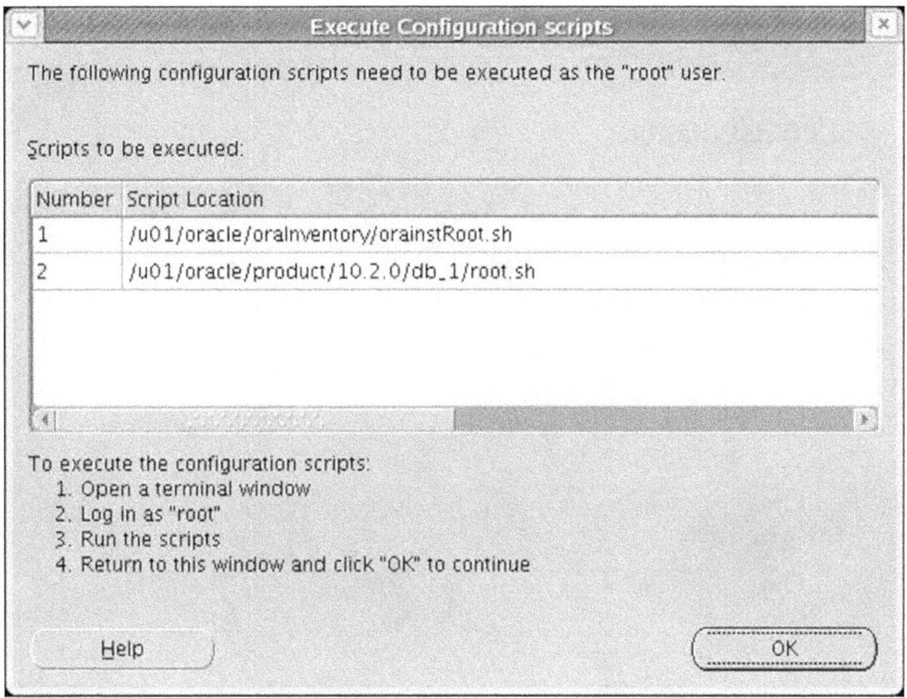

Figure 7.13: *Executing Two Scripts*

The last window informs that the Oracle installation was done successfully, and if the choice has been made to install the Enterprise Manager, it will contain the information on how to reach it.

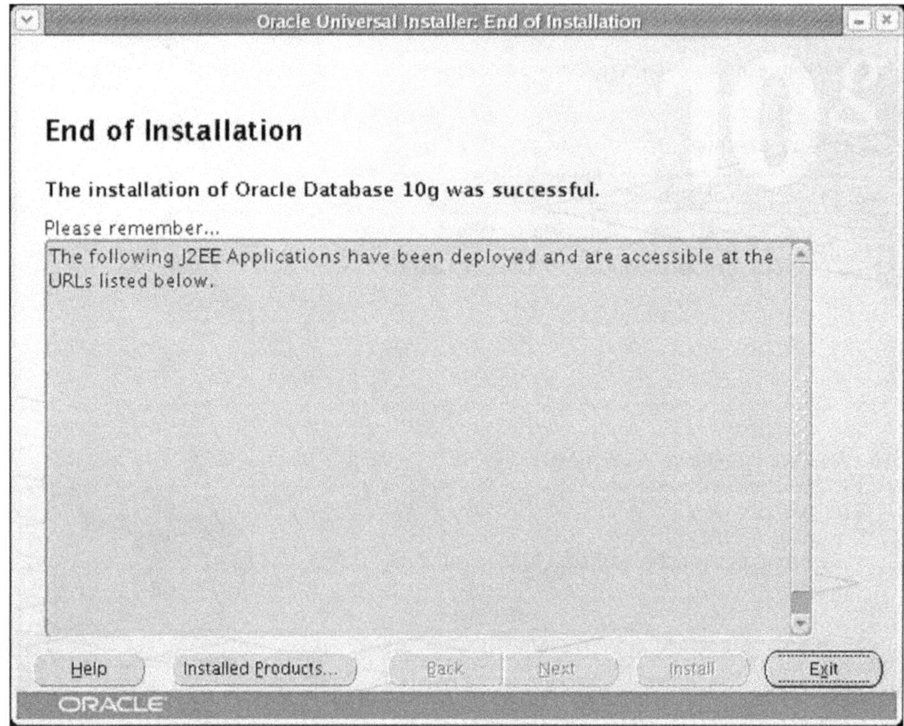

Figure 7.14: *Successful Installation Screen*

Oracle Universal Installer Log Files

Before the inventory location is defined, the OUI log files are located in the */tmp/OraInstall<date_time>* directory. But after the inventory is defined, the log files of the OUI are stored in the *$ORACLE_BASE/oraInventory/logs* directory. Every time the Oracle Installer is used, a file *installActions<date_time>.log* keeps usable evidences. The prerequisites checks are also stored in a log file available in the *$ORACLE_BASE/oraInventory/logs/results/db/ db_prereq_results.xml* file.

OPatch Utility

The OPatch tool helps the DBA apply one-off and temporary patches. The tool is installed in the *$ORACLE_HOME* in the directory *$ORACLE_HOME/OPatch/* and it helps to rollback the patches. With this tool, all the patches installed on the installation can be listed as well as all the installed Oracle components. The Oracle *patch* utility is installed by the OUI during the first installation.

In order to work *opatch*, the Java Runtime Environment is needed, which is installed with OUI on 10g Release 2, and the privileges to execute the Linux command */sbin/fuser* that controls if any processes are running on the binaries to patch are required. In addition, the write access to the Oracle inventory is needed to store the patch information and a Perl version minimum 5.005_3 interpreter working for the oracle user is a must.

To use the *opatch* commands, the *path* values should include the *$ORACLE_HOME/OPatch* in the list. After a description is obtained, here are some *opatch* commands to do the list, installation and rollback the patch on the Oracle installation.

To list the installed patches:

```
opatch lsinventory -oh $ORACLE_HOME -all
```

To install a patch:

```
opatch apply <patch_directory> $ORACLE_HOME
```

To rollback a patch:

```
opatch rollback -id <patch_id> $ORACLE_HOME
```

To get the help of the *opatch* utility:

```
opatch -help
```

Below is how to attach a new *$ORACLE_HOME* on the oraInventory. The software that is in the example is moved from another Linux server.

```
opatch attach -name <Oracle Home name> -oh $ORACLE_HOME
```

It is also possible to get help and options on specific commands by doing:

```
opatch lsinventory -help
```

Relink the Binaries

Oracle distributes objects, libraries and source files that must be linked by the DBA's specific operating system. With the link process, Oracle can do a consistent integration with the OS libraries. The link process also provides optimal performances as the binaries are produced with the OS libraries. The link or relink happens automatically when the product is installed or when an install is done on an Oracle patch set.

In the following situations, a manual relink of the Oracle binaries will have to be performed:

- When the operating system is upgraded
- When operating system libraries are updated. This can also be done with an OS upgrade.
- When the Oracle executables are producing core dumps during the startup
- When a single Oracle patch is installed and the readme instructions of the patch are describing the relink to be necessary

When a relink is executed, make sure that before performing it, the *$ORACLE_HOME* is correct, that the binaries have no running processes and *ld_library_path* contains the *$ORACLE_HOME/lib* in the arguments.

It is possible to perform the relink operation on the following parts:

- *relink oracle* : Relinks the database executables
- *relink utilities* : Relinks RMAN, TKPROF, impdp, expdp, imp, exp and SQL*Loader
- *relink all* : Relinks all the Oracle components
- *relink network* : Relinks only the network component as listener, names and cman
- *relink oemagent* : Relinks the Intelligent Agents
- *relink ctx* : That commands will relink the Oracle text

Solve Issues During the Installation

During the installation process, some mistakes or missing prerequisites can result in installation failures, i.e. wrong kernel values can generate ORA-3113 "End of file" messages, missing compiler in the path, wrong permission or misspelled variables. If this occurs, take time to ensure that the prerequisites values are correct for the kernel, that the environment variables are properly set, user rights for the installation and repository directory are correctly set and that all the required RPM packages are installed on the Linux server.

The DBA should also make sure that the log files produced by the Oracle Universal Installer can be a source to solve the issues, eventually following the installation in a second xterm window with a *tail –f* on the log file of the installer. In addition, it is possible to set traces on the OUI by doing the following command:

```
./runInstaller -logLevel trace -debug /-J-DTRACING.ENABLED=true -J-
DTRACING.LEVEL=2/
```

 Exam Advice: Be sure to know the Oracle installation operations, the locations of the Oracle Inventory files, roles of the files and the relink reasons and options.

Topics Not On Exam

Java NCOMP

Oracle includes a native compilation of Java that increases from two to ten times the speed of byte code interpretation, but the 10.2.0.1 Linux installation package is missing the NCOMP (Native Compiler) tool. To avoid ORA-29558 errors, Java NCOMP needs to be installed. The Java NCOMP tool is present on the Companion CD 10g Release 2. With the following procedures, it can be confirmed that the Java NCOMP error is present or not.

With the OUI of the Companion CD, select and install the option that contains the JAccelator (NCOMP).

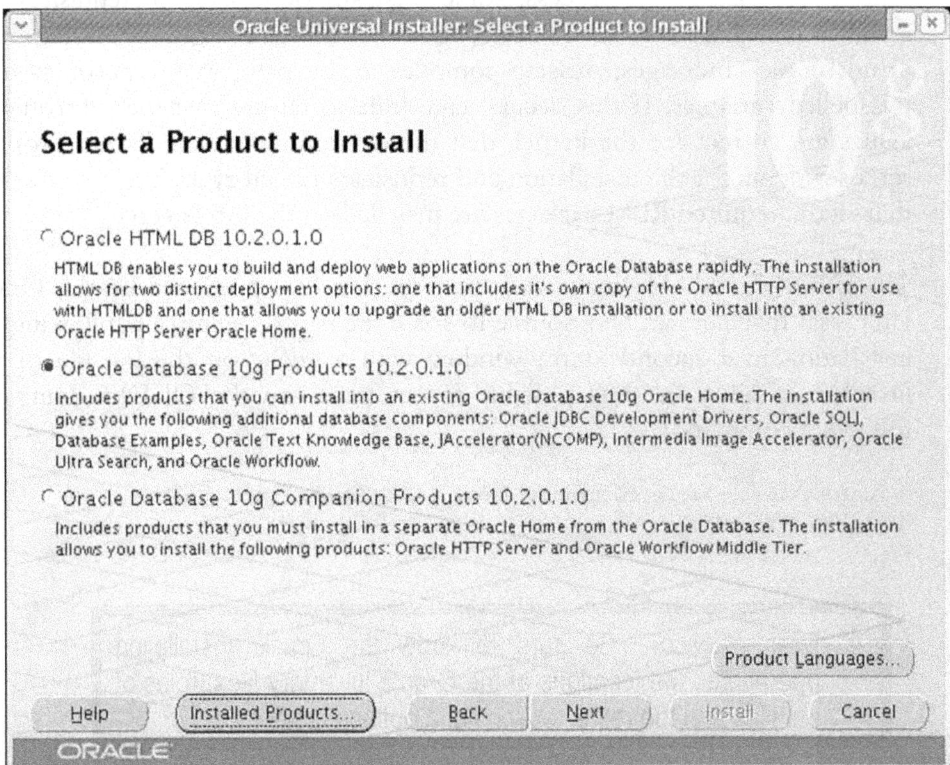

Figure 7.15: *Oracle Database 10g Products to Install*

Confirm in the summary that the JAccelator (COMPANION) is selected before performing the installation.

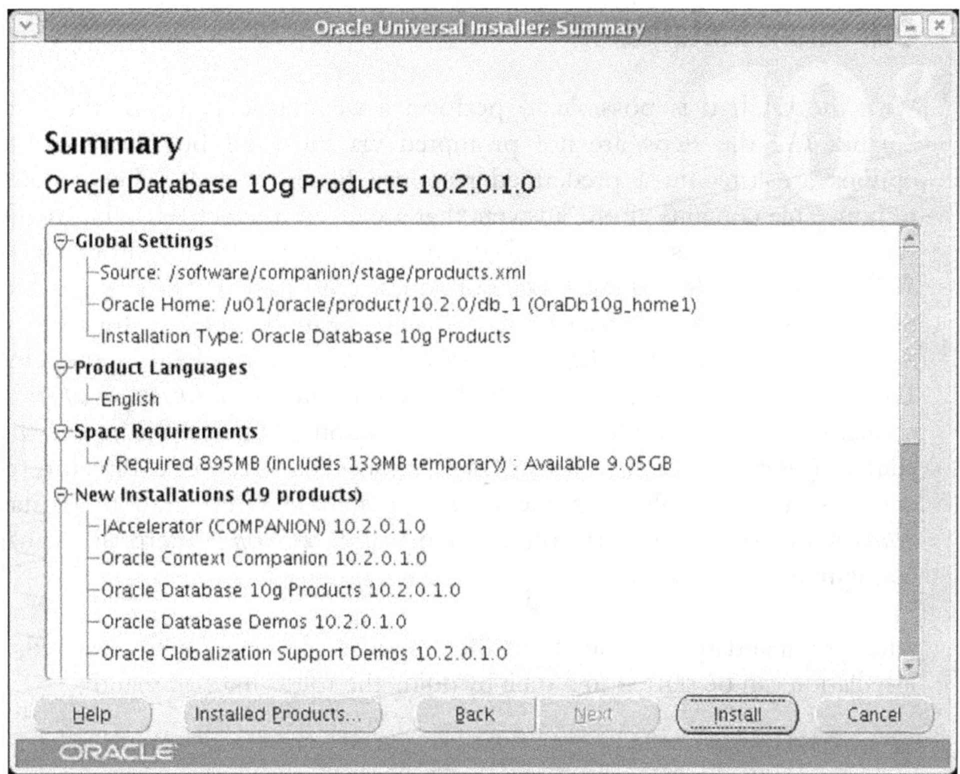

Figure 7.16: *Confirmation of JAccelerator (Companion) Product*

Here is the NCOMP error on an Oracle installation that does not have the 10g Companion NCOMP option installed.

```
SQL> select dbms_java.full_ncomp_enabled from dual;
select dbms_java.full_ncomp_enabled from dual

      *
ERROR at line 1:
ORA-29558: JAccelerator (NCOMP) not installed. Refer to Install Guide for
instructions.
ORA-06512: at "SYS.DBMS_JAVA", line 236
```

On a 10g R2 database with the 10g Companion option *SQL> select dbms_java.full_ncomp_enabled* installed from dual;

```
FULL_NCOMP_ENABLED
--------------------------------------------------------------------------------
OK
```

OUI Silent Installation

With the OUI, it is possible to perform a silent installation of the Oracle binaries. All the steps are not prompted via the GUI but the installation options are listed in a predefined response file in a shell. The predefined response file contains all the answers that are given interactively with the GUI such as the options to be installed, the location of the inventory and the *$ORACLE_HOME* values. Oracle provides templates of the response file in the installation package that can be found in *<root_of_the_installation_package>/response/ <installation_type>.rsp* in the Oracle 10g: *10201_database_linux32.zip*. The files are located in *Disk/response/*, which contains the response files for a standard edition (*standard.rsp*), the enterprise edition (*enterprise.rsp*) and custom installations. The response directory also contains response files for the *dbca.rsp* (database configuration assistant), *netca.rsp* (network configuration assistant) and *emca.rsp* (enterprise manager configuration assistant).

After the mandatory questions in the response file have been answered, the installation can be started in a shell by doing the following command:

```
cd Disk1/response
./runInstaller -silent -responseFile custom.rsp
```

If the DBA needs to create a specific response file, OUI can record the installation session from the GUI. It is possible to perform the installation while recording the response file or only record a response file; in that case, the operation will have to be stopped on the summary page. The response file recording can only be performed from the GUI, not from a character terminal without X Windows:

```
./runInstaller -record -destinationFile
/install/Disk1/response/mynewfile.rsp
```

In case the DBA is performing an Oracle installation on a server that does not have any Oracle product installed, the inventory can be created by doing the actions below:

```
# Values for
# $ORACLE_BASE=/u01/app/oracle
# group owner of the inventory is oinstall
#
su - root
```

```
cd /etc
vi oraInst.loc
     inventory_loc=/u01/app/oracle/oraInventory
     inst_group=oinstall
chown oracle:oinstall oraInst.loc
chmod 664 oraInst.loc
```

OUI Binaries Cloning

A database administrator may have to install and set up a lot of Oracle binaries for a project on the same server or on a different server within a very tight delivery schedule. Sometimes it is even necessary to migrate the databases on new servers. Oracle makes it possible to facilitate these installation tasks by using the cloning of the Oracle installation.

When cloning is used, it is not necessary to execute all the installation steps performed previously as all those steps will be present in the clone package. With cloning, it is possible to have a distribution image on the installation servers so the DBA is able to rapidly deploy the Oracle installation. It will also simplify the deployment methods of new patches or specific installation with, for example, a standard edition, customized or an enterprise edition clone. To accomplish the steps needed to clone an already installed Oracle 10g release 2 RDBMS, perform the following operations:

1. Make sure that all the components and patches are installed on the clone source. See the installation logs if any error is present.
2. Stop all the binaries of the *$ORACLE_HOME* that need to be cloned.
3. Verify that the directory *$ORACLE_HOME/clone/bin* contains the perl files and prepare *$ORACLE_HOME* to be cloned.
4. Copy the sources files in a recursive way or make a tar ball of all the files in *$ORACLE_HOME.*
5. Uncompress the tar or put the copied files in the new location.
6. Perform the *perl* script to do the cloning operation.
7. Run the *root.sh* script to finish the installation.
8. Perform a test on the new installation and control the log files.

Note that the cloning operation can also be performed with Grid or the Enterprise Manager DB console, but the tools use the *perl* scripts located in

$ORACLE_HOME/clone/bin. Therefore, do confirm that the files are present.

If it happens that the cloning operation is being perfromed on the same server where the source's files are, it is preferable to do a backup of the inventory before performing the cloning operations.

The detailed steps are:

1. Make sure that all the components and patches are installed on the clone source. See the installation logs if any error is present.
2. Stop all the binaries of the *$ORACLE_HOME* that need to be cloned. Make sure that all the processes related to *$ORACLE_HOME/* are stopped, i.e. fuser *$ORACLE_HOME/*.

```
dbshut
emctl stop dbconsole #if the OEM console is used
emctl stop agent #if you a using an agent and grid controller
```

3. Verify that the directory *$ORACLE_HOME/clone/bin* contains the perl files:

```
cd $ORACLE_HOME/clone/bin
ls
clone.pl    prepare_clone.pl
```

4. Execute the *prepare_clone.pl* perl script on the source directory. It will perform the preparation operations.
5. Copy the source's files in a recursive way or make a tar ball of all the files in *$ORACLE_HOME*:

```
export CLONE=/software/clone
cd $ORACLE_HOME
# prepare the exclude file
 find . -name *.log |grep -v "./log" >$ORA_CLONE/excludefromtar
 find ./network/admin >>$ORA_CLONE/excludefromtar
 find ./oc4j/j2ee/OC4J_DBConsole_*  >>$ORA_CLONE/excludefromtar
 find `hostname |cut -d "." -f 1`*_* >>$ORA_CLONE/excludefromtar
# Use the line below if the template shouldn't be included
 find ./assistants/dbca/templates >>$ORA_CLONE/excludefromtar

# Get the oracle software to clone from
tar -X $ORA_CLONE/excludefromtar -czvf $ORA_CLONE/10g_ora_custom.gz .
```

6. Uncompress the tar or put the copied files in the new location:

```
export ORA_CLONE=/software/clone
mkdir -p /u01/oracle/product/10.2.0/db_2
export ORACLE_HOME=/u01/oracle/product/10.2.0/db_2
cd $ORACLE_HOME
tar -xzvf $ORA_CLONE/10g_ora_custom.gz
```

7. After the decompression is performed, ensure that the permissions are properly set on the files in the new *$ORACLE_HOME/*. If not, align it with the source of the clone.

8. Perform the *perl* script to do the cloning operation:

```
cd $ORACLE_HOME/clone/bin
perl -version
perl clone.pl                          \
    ORACLE_BASE=/u01/oracle/           \
    ORACLE_HOME=/u01/oracle/product/10.2.0/db_2 \
    ORACLE_HOME_NAME=OraDb10g_home2
```

9. Verify that the *perl* version used is a minimum of 5.005_3 or higher. If the *perl* is not the correct one, set the variable *$perl5lib* to select the correct release of the *perl* needed.

If the server does not have an Oracle inventory existing, the clone action will create a new inventory location. If the server does have an existing Oracle inventory, be sure that the *oracle_home_name* is not already in use. To control this, take a look in the file *$ORACLE_BASE/oraInventory/ContentsXML/inventory.xml* and choose a name that is not in use in the XML variable *home_name*. When cloning a 10g standard edition Release 2 is attempted, a bug can be blocking that process. Therefore, use the Oracle Support Note 416255.1 to fix that issue.

10. Run the *root.sh* script to finish the installation with the root account.

11. Perform a test of the new installation and control the logs files by setting the listener and starting SQL*Plus.

Summary

This chapter focused on installing Oracle on a Linux server with a description of the variables available for the Oracle account and other components. Next to be covered was the installation itself using Oracle Universal Installer (OUI) with screen shots of the steps required to complete a successful installation. Then the log files of the OUI were examined. Finally, additional topics that are not part of the exam were illustrated including installing Java NCOMP and OUI's silent installation and binaries cloning.

Exercises

1. Do the installation of the Oracle binaries on the Linux server.
2. Relink all the Oracle components.

Q&A

Questions

1. Match the following variables with the correct description:

A. *$ORACLE_HOME* is
B. *$ORACLE_BASE* is
C. *$ORACLE_SID* is
D. *$ORACLE_HOSTNAME* is
E. *$ORACLE_DOC* is
F. *$ORA_NLS10* is
G. *$LANG* IS
H. *$TMPDIR* OR *TMP*
I. *$AGENT_HOME* is
J. *$LD_LIBRARY_PATH* is
K. *$ORACLE_OWNER*
L. *$ORACLE_TERM*

a. The Oracle instance name of the user's database
b. The location of the Oracle documentation
c. The home of the Oracle Enterprise Manager agent home
d. Used in case multiple network cards have been activated. That value of the Oracle hostname will need to be set.
e. A mandatory value that is present in the profile. It contains the Oracle binaries and software.
f. The path that contains the C libraries. The other user libraries are set in *$PATH, i.e. /usr/lib*
g. Is used to set the X Windows terminal windows. Typically is the value *xterm.*

h. Is used in case the */tmp* is too small and cannot be changed. The variable can be used to set an alternative temporary location for the installation.
i. The character set files location
j. The language of the Linux system
k. Is used to define what the Oracle Linux user is
l. The root directory for the Oracle binaries and software

2. What is most important when an Oracle installation is being done with OUI on the GUI? (Choose the correct answer)

A. Having the Oracle account that is unlocked
B. That the *%ORACLE_HOME%\bin\oradims* is working
C. That the X Windows display is set properly and working
D. That the operation group *oper* exists

3. What are the benefits of using OFA? (Choose all that apply)

A. It reduces the cost of disks and memory
B. It makes it possible to have multiple Oracle releases installed on the same server
C. It increases the reliability
D. It balances I/O

4. What does the file */etc/oratab* store? (Choose the correct answer)

A. This file does not exist in an Oracle installation
B. It stores the name of the database only
C. It contains the *$ORACLE_SID*, *$ORACLE_HOME* and a flag Y or N to start the database or not
D. It is not used by the scripts *oraenv* and *dbhome*

5. Which of the following variable values are setting the *oraenv* in an interactive mode? (Choose all that apply)

A. *oraenv_ask=*
B. *oraenv_ask =yes*
C. *oraenv_ask =no*
D. *oraenv_ask _interactive=yes*

6. What are the correct values of the groups osdba and osoper? (Choose all that apply)

A. oracle

B. *dba*
C. *oper*
D. nothing of the given values

7. Where is it possible to get the log files of the Oracle Universal Installer? (Choose all that apply)

A. *$ORACLE_BASE/oraInventory/logs*
B. *$ORACLE_HOME/oraInventory/logs*
C. */tmp/OraInstall<date_time> directory*
D. *$oracle_log/oraInventory/logs*

8. What will *opatch* do with the following command *opatch lsinventory –oh $ORACLE_HOME –all?* (Choose the correct answer)

A. It rebuilds the Oracle inventory and lists the results in *$ORACLE_HOME*
B. It will apply the new patch
C. it deletes all the entry in the Oracle inventory
D. It lists all the patches installed in the *$ORACLE_HOME.*

9. Jack, a junior DBA, needs to relink the Oracle binaries since the Linux server was recently patched. What should be done before doing that relink operation? (Choose all that apply)

A. Make sure that all the Oracle binaries are stopped
B. It is not necessary to stop all the Oracle binaries
C. It is not necessary to take a backup
D. Take a backup of the *$ORACLE_HOME*

10. What are the possible actions when the installation of Oracle with OUI is failing? (Choose all that apply)

A. Set the trace in OUI to debug and use the command *tail -f* to follow the logs
B. Control all the prerequisites such as memory and rpm
C. Do a complete reinstallation of the Linux server
D. Log a Service Request in Oracle Support

Answers

1. The correct matches are:

A-e
B-1

C-a
D-d
E-b
F-i
G-j
H-h
I-c
J-f
K-k
L-g
HINT: Read again the section on Oracle account settings.

2. The correct answer is: C. That the X Windows display is set properly and working.

HINT: Consult the section "Installation" to understand why.

3. The correct answers are: B. It makes it possible to have multiple Oracle releases installed on the same server; C. it increases the reliability; and D. It balances I/O.

HINT: Study again the OFA (Optimal Flexible Architecture) to get the correct answers.

4. The correct answer is: C. It contains the *$ORACLE_SID*, *$ORACLE_HOME* and a flag Y or N to start the database or not.

HINT: Study again the section about multiple Oracle versions on the same server, if your answer is incorrect.

5. The correct answers are: A. *oraenv_ask*=; and B. *oraenv_ask =yes*

HINT: Consult again the section on multiple Oracle versions on the same server to understand how the *oraenv* works.

6. The correct answers are: B. dba and C. oper

HINT: Read again the section "Installation" if this is a wrong answer.

7. The correct answers are: A. *$oracle_base/oraInventory/logs* and C. */tmp/OraInstall<date_time>* directory

HINT: Consult the Oracle Universal Installer log files.

8. The correct answer is: D. It lists all the patches installed in the *$ORACLE_HOME*.

HINT: Read again the section OPatch utility.

9. The correct answers are A. Control that all the Oracle binaries are stopped; and D. Take a backup of the *$ORACLE_HOME*.

HINT: Study the section Relink the binaries.

10. The correct answers are A. Set the trace in OUI to debug and use the command *tail -f* to follow the logs; B. Control all prerequisites such as memory and rpm and D. Log a Service Request in Oracle Support.

HINT: Consult the section on solving issues during the installation.

Solutions to Exercises

1. Before starting, confirm that all the prerequisites are met. Read the section about downloading the installation files and on installation to get the installation process. Follow all the given actions to succeed in the Oracle installation. After the installation is done, check out the log's files.
2. Verify that the *$ORACLE_HOME* of the binaries to be relinked is properly set. Ensure that no processes are running in the *$ORACLE_HOME* with the */sbin/fuser $ORACLE_HOME* and that *the ld_library_path* contains the *$oracle_home/lib* directory. When all those controls and verifications are done, execute the following commands:

```
cd $ORACLE_HOME/bin
./relink all
```

Managing Storage

CHAPTER

This chapter covers the following exam objectives:

4. Managing Storage
4.1. Distinguish the differences between certified and supported file systems
4.2. Select a file system

This chapter will cover the aspects related to a file system that are in the exam and also what are the supported and certified file systems. This is a continuation of Chapter 3, which is about file systems with more details that are required to know in order to pass the exam.

File System Features

The most important features of a file system are ensuring the security of the data, write acknowledgement, write via a cache, and having high performances and a record in a journal to restore very quickly the integrity of the file system. The journal can be compared to the redo logs of the database that helps to keep track of the changes performed. It also helps particularly in the boot sequence by boosting the *fsck* command when the command controls perform the controls of the file system. When the file system is not journalized, the *fsck* command uses much more time to control the file systems. In case the user's system crashes or is shutdown without doing the synchronization of the disks, the journal file can be useful by doing the restore of the file system integrity.

Linux is able to support different file systems type-mounted on the same server and the operating system is completely independent of which file systems are used. The most frequently used file system in Linux is the ext3 file system that includes the journalizing feature. It is the extension of the previous version ext2. The fourth version, ext4, was released on December 25, 2008. The other file systems that have the journal included are JFS and reiserfs. Oracle provides a cluster file system that is meant to be used with the

Oracle Real Application Cluster (RAC). The Oracle Cluster File System (OCFS) can both store database physical files and also binaries, files, and configuration files. It is possible to share across the servers in the cluster with this file system by sharing the disks. OCFS supports 32 nodes and allows very large files up to 2 TB. The OCFS2 is the POSIX compliant file system with high performances and availability that also includes the journaling with write-back and ordered data modes. To get more information about OCFS and OCFS2, consult the websites http://oss.oracle.com/projects/ocfs/and http://oss.oracle.com/ projects/ocfs2/. It is under General Public License.

The benefits of OCFS2 are that the commands used to navigate in the file system are standard (cd, mkdir, rm, ls, and such). There are no limits on the number of files, but OCFS2 allows up to 32000 subdirectories. It can store database fies as well as other files such as binaries, configuration and text files and it is freeware.

The release 2 of OCFS can be downloaded at the following webpage: http://oss.oracle.com/projects/ocfs2/files/. The website includes the sources and the compiled version in RPM format for the RHEL 4 and 5 for the different platforms.

Automatic Storage Management is recommended by Oracle to store all the database physical files. ASM and its features will be described in more detail in Chapter 9.

 Exam Advice: Be able to describe all the benefits of the file system related to the journalizing. Focus on ext3 and OCFS, but also know the other files systems that are journalized.

Partitions in Linux

Disk partition is an important topic that should not be forgotten as it can improve the upgrades, backup, restore and recovery operations. When there are huge partitions, the *fsck* will take much longer than when the partitions are smaller. Therefore, it would be best to keep the directories listed next on separate specific partitions. By splitting the partition into smaller entities, it will also significantly reduce the backup and restore operation.

Directories

- /
- /boot
- /home
- /var
- /var/log
- /tmp
- /u01/oracle
- /u01/oracle/oradata

The partition */var/log* and */tmp* should be separated from / to reduce the effects of runaway shells and log files. It is possible to see the partitions with the command *fdisk -l*, which will list all the partitions.

Exam Advice: Know why the file systems are faster with the proper option and be able to explain what can be done to have a faster *fsck* command.

Supported and Certified File Systems by Oracle

Oracle certifies specific file systems based on the criteria of security, performance and reliability. When a file system is chosen that is certified, this entitles the DBA to get support from Oracle. However, if the file system is only supported and not certified, the specific vendor of the file system will need to be contacted.

The three file systems on Linux that are certified are:

- ASM (Automatic Storage Management)
- OCFS /OCFS2 (Oracle Cluster File System)

- Ext3

File systems like reiserfs, JFS and XFS are supported, but file systems like VFAT and XFS are not acceptable to store database files due to a lack of file permission definition.

> Exam Advice: Know what the differences are between supported and certified. It is also important to be able to enumerate the certified file systems.

Raw Device

The raw device is the alternative to a file system to store the database files. The raw devices are not buffered; this means that it is a direct I/O operation that can give better performances. The configuration of the raw devices can be obtained in the file */etc/sysconfig/rawdevices* that is used to configure the raw device binding. However, keep in mind that the raw devices are much more difficult to administrate than the file systems.

Ext2 and Ext3

The file system ext2 was present for a long time on Linux. It is now replaced by ext3 since it is possible to convert with the command *tune2fs -j <device_name>*. The file system ext3 also brings the journaling and faster performances. The DBA is able to set one of the three journalizing levels in an ext3 file system by editing the */etc/fstab* file. The three levels are given with the option in */etc/fstab*:

- Lowest level: *data=writeback* means that only the metadata are written.
- Default level: *data=ordered* means that the metadata are written with an increased integrity over the lowest level.
- Highest level: *data=journal* means that it writes in the journal all the data and metadata changes. It is advised that the high level be used as it is the most reliable journaling option.

> Exam Advice: Know the differences between ext2 and ext3 and be capable of describing the different levels of journaling in ext3.

NFS and Oracle

The Network File System (NFS) is supported by Oracle only with network file servers. The CIFS (Common Internet File System) is not a supported protocol because the data commit and write block size are not guaranteed.

Summary

File systems, disk partitions and their features were covered in this short chapter as well as an explanation of certified versus supported file systems. The next chapter will cover Automatic System Management (ASM).

Exercises

1. Create an ext2 mount point.
2. Convert the ext2 file system to ext3.

Q&A

Questions

1. What is Linux able to support on the file systems? (Choose all that apply)

A. Different file systems can be type-mounted on the same server
B. Only one type of file system is supported
C. Support only ext2 for the /
D. Is completely independent of which file system is used

2. Which of the following file systems have the journaling feature? (Choose all that apply)

A. ext2
B. jfs
C. reiser

D. ext3

3. What file systems can be chosen to store both database files and Oracle binaries so that Oracle provides support? (Choose all that apply)

A. OCFS2
B. OCFS
C. reiserfs
D. ext3
E. jfs

4. Oracle has certified three file systems (ext3, OCFS and ASM), but which file system can only store Oracle database physical files? (Choose the most correct answer)

A. ext3
B. OCFS
C. OCFS2
D. ASM

5. What are the actions that should be done during the installation of the Linux systems in order to make the *fsck* and the mount operations much shorter? (Choose all that apply)

A. Have only one partition that contains all the directories
B. Have multiple partitions and, if possible, small partitions
C. Do not use a file system with journaling
D. Use a file system with journaling

6. What are the benefits of using the raw devices? (Choose the correct answer)

A. There is no benefit in using the raw device instead of the OS file system
B. It is using the journaling
C. The raw devices are much easier to manage than file systems
D. It is much faster as it bypasses the Linux I/O buffers

7. What partitions are separated from / to avoid runaway file issues? (Choose all that apply)

A. */boot*
B. */var/log*
C. */tmp*
D. */temp*

8. What journaling level on ext3 is the default level? (Choose all that apply)

A. *data=order*
B. *data=journaling*
C. *data=journal*
D. *data=ordered*

9. What journaling level on ext3 should be chosen to write only the metadata in the file */etc/fstab*? (Choose the correct answer)

A. None, it is default
B. data=order
C. data=writeback
D. data=journaling

10. What command enables converting the ext2 file system to ext3? (Choose the correct answer)

A. *tune3fs -j <device_name>*
B. *tune2fs -j <device_name>*
C. *convert2fs -j <device_name>*
D. *conver2fs3 -j <device_name>*

Answers

1. The correct answers are: A. Different file systems can be type-mounted on the same server; and D. Is completely independent of which file systems are used.

HINT: Consult again the section on file system features.

2. The correct answers are: B. jfs; C. reiser; and D. ext3

HINT: Consult again the section on file system features.

3. The correct answers are: A. OCFS2; B. OCFS and D. ext3

HINT: In case the answers are not correct, read again about supported and certified file systems by Oracle.

4. The correct answer is: D. ASM

HINT: All the other file systems can store both binaries and Oracle database files.

5. The correct answers are: B. Have multiple partitions and, if possible, small partitions; and D. Use a file system with journaling.

HINT: Review the section on partitions in Linux to know why these are the correct answers.

6. The correct answer is: D. It is much faster as it bypasses the Linux I/O buffers.

HINT: Read again the short section concerning raw devices.

7. The correct answers are: B. */var/log* and C. */tmp*

HINT: Review the section "Partitions in Linux".

8. The correct answer is: D. *data=ordered*

HINT: Consult again the section on ext2 and ext3.

9. The correct answer is: C. *data=writeback*

HINT: Study again the section about ext2 and ext3.

10. The correct answer is: B. *tune2fs -j <device_name>*

HINT: Read again the section about ext2 and ext3.

Solutions to Exercises

1. Create an ext2 mount point: Login as root, then create a partition with *fdisk*. When the partition is created, use the command *mke2fs /dev/sda2* and mount the file system *mount -t ext2 /dev/sda2 /mnt/ext2*. Login as root. Make sure that the device is */dev/sda2* mounted as read write in the file */etc/fstab*. Unmount the device to be converted: *umount /dev/sda2*.
2. Convert the ext2 file system to ext3: *tune2fs –j /dev/sda2*. Change the file system type in the file */etc/fstab*. Change it from ext2 to ext3 and finally mount the converted device *mount /dev/sda2*. Find the file system type by typing *mount | grep /dev/sda2*.

Automatic Storage Management

CHAPTER

This chapter covers the following exam objectives:

5. Automatic Storage Management
5.1. Install and initialize Automatic Storage Management Library Driver (ASMLib)
5.2. Mark disks for ASMLib
5.3. Create an Automatic Storage Management instance

What is ASM?

Oracle introduced Automatic Storage Management (ASM) in the Oracle 10g release with the purpose of having both a file system and a volume manager for Oracle database files. ASM includes features related to the stripping, mirroring and optimizing of the performance on the DBA's storage. ASM does away with the needs of I/O tuning with Oracle databases that are stored in the ASM storage area. ASM storage can only be viewed with the RMAN, database instances and Oracle command tools like *asmcmd*. It is transparent for the OS how the ASM storage structure is built.

ASM manages the disk devices in disk groups. A disk device can consist of individual or multiple disks from NAS, SAN or a RAID. To be able to use the ASM balance I/O, it would be better to have disk groups with similar storage size and performances. It is possible to create disk groups that can be dedicated to specific actions such as recovery and backup, flashback and database storage.

In ASM, it is possible to store data in a mirroring and stripping manner. Ideally with ASM, the OMF (Oracle Managed Files) are used depending on the redundancy chosen. The extends in ASM are about 1 MB and are spread across the disks in the disk group. By doing this, it optimizes the disk utilization and performance. The redundancy level in ASM is specified on a file basis. The mirroring of the files is performed on the extent level; this depends on the redundancy level set for the files. The ASM redundancy options that can be used are:

- External: Means that ASM is not in charge of the mirroring, but it is performed by the hardware on which the disks are residing.
- Normal: Means that 2-way mirroring is done by ASM, so the extent has one copy mirrored.
- High: Means that ASM is doing a 3-way mirroring so each of the extents has two copies that are mirrored. However, it is necessary to have at least three disks.

ASM is managing the group of disks in a disk group and the product also manages the redundancy with the disk groups. ASM provides an optimal I/O balancing without requiring any manual tuning phases. The database objects do not have any mount points and it supports very large files.

What is ASM Able to Store?

ASM is able to store most of the database files:

- Data files
- Data files copies
- Temp files
- SPFILE (Persistent initialization parameter file)
- Control files
- Redo log files
- RMAN backup files
- Archived redo log files
- Temporary files
- Data files' backup pieces
- Incremental data files' backup pieces
- Flashback logs
- Data pump dump sets
- Auto backups of the control files

- Data files cross-platform transportable
- Change tracking files
- Backup piece of archive redo logs
- Dataguard disaster recovery configurations

However, it is not possible to store the Oracle binaries, trace files and OS files.

ASM Installation, Settings and Best Practices

Installation of ASM is performed with the same binaries' source as the Oracle RDBMS database since ASM is also a special instance that handles disks in disk groups. The ASM instances are only found in a mounted mode that makes the disks reachable by other Oracle databases. Use the Oracle Manage File (OMF) to manage the database files in ASM.

ASM binaries should have their own *$ORACLE_HOME*. This will split the Oracle RDBMS binaries from the ASM binaries and by doing this, it will be possible to upgrade both entities without disturbing the other, i.e. the de-installation or upgrade of the Oracle RDBMS binaries can have the ASM instance modified. Only one ASM instance can be created and up on one server node as the ASM instance will manage the user's storage for this node. When the Oracle Cluster option is being used only with ASM, the CRS (Cluster Ready Services) will not be licensable.

Note that when patches are being applied on the Oracle database's binaries, it is important that the patches also be applied on the ASM binaries, i.e. the patch set 10.2.0.4 shall both be installed on the ASM binaries and on the databases using the ASM instance.

For the disk groups, there should at least be a dedicated database disk group area and also another for the flashback recovery operations. The disks used for the ASM disk groups should have the same sizes and performances so the ASM load balancing feature will work properly.

> Exam Advice: Be able to describe and explain all the best practices that shall be used for ASM.

Download of ASM Lib Packages

It is possible to download the RPM packages for Redhat and Suse of the ASM library at the Oracle website http://www.oracle.com/technology/tech/linux/asmlib/index.html. Verify which package fits the user's Linux kernel.

ASM Library Install and Setup

The purpose of the Automatic Storage Management Library (ASMLib) is to make the configuration of the disk devices much easier than binding each disk device to be used by ASM to a raw device since this is eliminated by the ASMLib. Oracle recommends the usage of the ASMlib for all the Linux systems.

After the proper ASMLib RPM installation package for the kernel is obtained, it is time to perform the installation as root by using the RPM upgrade installation command. The packages needed are *oracleasmlib*, *oracleasm-support* and *oracleasm*. Eventually, the debug package can also be acquired. For the Red Hat Kernel, the proper files will need to be downloaded. If the kernel version is unknown, do a *uname –r* and this will give the release of the kernel. The following matrix will inform what ASMLib should be chosen.

	For Linux 2.4 Kernel	**For Linux Kernel 2.6**
Linux versions	Red Hat Advanced Server 2.1 Red Hat Enterprise Linux 3 United Linux 1.0 Suse Linux Enterprise Server 8	Red Hat Enterprise Linux 4 SuSE Linux Enterprise Server 9
Kernel Driver release	oracleasm-1.0 (1.0.4 or higher)	oracleasm-2.x
ASMLib release	oracleasmlib-2	oracleasmlib-2
Support Tools release	oracleasm-support-2.	oracleasm-support-2.

Table 9.1: *Possible ASMLib Versions Depending on Kernel Version*

For the kernel 2.6.9-55.EL, the packages needed are:

```
rpm -Uvh oracleasm-support-2.1.3-1.el4.x86_64.rpm \
    oracleasmlib-2.0.4-1.el5.x86_64.rpm \
    oracleasm-2.6.9-55.EL-2.0.3-1.x86_64.rpm

Preparing...                ###########################################
[100%]
   1:oracleasm-support      ########################################### [
34%]
   2:oracleasm-2.6.9-55     ########################################### [
68%]
   3:oracleasmlib           ###########################################
[100%]
```

When the RPM packages are installed successfully with the root account, it is necessary to perform the setup of the ASMlib component with the root account. The ASMLib configuration script will ask:

1. What will be the default user that will own the driver?
2. What will be the default group that will own the driver?
3. Will the start of the ASMLib be automatic?
4. Will the permission of the ASM disks be fixed on the boot?

Note that the values between the brackets ([ ]) are the default values. Following are the default values when the user that owns the ASM binaries is oracle and the group is dba.

```
/etc/init.d/oracleasm configure
 Configuring the Oracle ASM library driver.
```

This will configure the on-boot properties of the Oracle ASM library driver. The following determines whether the driver is loaded on boot and what permissions it will have. The current values will be shown in brackets ('[ ]'). Hitting without typing an answer will keep that current value. Ctrl-C will abort.

```
Default user to own the driver interface []: oracle
Default group to own the driver interface []: dba
Start Oracle ASM library driver on boot (y/n) [n]: y
Fix permissions of Oracle ASM disks on boot (y/n) [y]: y
Writing Oracle ASM library driver configuration            [  OK  ]
Creating /dev/oracleasm mount point                        [  OK  ]
Loading module "oracleasm"                                 [  OK  ]
Mounting ASMlib driver filesystem                          [  OK  ]
Scanning system for ASM disks                              [  OK  ]
```

It is possible to enable or disable the ASMLib utility:

```
/etc/init.d/oracleasm enable

 Writing Oracle ASM library driver configuration          [  OK  ]
  Loading module "oracleasm"                              [  OK  ]
  Mounting ASMlib driver filesystem                       [  OK  ]
  Scanning system for ASM disks                           [  OK  ]
```

Perform the Disk Configuration

As a best practice, Oracle recommends that the entire disk's partitions should be used for ASM. This can be performed by using the command *fdisk <name of the disk device>*. After that, select the entire partition with the *fdisk* utility. It is necessary to tell the kernel the partition changes by doing a */sbin/partprobe* as root. This command will investigate what new partitions are available.

The entire disk will be allocated to ASM by using the */sbin/fdisk* command. If more details on that command are needed, read Chapter 3 or consult the man pages.

Mark Disks to be Used by ASM

When the disk to be used as ASM disks is marked, it is best to give the disk group names in relation with the type of data store on the disks and remember to separate the data from the flashback area.

- /etc/init.d/oracleasm createdisk DATA1 /dev/hdb1
- /etc/init.d/oracleasm createdisk DATA2 /dev/hdc1
- /etc/init.d/oracleasm createdisk FLSH1 /dev/hde1

After the disks to be used by ASM are marked, it is important to have the disks available for ASM. This operation is performed with the *scandisks* option of the *oracleasm* command.

```
/etc/init.d/oracleasm scandisks
```

The */etc/init.d/oracleasm* command does have other parameters that are not mandatory for the OCE exam, but they should be given for future use:

- */etc/init.d/oracleasm enable/disable* is used to define whether the ASM driver should be started at the system boot or not.
- */etc/init.d/oracleasm start/stop/restart* enables to start, stop or restart the oracleasm.
- */etc/init.d/oracleasm deletedisk name* makes it possible to delete the disks from the ASM association.
- */etc/init.d/oracleasm status* gives the status of the ASM library driver.

Create the ASM Instance

After the installation, setup and disk preparation have been finished, it is necessary to create an ASM instance and perform that with the *dbca* (Database Configuration Assistant Client). Consult Chapter 10 for more details about the *dbca*. Remember that only one ASM instance is needed on each node to handle all the disks used by several instances on the DBA's node. In case the *cssd* (*ocssd.bin*) daemon is not running, the *$oracle_home/bin/localconfig add* will have to be executed as the user root. This will add the *cssd* start in the *inittab* file. *Cssd* is a daemon that controls the communication between both the ASM instance and database instance.

Concerning the initialization parameters, only the default parameters that a normal Oracle instance requires to start are needed. The important parameters in ASM are:

- *Instance_type*: Has the value *asm* instead of *rdbms*
- *Asm_power_limit*: Concerns the power given for doing the rebalancing on the Oracle ASM instance. The value can be from 1 up to 11 (default is 1). When a higher value is chosen, be prepared for more resources to be required.
- *Asm_diskgroups*: This is about the diskgroups that will be mounted during the instance startup of the ASM instance. It is also used by the command *alter diskgroup all mount*.
- *Asm_diskstring*: Related to the discovery of the ASM disks.

ASMLib and ASM Digest

The following steps should be performed to get ASMlib and ASM working:

1. Download the ASMLib packages.
2. ASM library install and setup by executing *oracleasm configuration* and after that, *oracleasm enable*.
3. Perform the disk configuration by creating an entire partition of each disk and run the *partprobe* as the root user so the kernel will deal with the new partition.
4. Mark disks to be used by ASM with the command *oracleasm createdisk disk_name device_name*. Disks that are marked can be verified by *oracleasm listdisks*.
5. Perform an *oracleasm scandisks* to make the disks usable by ASM. It has to be executed on all the nodes if a cluster is being used, so all the nodes recognize the new volumes created.
6. Create the ASM instance manually or by using the Oracle database configuration assistant utility DBCA.

> Exam Advice: Be capable of giving the benefits of using the ASM Library drivers, explain how to perform the installation ASMLib and know all the necessary steps to get the ASM instance working with disks allocated.

Summary

Automatic Storage Management (ASM), introduced in Oracle 10g, was explained in this chapter. ASM offers a file system and a volume manager for a whole list of Oracle database files. Installation of ASM and its library, ASMLib, were described in detail as well as setup and disk preparation. The next chapter will involve creating an Oracle database.

Exercises

1. Install and setup the ASM RPM.
2. Perform the disk creation and the instance creation.

Q&A

Questions

1. Richard, a junior DBA, would like to install the Oracle RDBMS and ASM in the following directory: (Select the correct answers)

   $ORACLE_HOME: /u01/oracle/product/10.2/db_1
   $ORA_ASM_HOME: /u01/oracle/product/10.2/db_1

A. Doing the installation like that will not cause issues with the example of the Oracle patches
B. To avoid issue with the Oracle patches, the ASM and Oracle RDBMS binaries can use the same home
C. *$ORACLE_HOME* and *$ORA_ASM_HOME* should not be identical, so the patches can be installed separately
D. It is impossible to share the same home for ASM and *$ORACLE_HOME*

2. What are the correct best practices in the following list? (Choose all that apply)

A. *$ORACLE_HOME* and *$ORA_ASM_HOME* should be the same
B. Have multiple ASM instances running on one node to split the load and data
C. The data files and flashback can be stored on different disk groups
D. ASM should not be installed on Linux as it only works on Windows

3. Select the initialization parameters that have the correct values for an ASM instance. (Choose all that apply)

A. *instance_type = rdbms*
B. *instance_type = asm*
C. *asm_power_limit = 0*
D. *asm_power_limit = 1*

4. Select the correct options for the *oracleasm* command. (Choose all that apply)

A. *createstorage*
B. *createdisk DATA2 /dev/hdc1*
C. *scandisks*
D. *disks*

5. How can Andrew get the disks in a disk group so ASM can use the disks? (Choose all that apply)

A. Use the *fdisk* utility to make a partition with the entire disks.
B. Doing a */sbin/partprobe* as root
C. Doing a */sbin/partprobe* as the oracle user
D. Create the disks with */etc/init.d/oracleasm createdisk DATA1 /dev/hdb1*

6. Below are the steps to perform the installation for ASM. Choose the order the steps need to be in. (Choose the correct answer)

A. Download of ASM lib packages. ASM library install and setup by executing *oracleasm configuration* and after that, *oracleasm enable.*
B. Mark disks to be used by ASM with the command *oracleasm createdisk disk_name device_name.* Disks that are marked can be verified by *oracleasm listdisks.*
C. Perform the disk configuration by creating an entire partition of each disk and run the *partprobe* as the root user so the kernel will deal with new partition.
D. Create the ASM instance manually or by using the Oracle database configuration assistant utility (DBCA).
E. Perform an *oracleasm scandisks* to make the disks usable by ASM. It has to be executed on all the DBA's nodes if a cluster is being used, so all the nodes recognize the new volumes created.

1. A – B – C – D – E
2. A – C – B – E – D
3. C – D – E – A – B
4. D – E – A – B – C

7. Choose the correct description for the *cssd* daemon process. (Choose the correct answer)

A. *cssd* is a daemon that controls the communication of only the ASM instance and the disks
B. *cssd* is a daemon that controls the communication of only the database instance and the disks
C. *cssd* is a daemon that controls the communication of only the ASM instance
D. *cssd* is a daemon that controls the communication between both the ASM instance and database instance

8. What needs to be considered when working with ASM disks? (Choose all that apply)

A. Only half disks can be used when working with ASM for performance reasons
B. All the disks used for the group can have the same size and performances
C. The disks used for the group should not have the same size and performances
D. ASM disks groups should exist for the database area and also another for the flashback recovery operations

9. In the following list, what is not correct about the ASM product? (Choose all that apply)

A. Normal redundancy is 2-way mirroring done by ASM, so the extent has one copy mirrored
B. It is quite important to do manual tuning of the ASM instance
C. ASM cannot be installed on Linux
D. High means that ASM is doing a 3-way mirroring, so each of the extents have two copies that are mirrored. However, it is necessary to have at least three disks

10. Why should the disk probe */sbin/partprobe* be performed on the Linux server? (Choose the correct answer)

A. The command is investigating what new partitions are available and informs the kernel about it
B. The command is making a list of the partition and displays it to the user
C. The command does not exist on Linux
D. The command is making a list of the ASM disks partitions

Answers

1. The correct answer is: C. $*ORACLE_HOME* and $*ORA_ASM_HOME* should not be identical, so the patches can be installed separately.

HINT: Read again the section ASM Installation, settings and best practices.

2. The only correct answer is: C. The data files and flashback can be stored on different disk groups.

HINT: Consult again the section about ASM installation, settings and best practices

3. The correct answers are: B. *instance_type* = *asm* and D. *asm_power_limit* = *1*

HINT: Read again "Create the ASM Instance".

4. The correct answers are: B. *createdisk DATA2 /dev/hdc1* and C. *scandisks*

HINT: The mark disks to be used by ASM need yo be reviewed.

5. The correct answers are: A. Use the *fdisk* utility to make a partition with the entire disks; B. Doing a */sbin/partprobe* as root and D. Create the disks with */etc/init.d/oracleasm createdisk DATA1 /dev/hdb1*

HINT: Read again the section "Mark Disks to be Used by ASM".

6. The correct answer is: 2. A – C – B – D – E

HINT: Study the section ASMlib and ASM Digest.

7. The correct answer is: D. *Cssd* is a daemon that controls the communication between both the ASM instance and database instance.

HINT: Read again the section on creating the ASM instance to understand why this answer is correct.

8. The correct answers are: B. All the disks used for the group can have the same size and performances and D. ASM disks groups should exist for the database area and also another for the flashback recovery operations.

HINT: Consult the section about ASM installation, settings and best practices.

9. The answers that are not true about ASM are: B. It is quite important to do manual tuning of the ASM instance; and C. ASM cannot be installed on Linux.

HINT: Consult again the "What is ASM?" section.

10. The correct answer is: A. The command is investigating what new partitions are available and informs the kernel about it.

HINT: Study the section on performing the disk configuration once again.

Solutions to Exercises

1. Install and setup the ASM RPM. Consult the section on ASM installation, settings and best practices and perform all the steps given.
2. Perform the disk creation and the instance creation. Follow the action given in the chapters concerning the installation setup and ASM instance creation.

Creating An Oracle Database

CHAPTER

This chapter covers the following exam objectives:

6. Creating a Database
6.1. Create an Oracle database that uses ASM
6.2. Identify the location of various Oracle files
6.3. Implement OS authentication

How to Create an Oracle Database

It is possible to create an Oracle database by using the utility *dbca* (Database Configuration Assistant). With the *dbca* utility, it is possible to set the password and perform the configuration of the database setup and the storage type of the DBA's database (file system, RAW devices and Automatic Storage Management). The following describes the steps used to create a database with the *dbca* GUI (Graphical User Interface).

Before starting the *dbca* under Linux, the DBA needs to make sure that the *$ORACLE_HOME*, *$DISPLAY* and *$PATH* are properly set:

- $ORACLE_HOME=$ORACLE_BASE/product/10.2.0/db_1
- *$DISPLAY=localhost:0.0* or the X11 host values
- *$PATH* contains the *$ORACLE_HOME/bin*

After that, the environment variables are set properly and it is possible to run the *dbca*:

```
[oracle@orion ~]$ dbca&
```

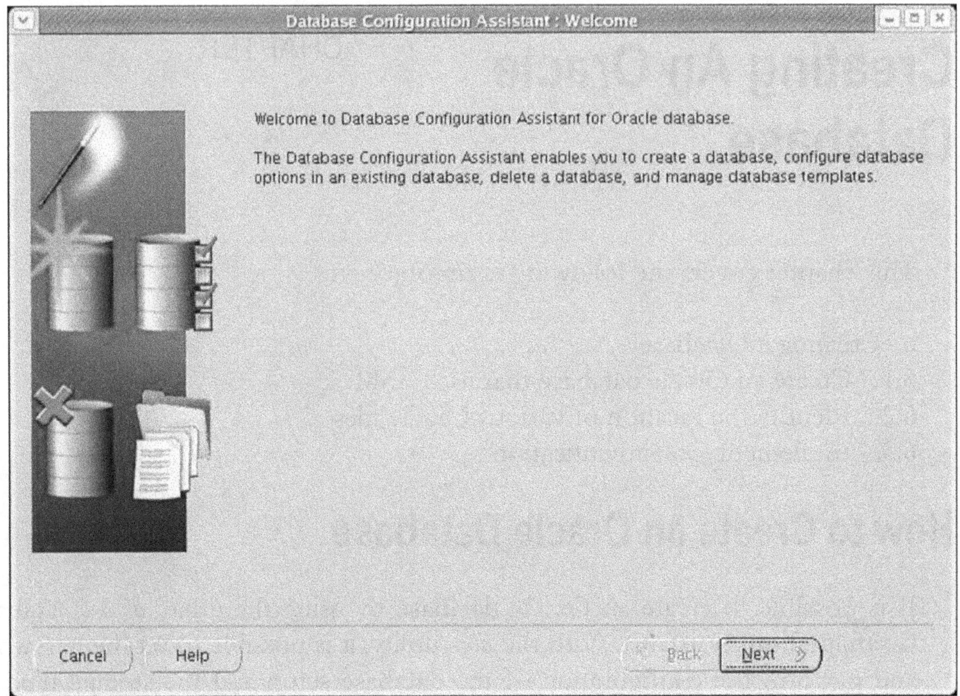

Figure 10.1: *Introduction to Database Configuration Assistant*

To continue the execution of the *dbca* wizard, click on Next, and the options to create the database will appear. The templates or the ASM storage can then be managed.

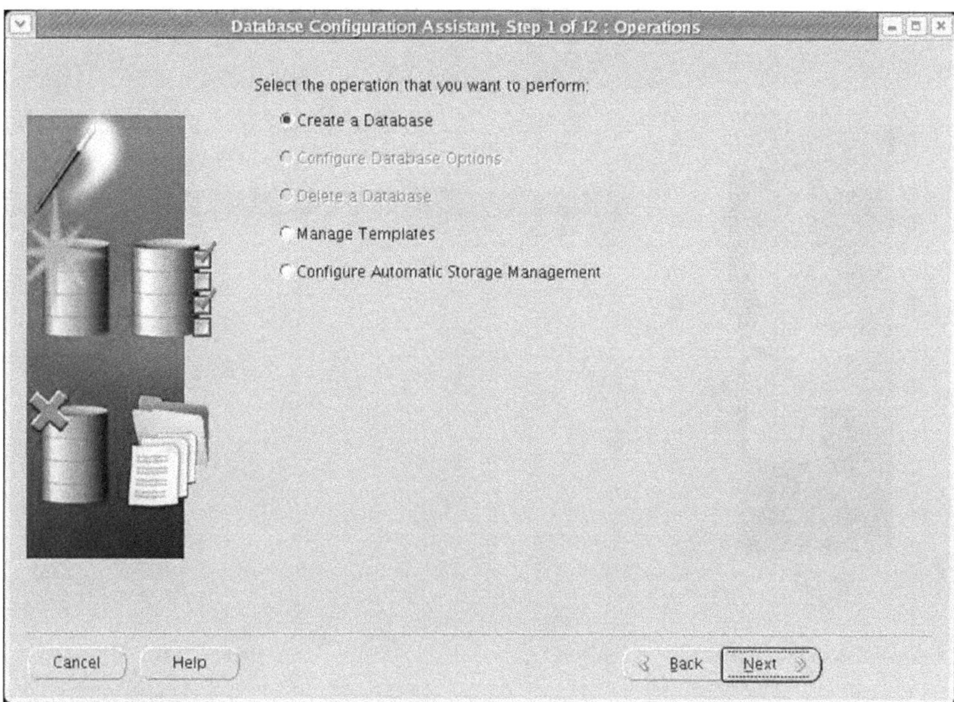

Figure 10.2: *Create a Database Screen*

In this case, choose the Create a Database option and continue to the next screen.

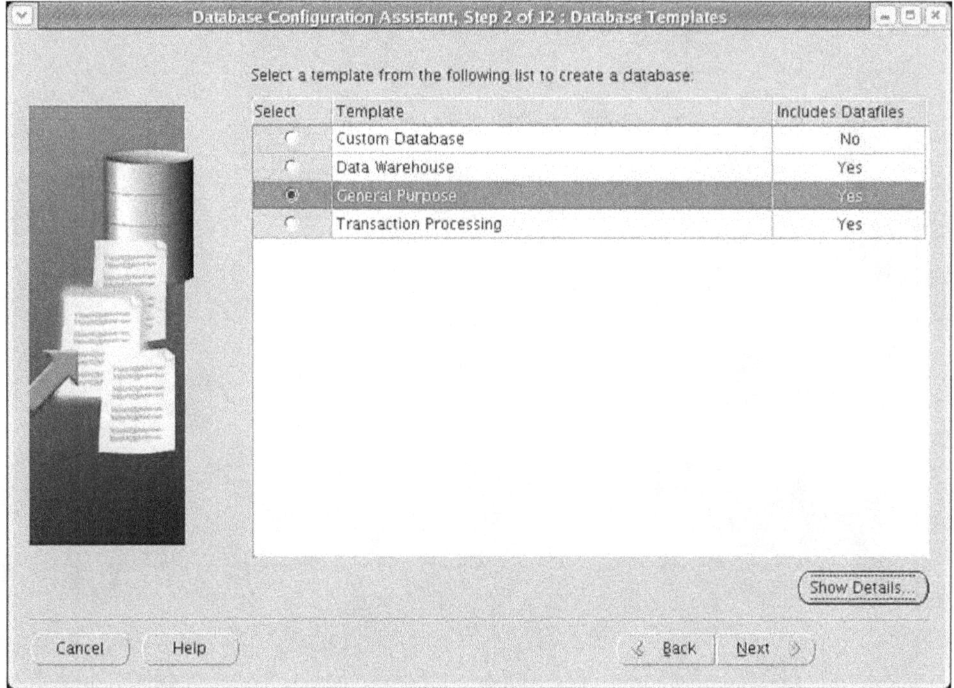

Figure 10.3: *Choosing a Template for the Database*

In *dbca*, it is possible to create a database based on templates. The templates contain specific settings that are optimized for the type of work the database will be in charge of doing. If the DBA is unsure what kind of workload will be on the database, the General Purpose should be chosen.

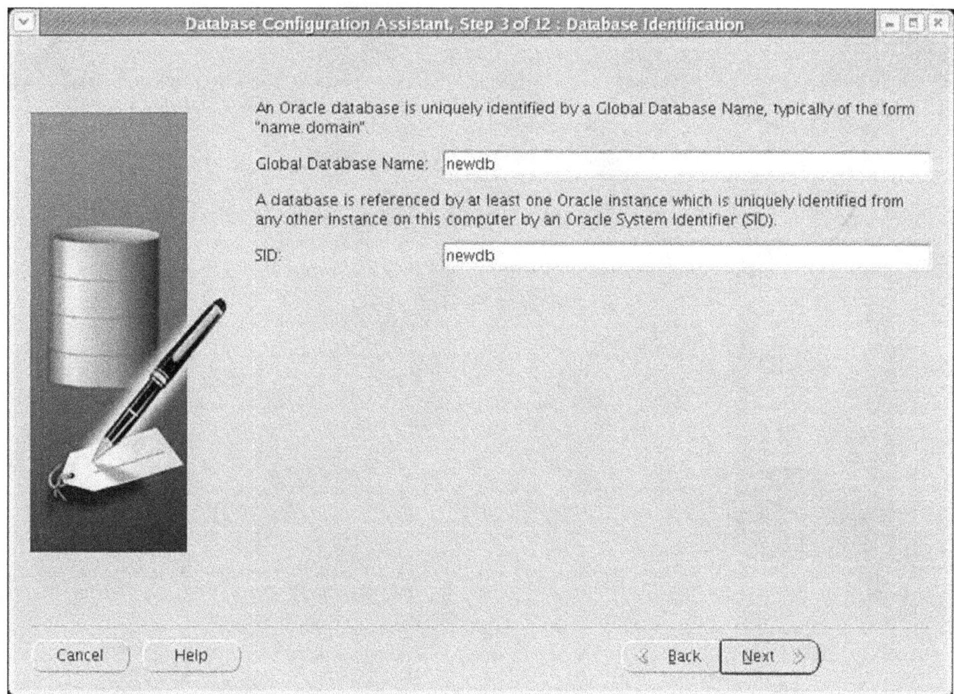
Database Configuration Assistant, Step 3 of 12 : Database Identification
An Oracle database is uniquely identified by a Global Database Name, typically of the form "name domain".
Global Database Name:
newdb
A database is referenced by at least one Oracle instance which is uniquely identified from any other instance on this computer by an Oracle System Identifier (SID).
SID:
newdb
Cancel
Help
Back
Next

Figure 10.4: *Database Identification*

On the screen Database Identification, the SID of the database and also the Global Database Name can be set. Oracle System ID (SID) is a unique identifier for the database on a Linux system, so it is not possible to have the same SID for different databases on the same server. The Global Database Name should also be unique on the user's network; the name is composed by the database name and the domain name.

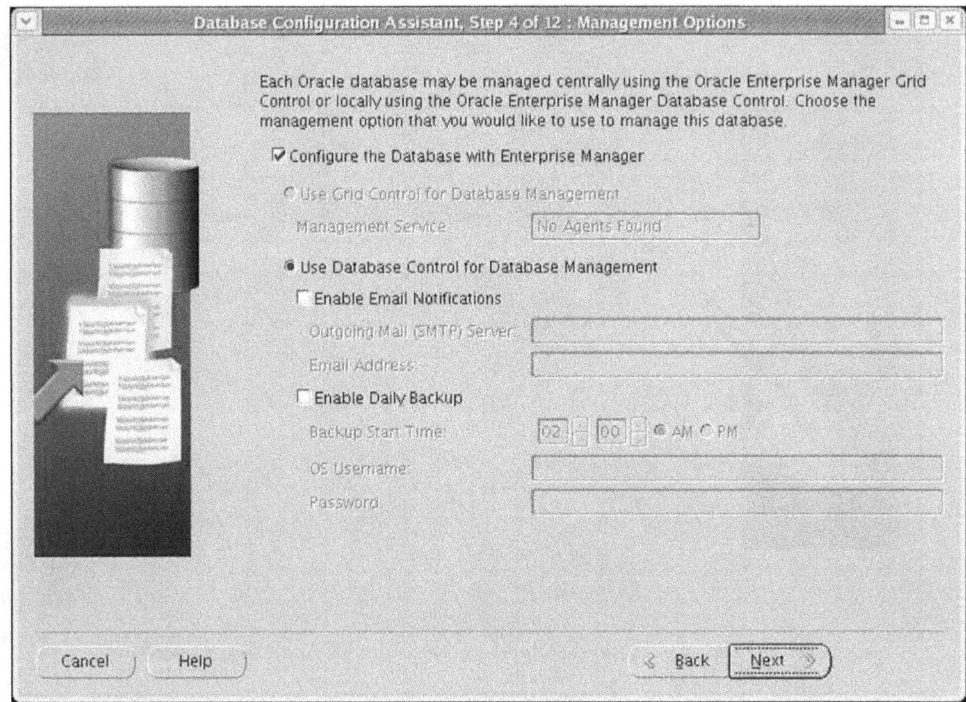

Figure 10.5: *Management Options*

In the Management option, it is possible to choose the type of Enterprise Manager management that will be on the new database. Use the Grid controller to perform the management centrally or have a dedicated database control to do the management locally on the Linux server.

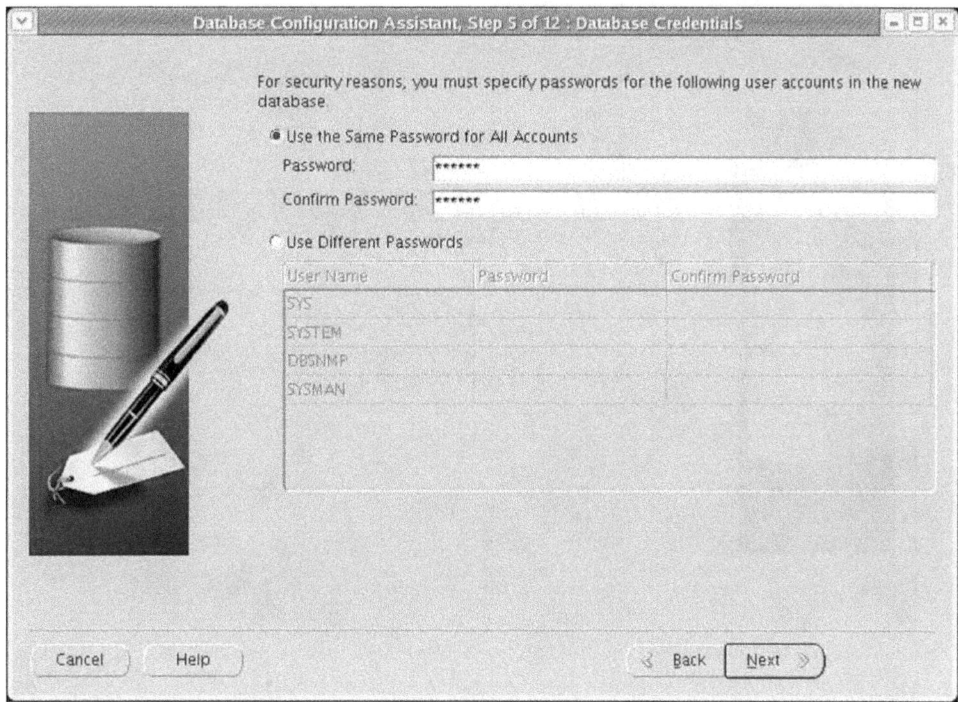

Figure 10.6: *Database Credentials Screen*

In the Database Credentials window, the password can be set for the user's SYS, SYSTEM, DBSNMP and also for the SYSMAN. It is possible to set the same password on all the accounts or set the password individually for each user.

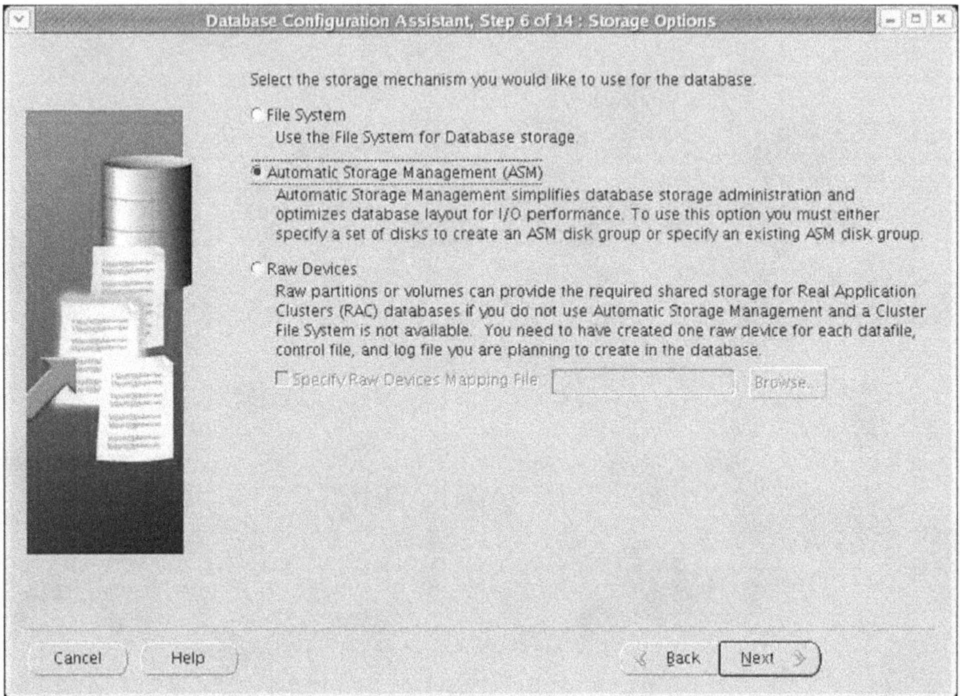

Database Configuration Assistant, Step 6 of 14 : Storage Options
Select the storage mechanism you would like to use for the database.
File System
Use the File System for Database storage.
Automatic Storage Management (ASM)
Automatic Storage Management simplifies database storage administration and optimizes database layout for I/O performance. To use this option you must either specify a set of disks to create an ASM disk group or specify an existing ASM disk group.
Raw Devices
Raw partitions or volumes can provide the required shared storage for Real Application Clusters (RAC) databases if you do not use Automatic Storage Management and a Cluster File System is not available. You need to have created one raw device for each datafile, control file, and log file you are planning to create in the database.
Specify Raw Devices Mapping File
Browse...
Cancel
Help
Back
Next

Figure 10.7: *Database Storage Options - ASM*

In the Storage Options window, configure the storage type the database will use. Choose to create the database to use file systems, ASM or raw devices. In this case, ASM storage will be used as this is a mandatory exam objective.

Note that when the raw devices are used, it is possible to have a raw device mapping file that can contain all the raw devices that are desired on the database.

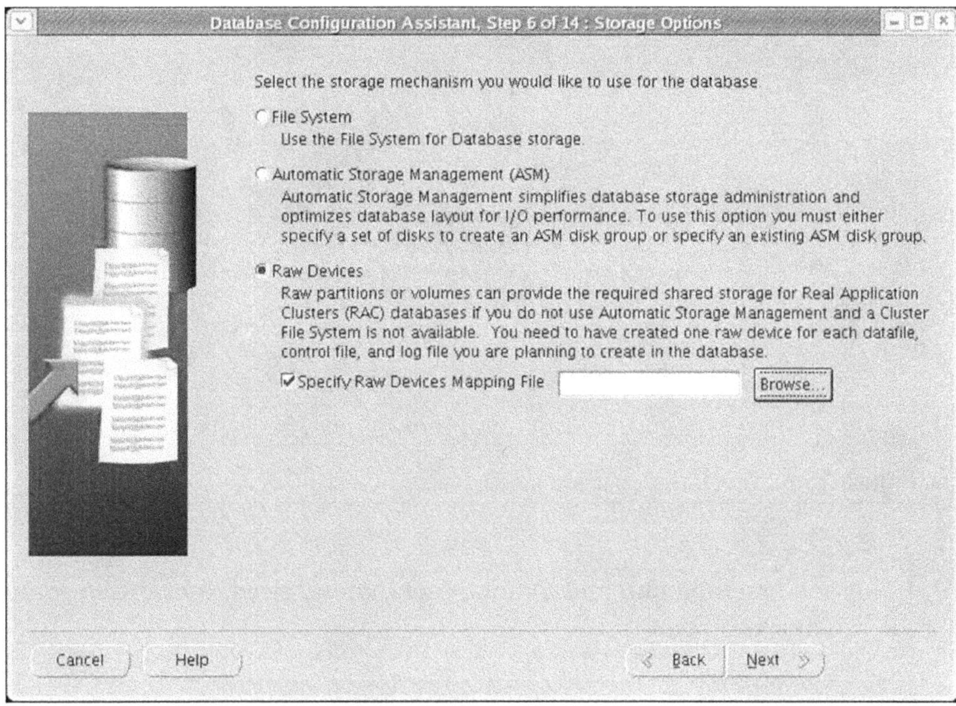
Database Configuration Assistant, Step 6 of 14 : Storage Options
Select the storage mechanism you would like to use for the database
File System
Use the File System for Database storage.
Automatic Storage Management (ASM)
Automatic Storage Management simplifies database storage administration and optimizes database layout for I/O performance. To use this option you must either specify a set of disks to create an ASM disk group or specify an existing ASM disk group.
Raw Devices
Raw partitions or volumes can provide the required shared storage for Real Application Clusters (RAC) databases if you do not use Automatic Storage Management and a Cluster File System is not available. You need to have created one raw device for each datafile, control file, and log file you are planning to create in the database.
Specify Raw Devices Mapping File
Browse...
Cancel
Help
Back
Next

Figure 10.8: *Database Storage Options – Raw Devices*

```
i.e.: newdb_raw.conf

system=/dev/raw/raw_1
sysaux=/dev/raw/raw_2
example=/dev/raw/raw_3
users=/dev/raw/raw_4
temp=/dev/raw/raw_5
undotbs1=/dev/raw/raw_6
redo1_1=/dev/raw/raw_8
redo1_2=/dev/raw/raw_9
control1=/dev/raw/raw_10
control2=/dev/raw/raw_11
spfile=/dev/raw/raw_12
pwdfile=/dev/raw/raw_13
```

When the ASM storage type has been selected, the *dbca* utility makes sure that the necessary daemon to run the ASM is running on the system. If the daemon process is not running on the system, the following window will appear.

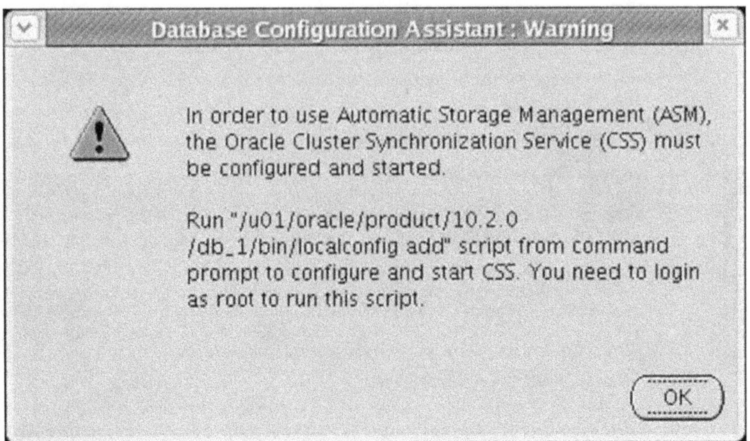

Figure 10.9: *Configuration Warning*

If this window shows up, the command as root will need to be run to continue the database creation.

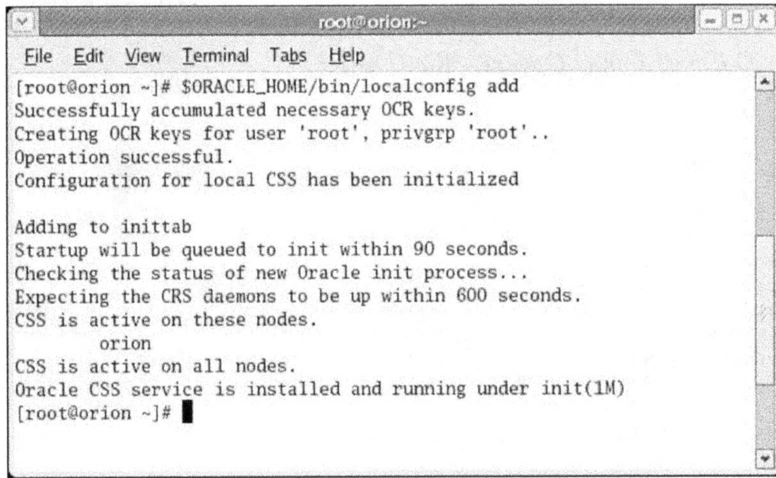

Figure 10.10: *Running Command as Root*

After that, the prompt back in the shell that executed the css creation comes back. Make sure that the process is running with the command *ps –efd | grep d.bin* as this will show all the dæmons that are running. The *localconfig* command also creates a script in */etc/init.d/init.cssd* that makes it possible to stop/start the CSS daemon manually or automatically during the system stop/start.

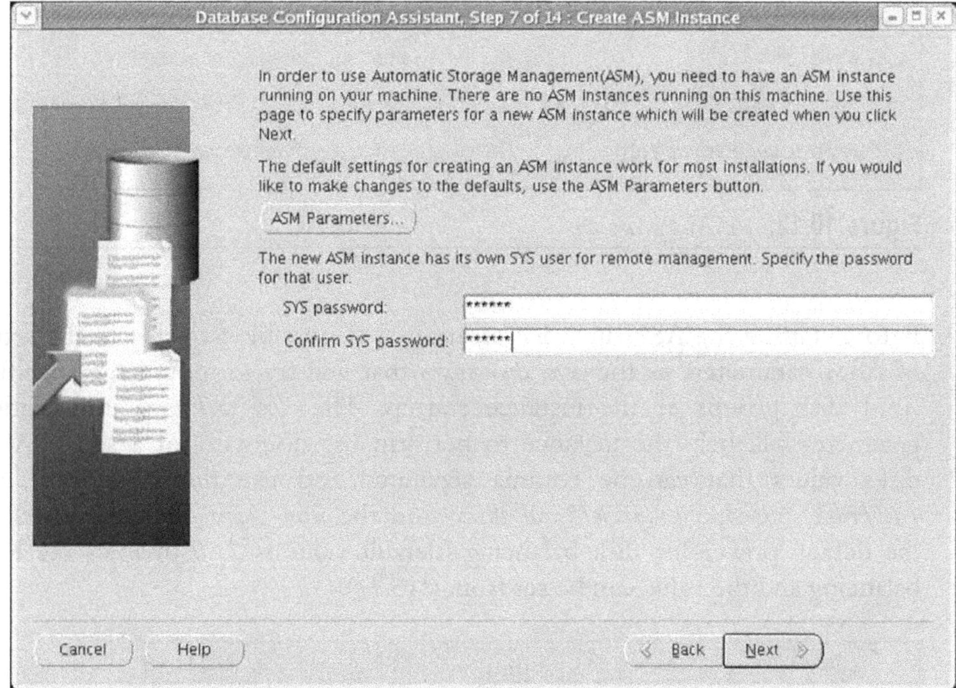

Figure 10.11: *Creating ASM Instance*

When the Oracle Cluster Synchronization Services (CSS) daemon is running, the DBA's work in the *dbca* wizard can be continued, so the next step is to create the ASM instance.

Name	Value	Override Default	Category
asm_diskgroups			Automatic Storage Management
asm_diskstring			Automatic Storage Management
asm_power_limit	1		Automatic Storage Management

Show Advanced Parameters | Close | Show Description | Help

Figure 10.12: *ASM Parameters*

Before starting the ASM instance creation, it is possible to perform the setup of ASM parameters as the *asm_diskgroups* that will try to mount the specified ASM disk groups at the instance startup. The *asm_diskstring* initialization parameter will help the instance to perform the discovery of a set of ASM disks values that can be comma separated and use the * wildcard, i.e. */dev/rdsk/*disk5*, */dev/rdsk/*asm_disk8* and the *asm_power_limit* that specifies the default power for disk balancing (default value is *1*, *0* disables the load balancing and the value can be set from *0* to *11*).

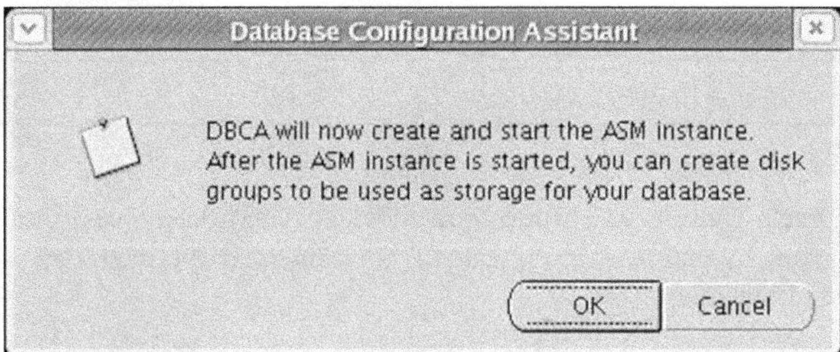

Database Configuration Assistant
DBCA will now create and start the ASM instance.
After the ASM instance is started, you can create disk
groups to be used as storage for your database.
OK
Cancel

Figure 10.13: *Creating ASM Instance*

After doing all the settings and clicking on the next button, a message will ask if the database should be created, so select OK and while the database is in creation, the following window will be in view.

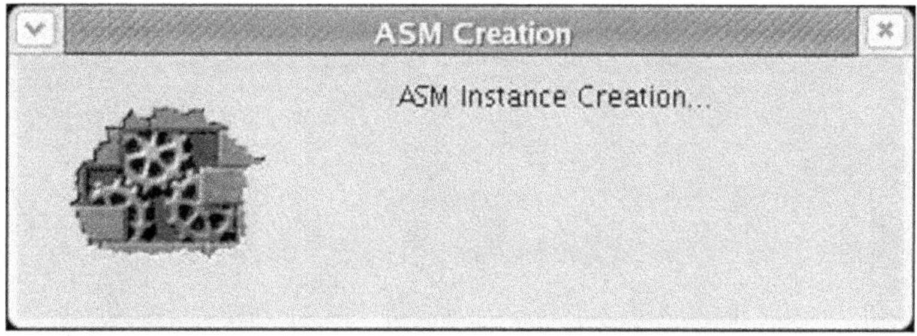

Figure 10.14: *Creating ASM Instance – In Progress*

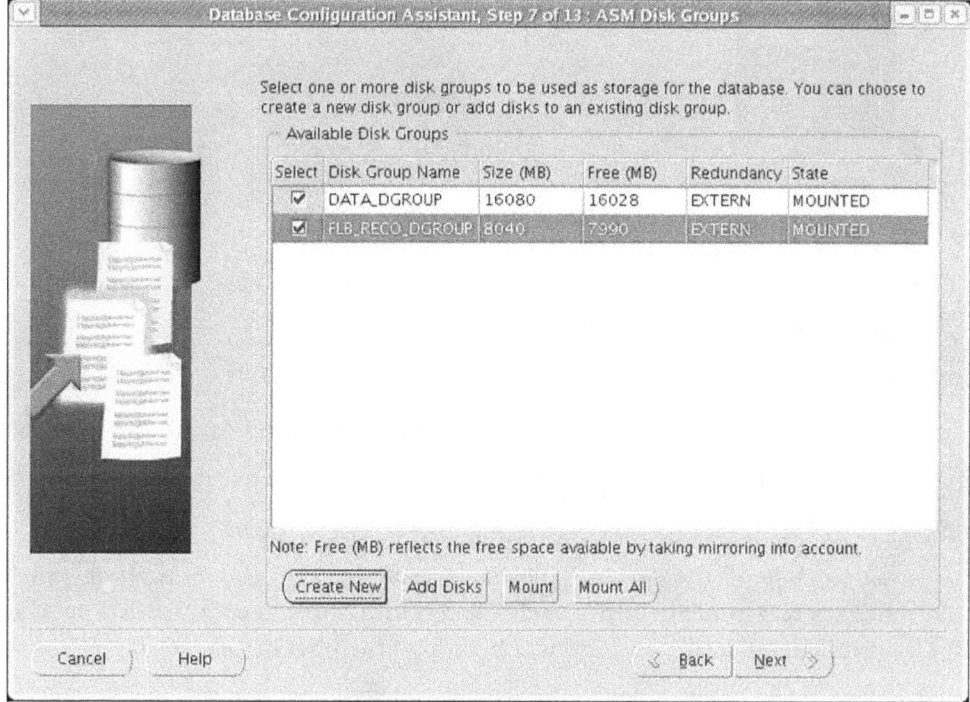

Figure 10.15: *ASM Disk Groups Screen*

After the ASM database has started, it is possible to allocate the disk storage for the database. In this example, the disk group is *data_dgroup* for the datafiles and disk group *flb_reco_dg_group* for the flashback recovery area.

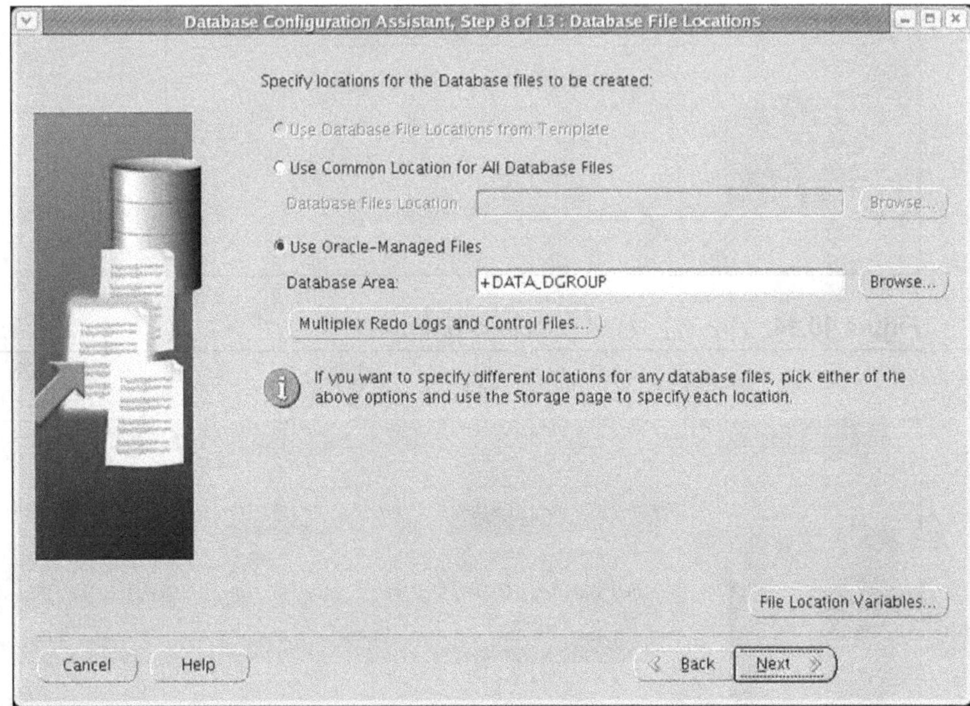

Figure 10.16: *Choosing Database File Location*

After the disk groups are created, it is necessary to select the location of the database files, and as preferred when using the ASM, select the Oracle Managed Files. Oracle will manage these database files, so the location of the files can then be set with the initialization parameter *db_create_file_dest.* The multiplexing of the control files and redo logs is also a part of the best practices recommended by Oracle. Therefore, those recommendations should be applied, especially on production or high SLA databases.

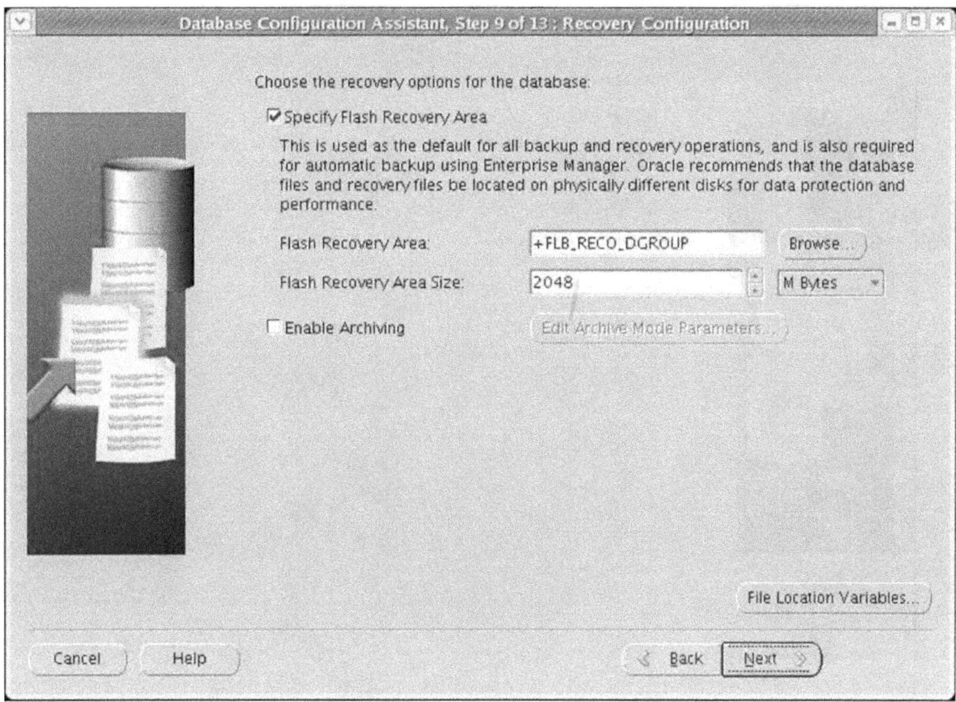

Figure 10.17: *Choosing Recovery Options*

After the location of the database files is configured, the configuration of the flashback recovery area will have to be performed on a different disk group. After the database is created, those settings can be managed with the initialization parameters *db_recovery_file_dest* and *db_recovery_file_dest_size* and the given settings can be managed in the database.

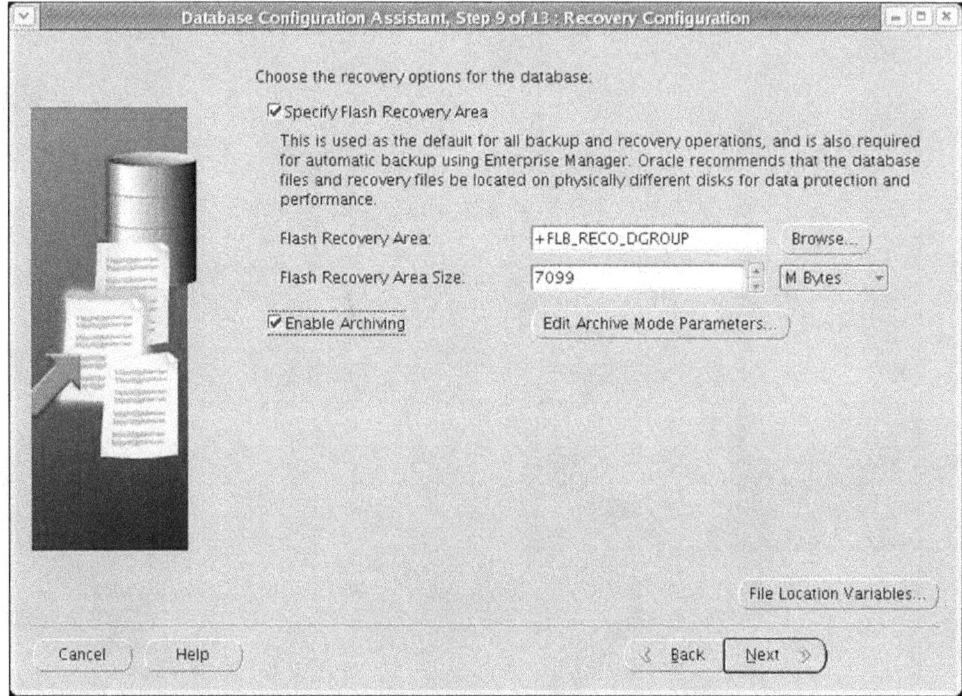

Figure 10.18: *Enabling Archiving*

On the database, it is important to enable the archiving of the redo logs. This can be made in the screen by selecting the Enable Archiving option and editing the archive mode parameters.

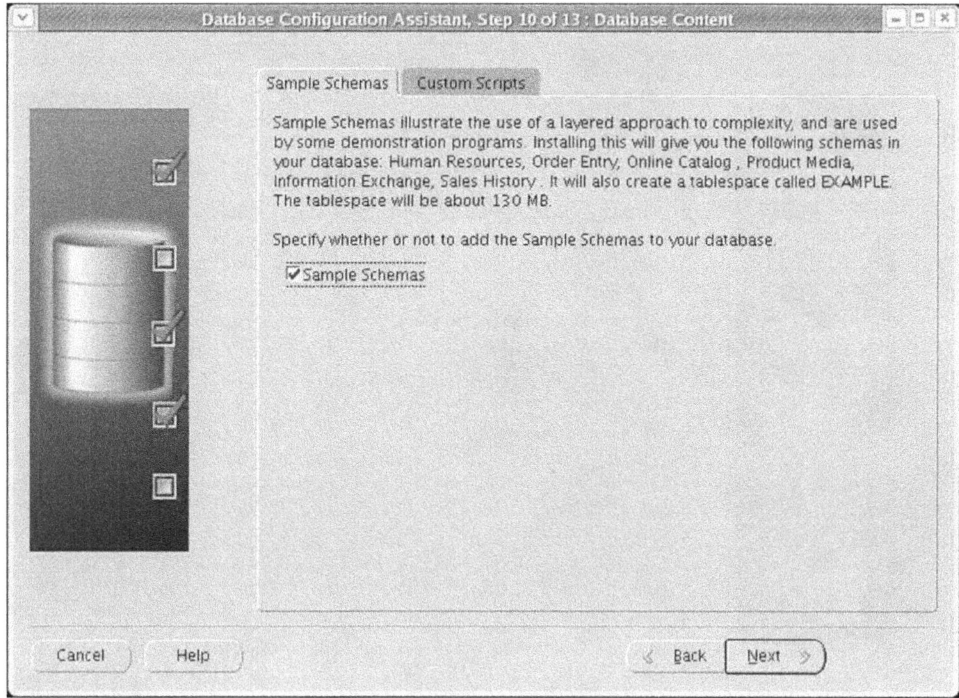

Figure 10.19: *Database Content Screen*

In the database content, it is possible to have sample schemas in the database and it is possible to run custom scripts after the database is created. The sample schemas should not be present on production databases unless it is required to perform some tests; otherwise, they should not be created. The following schemas are available:

- Scott/tiger schema with the *emp* and *dept* tables
- Human Resources (HR) suits for learning the basic features of an Oracle database
- Order Entry (OE) with a lot of data types include the non-scalar
- Online Catalog (OC) with object-relational database objects
- Product Media (PM) with multimedia data types
- Information Exchange (IX) that demonstrates Oracle Advanced Queuing capabilities

- Sales History (SH) as demo for large amounts of data

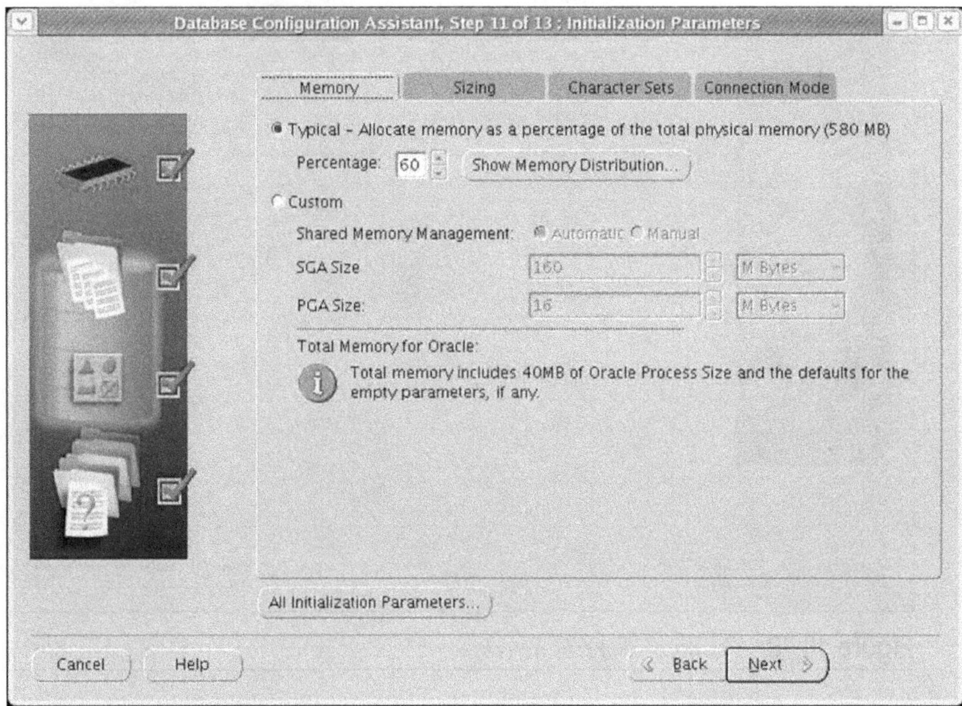

Figure 10.20: *Initialization Parameters*

With the Initialization Parameters window, the memory usage of the database can be set, the sizing of the database block size can be performed, the character set, national character set, default language and date format can be chosen and the connection mode can be set up. All the initialization parameters can be displayed with that window.

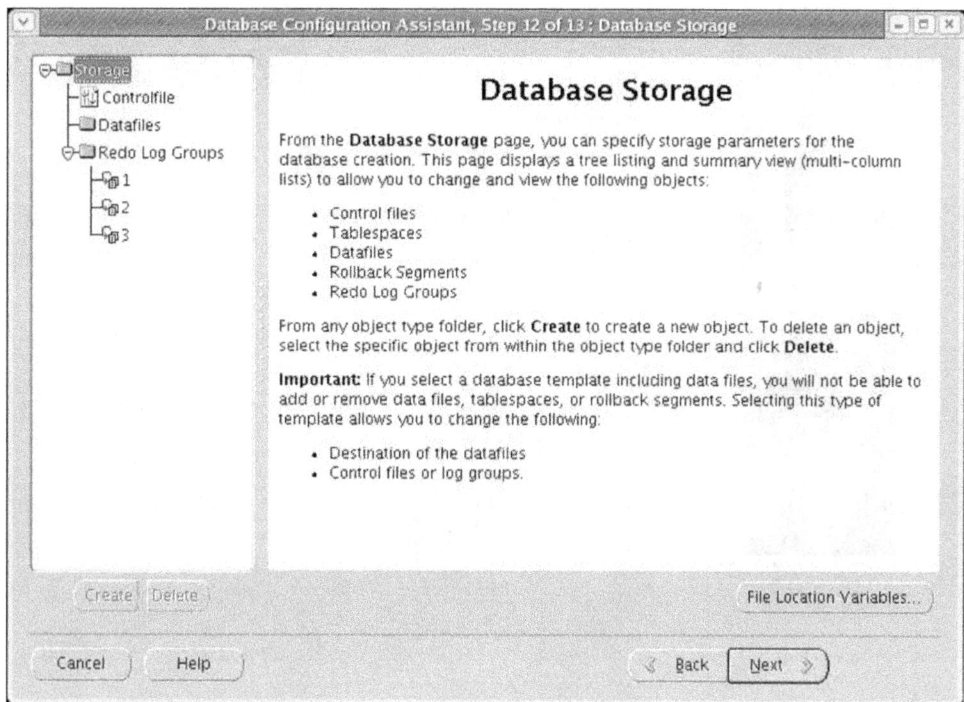

Figure 10.21: *Database Storage*

In the database storage window, the DBA can review, create and delete the database control files, redo log groups, tablespaces, and datafiles of the database.

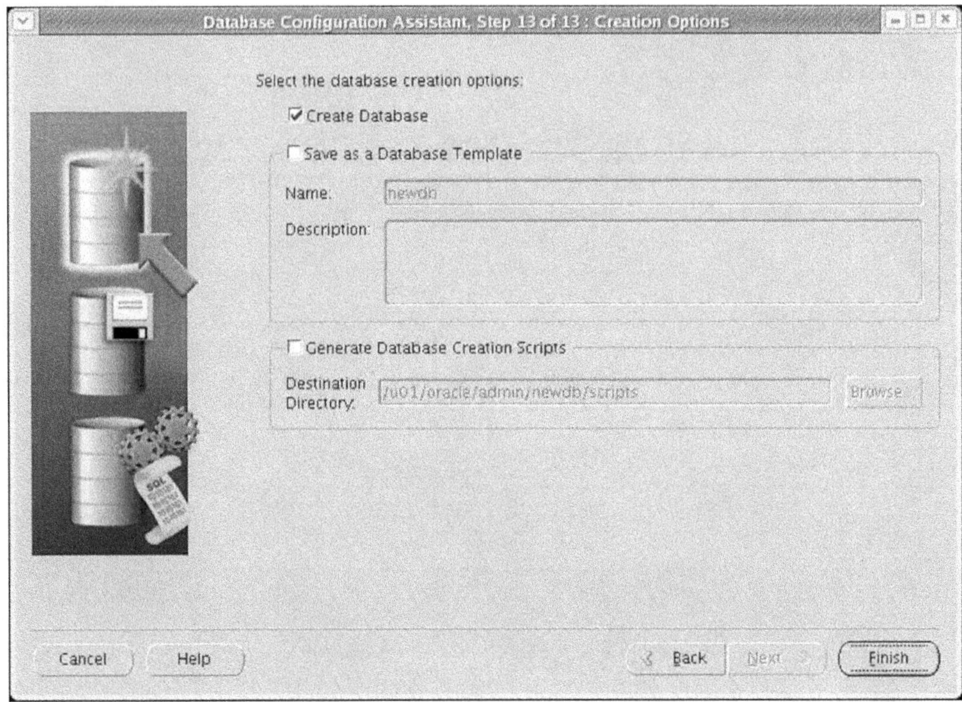

Figure 10.22: *Final Step of Database Configuration Assistant*

After that, in the Creation Options window where the database can be created, save the settings in a new database template for creating other databases with it and also get all the database creation scripts generated.

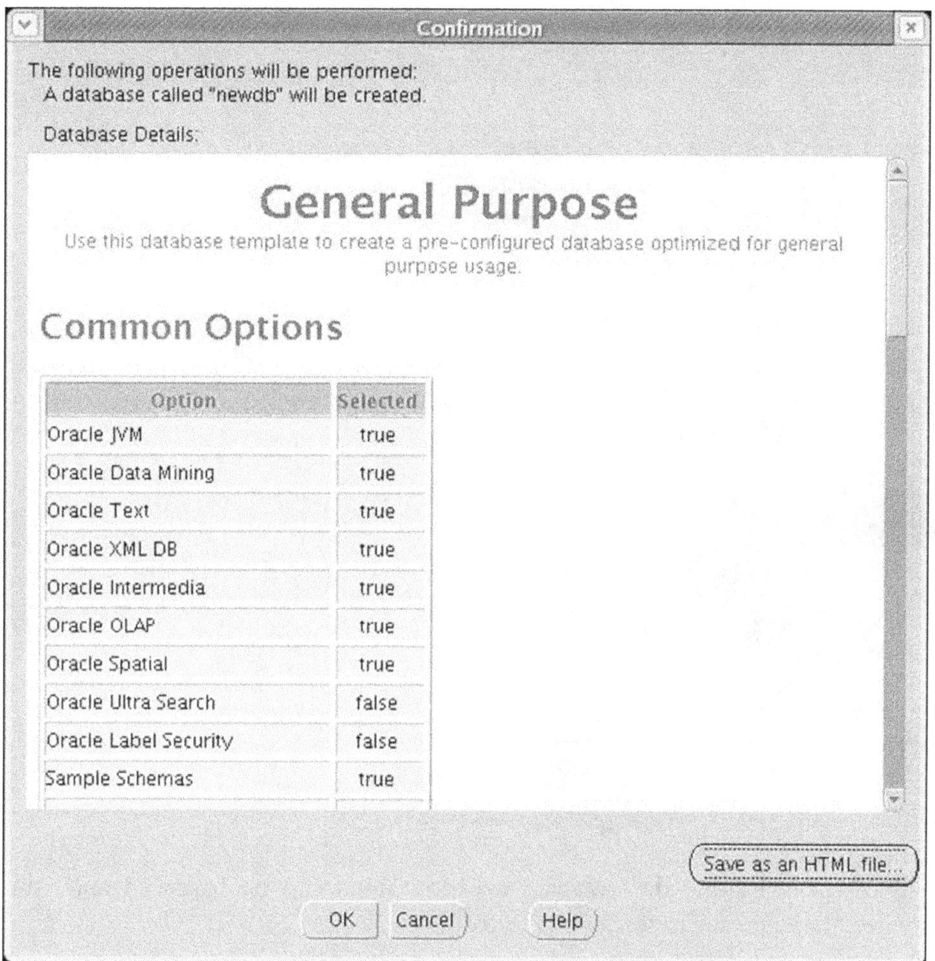

Figure 10.23: *Confirmation Screen*

With the Confirmation window, an overview and summary of the created database can be seen and the output can be kept in an HTML file for further documentation of the database creation.

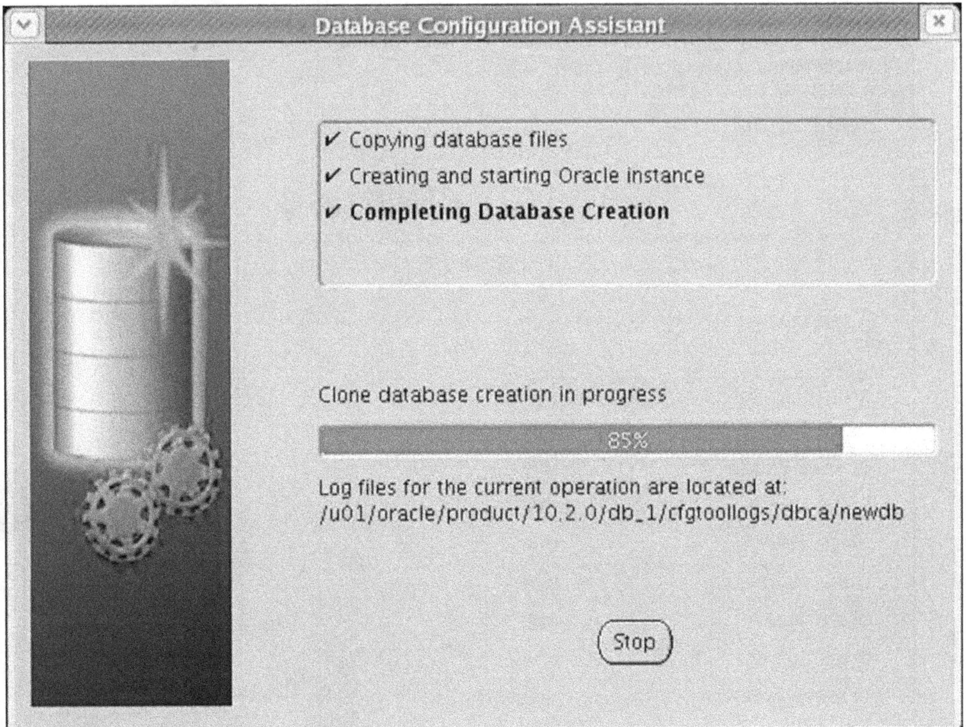

Figure 10.24: *Clone Database Creation in Progress*

With this window, the database creation steps can be followed and will tell when the database is ready to be used.

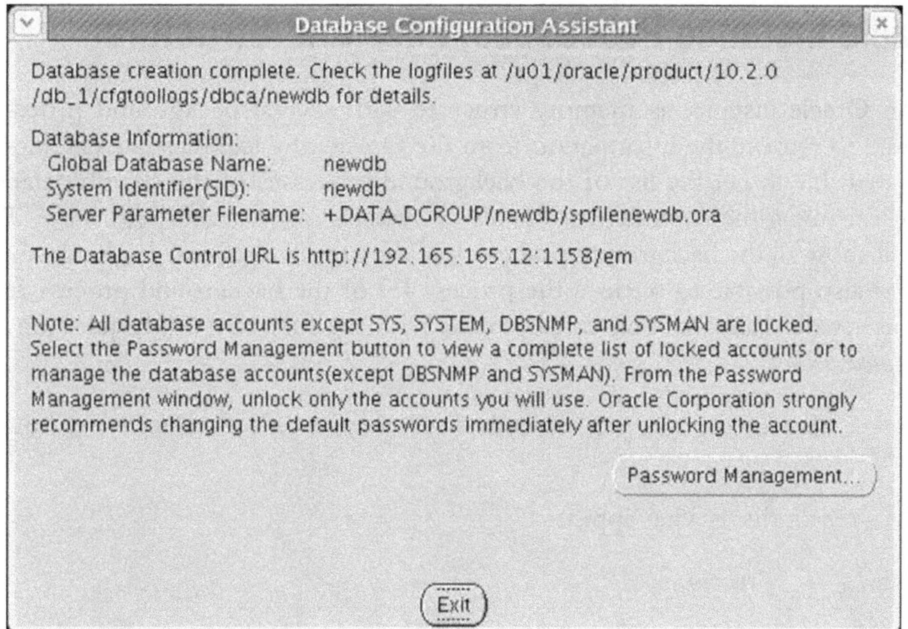

Figure 10.25: *Database Creation Successful*

This last window informs that the database is created successfully and also provides the database information and the URL of the database control.

NOTE: The *dbca* utility creates or updates the */etc/oratab* file that contains the information about the *ORACLE_SID*, *ORACLE_HOME* and the flag if the database is started. The update is performed the next time *dbca* is being used to create a new database or delete it.

The utility *dbca* is a Java-based application that can produce logs and the produced files can be found in the directory *$ORACLE_HOME/cfgtoollogs/dbca/<oracle_sid>*. The directory contains the log files of the database object's creation, configuration of the Enterprise Manager and schema imports logs of the examples (*tts_example_imp.log*).

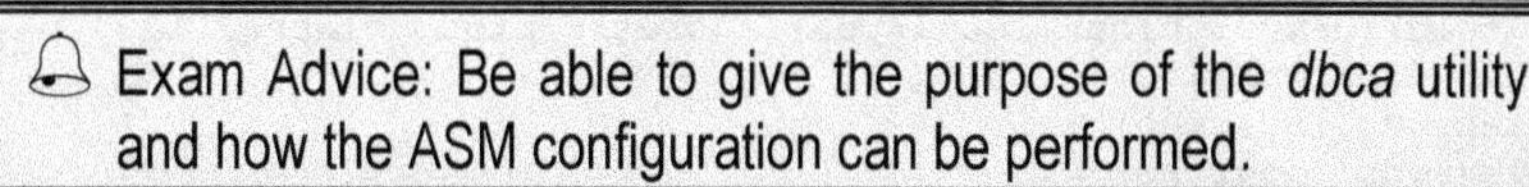

Oracle Instance Processes, Files and Structures

An Oracle instance is memory structure with several background processes used to retrieve the information from the Oracle physical files like datafiles. It is possible to get the list of the background processes of the newdb database by executing the command *ps –eo pid –o command | grep newdb | grep ora_*. This will show all the background processes of the newdb database. In the database, it is also possible to retrieve the process ID of the background process from the newdb database. This can be made with the following SQL query on the *v$process* view.

```
Select spid, program from v$process where program like '%(PMON)' or program
like '%(SMON)';
```

As a result, this is what appears:

```
SPID         PROGRAM
------------ ------------------------------------------------
123122       oracle@newdb (PMON)
426048       oracle@newdb (SMON)
```

It is also possible to get an entire list of all the background processes existing for the DBA's Oracle release by using the following SQL query on the *v$bgprocess* view:

```
select name, description from v$bgprocess
```

An Oracle instance also has server processes when the database is running in dedicated server mode. The server processes start with the database connections. Depending on how the DBA is connecting to the database, the session can be *local=yes* or *local=no*. When the connection is done with the service name *sqlplus scott/tiger@newdb*, it will have the *local=no* value and the *local=yes* will be given when the connection string is not using the service name like *sqlplus scott/tiger*. A complete list of the connections can be displayed with the Linux command *ps kpid -oe pid -o args | grep oracle*. This command will give all the exiting connections:

```
2008 oraclesid (description=(local=yes)(address=(protocol=beq)))
1912 oraclenewdb(local=no)
4006 oraclenewdb(local=no)
4006 oraclenewdb(local=no)
```

For the shared server, the processes involved are called dispatchers.

Note that the processes on Linux do have a hierarchy that can be shown with the commands *pstree* and *ps*. With the PPID value, the Parent Process ID of the processes can be seen.

In the *portlist.ini*, the DBA can get all the port numbers' information for the Oracle related application like iSQL*Plus and the port for the Enterprise Manager console. The file can contain the following information:

```
[oracle@orion install]$ cat $oracle_home/install/portlist.ini
iSQL*Plus HTTP port number =5560
Ultra Search HTTP port number =5620
Enterprise Manager Console HTTP Port (newdb) = 1158
Enterprise Manager Agent Port (newdb) = 3938
```

Dump files and parameter files are stored in the following sub-directories in the *$ORACLE_BASE* and *$ORACLE_HOME*.

In the *$ORACLE_BASE/admin*, the dump files are stored, and the location can be found in the initialization parameters:

- *audit_file_dest* stores all the audit files.
- *background_dump_dest* stores the *alert<$ORALCE_SID>.log* and the background processes' log files.
- *core_dump_dest* contains the core dump files.
- *user_dump_dest* stores the user process trace files.

The *$ORACLE_BASE/admin* contains the following directories:

```
[oracle@orion ~]$ ls -al $oracle_base/admin/*
/u01/oracle/admin/+ASM:
total 24
drwxr-x---   6 oracle oinstall 4096 Apr 21 02:41 .
drwxr-x---   4 oracle oinstall 4096 Apr 21 04:34 ..
drwxr-x---   2 oracle oinstall 4096 May 23 14:46 bdump
drwxr-x---   2 oracle oinstall 4096 Apr 21 02:41 cdump
drwxr-x---   2 oracle oinstall 4096 Apr 21 02:41 pfile
drwxr-x---   2 oracle oinstall 4096 May 23 14:46 udump

/u01/oracle/admin/newdb:
total 32
drwxr-x---   8 oracle oinstall 4096 Apr 21 04:34 .
drwxr-x---   4 oracle oinstall 4096 Apr 21 04:34 ..
drwxr-x---   2 oracle oinstall 4096 May 23 14:45 adump
drwxr-x---   2 oracle oinstall 4096 Apr 21 07:06 bdump
```

```
drwxr-x---  2 oracle oinstall 4096 Apr 21 04:34 cdump
drwxr-x---  2 oracle oinstall 4096 Apr 21 04:34 dpdump
drwxr-x---  2 oracle oinstall 4096 Apr 21 04:40 pfile
drwxr-x---  2 oracle oinstall 4096 May 23 14:45 udump
```

In the *$ORACLE_BASE/admin/$ORACLE_SID/* directory, it is also possible to store the dump files in *dpdump* and the *pfile* of the database. The *$ORACLE_HOME/dbs* can contain the *spfile* and the database *password* file.

> Exam Advice: Be able to make a list of the different processes, directories, files and structures that are making an Oracle instance. Also know the purpose of each directory and what kind of files are stored in that structure.

URL Information

Information about the URL can be found in the file *$ORACLE_HOME/install/readme.txt.* This will inform the DBA about the *hostname:port* of the Oracle application like iSQL*Plus ultra search and Enterprise Manager dbconsole. On the Linux server, the Enterprise Manager console can be started with the command *emctl start dbconsole.* It is possible to substitute the *start* with *status*; in this case, the *status* of the dbconsole on the server is obtained.

```
[oracle@orion admin]$ cat $oracle_home/install/readme.txt
Ultra Search URL:
http://orion.ibm.dk:5620/ultrasearch

Ultra Search Administration Tool URL:
http://orion.ibm.dk:5620/ultrasearch/admin

http://orion.ibm.dk:1158/em
```

OS Authentication

In Oracle, OS authentication can be made. That means that access to the databases can be provided to specific users rather than to a dedicated database user account. The following steps can be used to do that kind of authentication:

1. Create the user account under Linux.
2. Give the Linux user account the group *osdba* or *osoper* OS group, i.e. *dba* group to the Linux user.
3. Set the initialization parameter *remote_login_password* to the value *none.*
4. Test that the user is able to connect with the string *sqlplus / as sysdba.*

Note that the Linux group oper can be chosen. If the DBA would like to connect with the *sysoper* privileges, the connection can be made with *sqlplus / as sysoper.*

> Exam Advice: Be able to describe the steps needed to make the Linux user authenticated by the OS and what are the benefits.

Oracle Diverse Commands and Files

oraenv and *dbhome* are shell commands that enable the DBA to get the Oracle environment setup and to get the values of the current *$ORACLE_HOME*. It is mandatory to have the file */etc/oratab* filled with the correct value to have those commands working. The scripts are located in the *$ORACLE_HOME/bin* directory, but the *oraenv* is typically also present in */usr/local/bin/oraenv* as that command can be used to easily switch from different Oracle databases. The command *oraenv* can be run with the following method, *oraenv.* This will make value changes in the parent shell.

With the file */etc/oraInst.loc*, it is possible to locate the Oracle inventory that contains all the information about the Oracle installation on the servers and what group is the owner of the installation. The Oracle inventory is automatically created by the Oracle Universal Installer.

> Exam Advice: Be able to list the location of the Oracle inventory file and what the purpose is of the commands *oraenv* and *dbhome*.

Summary

The ins and outs of creating an Oracle database were covered in this chapter using the Database Configuration Assistant, or *dbca*, utility. The *dbca* wizard was shown step-by-step to assist in successfully creating the database by first choosing a template, then identifying the database and continuing with other options. Next came choosing storage options such as Automatic Storage Management (ASM) and raw devices. The wizard continued with specifications for creating an ASM instance as well as choosing the database file location and recovery options, among other steps. The database creation finished with a confirmation screen. The chapter ended with an explanation of Oracle processes and what they entail.

Chapter 11 will delve into customizing Oracle databases in Linux.

Exercises

1. Create a database that is using ASM as storage.
2. Configure the OS authentication on a new Linux user.

Q&A

Questions

1. In the following list, what are the correct prerequisites to start *dbca*? (Choose all that apply)

A. The oracle alias *dbca* is set
B. The *$DISPLAY* is set properly and works
C. The *$ORACLE_HOME* environment variable is set
D. The *$ORACLE_HOME/bin* is present in the *$path* environment variable

2. The database newdb is created by *dbca*. What files are created or updated besides the database creation? (Choose all that apply)

A. *spfile* file in *$ORACLE_HOME/dbs*
B. password file in *$ORACLE_HOME/dbs*

C. spfile file in *$ORACLE_HOME/dbs*
D. The file *oratab* in */etc/*

3. On a server that does not have any database created yet, the databases will be stored on ASM and the *dbca* utility can be used. What action can be performed to create the ASM storage database? (Choose all that apply)

A. Run as the user oracle the command *$ORACLE_HOME/bin/localconfig add*
B. Run as the user root the command *$ORACLE_HOME/bin/localconfig add*
C. Run as the user root the command *$ORACLE_HOME/bin/localconfig update*
D. Have the ASM instance created manually or by *dbca*

4. What action needs to be performed to have the Oracle Cluster Synchronization Services daemon running? (Choose the correct answer)

A. Service start *cssd*
B. *$ORACLE_HOME/bin/cssd_start*
C. */etc/init.d/init.cssd_start*
D. */etc/init.d/init.css_start*

5. For the database odb10g, in what directory are the files *alertodb10g.log* and the background process logs located? (Choose all that apply)

A. It depends on the value of the initialization parameter *background_dump_dest*
B. *$ORACLE_HOME/admin/*
C. *$ORACLE_BASE/install/odb10g/bdump/*
D. *$ORACLE_HOME/install/*

6. What shell command can be used to change both the $*ORACLE_SID* and the $*ORACLE_HOME*? (Choose all that apply)

A. *oratab*
B. *oraenv*
C. *oraenv*
D. *oratab*

7. Where is the Oracle inventory location (*oraInst.loc*) stored on a Linux server? (Choose the correct answer)

A. *$ORACLE_HOME*
B. *$ORACLE_BASE/admin*
C. */var/opt/oracle*
D. */etc/*

8. The initialization parameter *remote_login_password* is set to the value *none.* What kind of Oracle authentication can be performed? (Chose the correct answer)

A. An Oracle privileges authentication
B. An Oracle OID (Oracle Internet Directory) authentication
C. An OS authentication can be made
D. An Oracle Identity Management authentication

9. Select the correct operations that can be made to have the Linux user thomas to connect with *sqlplus/as sysdba* using the OS authentication. (Choose all that apply)

A. Give the Linux user account the group osoper OS group
B. Give the Linux user account the group osdba in the Linux user group
C. Set the initialization parameter *remote_login_password* to the value *yes*
D. Set the initialization parameter *remote_login_password* to the value *none*

10. What actions are required to have users other than oracle that can connect with SQL*Plus having the following strings / as *sysoper*? Choose the correct group in which to add the new Linux user:

A. dba
B. oper
C. sys
D. admin

Answers

1. The correct answers are: B. The *$DISPLAY* is set properly and works; C. The *$ORACLE_HOME* environment variable is set and D. The *$ORACLE_HOME/bin* is present in the *$path* environment variable.

HINT: Read again the section "How to Create an Oracle Database".

2. The correct answers are: A. *spfile* file in *$ORACLE_HOME/dbs*; B. *password* file in *$ORACLE_HOME/dbs* and D. The file *oratab in /etc/*.

HINT: Again, consult the "How to Create an Oracle Database".

3. The correct answers are: B. Run as the user root the command *$ORACLE_HOME/bin/localconfig add* and D. Have the ASM instance created manually or by *dbca.*

HINT: Study the section on creating an Oracle database.

4. The correct answer is: C. */etc/init.d/init.cssd start*

HINT: Consult the section "How to Create an Oracle Database".

5. The correct answers are: A. it depends on the value of the initialization parameter *background_dump_dest* and C. *$ORACLE_BASE/install/odb10g/bdump/*

HINT: Read again the section on Oracle instance processes, files and structures.

6. The correct answer is: C. *oraenv*

HINT: Study the section "Oracle Diverse Commands and Files".

7. The correct answer is: D. */etc/*

HINT: Consult the Oracle Diverse commands and files.

8. The correct answer is: C. An OS authentication can be made.

HINT: Read again the OS authentication.

9. The correct answers are: B. Give the Linux user account the group osdba in the Linux user group and D. Set the initialization parameter *remote_login_password* to the value *none.*

HINT: Study the section OS authentication

10. The correct answer is: B. oper

HINT: Consult again the section on OS authentication.

Solutions to Exercises

1. Create a database that is using ASM as storage.

   Follow the steps given in the section "How to Create an Oracle Database".

2. Configure the OS authentication on a new Linux user.

   Use the steps given in the section "OS Authentication".

Customizing Oracle Databases Under Linux

CHAPTER

The chapter covers the following exam Objectives:

7. Customizing Oracle on Linux
7.1. Create automated startup/shutdown scripts
7.3. Configure Linux startup and shutdown sequence

Why Customize Oracle Databases under Linux?

The system administrator and database administrator jobs imply that maintenance and BAU (Business As Usual) work should be performed outside the normal working or application usage peak hours as the services become available for the users. It is, therefore, important that the databases can be up rapidly in case the Linux servers are rebooting, a disk is defective, there are power failures and such.

In order to perform a system recovery, there should be reliable backups that are taken outside the peak hours. Monitoring of the systems is also important in order to collect and inform about software and hardware issues and performance problems since the DBA must be kept informed about the database and system health.

In this chapter, the customization of the Linux system in order to perform an appropriate shutdown and startup of the Oracle databases is covered since this is an exam requirement. In Chapter 3, information can be found about startup sequences of Linux, *init* modes and details about a startup script. Concerning other tools used to perform scheduling of tasks, refer to Chapter 4 in the section on scheduling tools that describes the Linux utilities *cron*, *at*, *batch* and *anacron*. The backup of Oracle and Linux is not an exam requirement, but information about the backup is found in Chapter 14.

This chapter also covers customization of Oracle under Linux that can be performed within the initialization parameters of Oracle and gives an overview of the Enterprise Manager dbconsole, mentioned in the previous chapter, that can help in performing automatic tasks.

Automatic vs. Manual Oracle Stop and Start

It is possible to start the Oracle database instances manually or automatically. The services that are making the Oracle database can be the Enterprise Manager agents or dbconsole, the Oracle listener, the ASM instance, the graphical SQL*Plus (iSQL*Plus) and the database's instances. With the oracle user, the following commands can be used to stop or start the services:

```
$ORACLE_HOME/bin/emctl {start|stop} agent
$ORACLE_HOME/bin/emctl {start|stop} dbconcole
$ORACLE_HOME/bin/lsnrctl {start|stop}
$ORACLE_HOME/bin/sqlplus /nolog <<EOF
connect / as sysdba
{startup|shutdown immediate}
EOF
$oracle_home/bin/isqlplusctl {start|stop}
```

The next section will describe how to configure the automatic stop and start of Oracle database services.

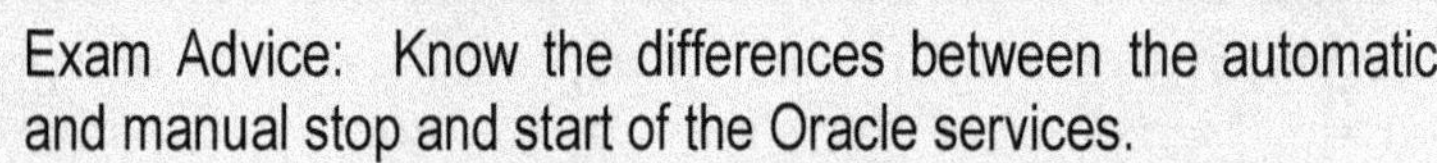

Exam Advice: Know the differences between the automatic and manual stop and start of the Oracle services.

Script to Perform Stop and Start of an Oracle Database

On a UNIX-like system like Linux, it is possible to have the software product customized to stop and start up automatically by choosing the *init* mode that will be running in the user's system.

The steps to perform an automatic stop and start of Oracle on Linux are:

1. Prerequisite: Have a */etc/oratab* filled properly with the flag *Y*.
2. Create a script, i.e. *dbora,* which will call the *dbstart* and *dbshut* script that is located in the */etc/rc.d/init.d* directory.
3. Have the correct permission set on the *dbora* file (ideally 750).

4. Make sure that the script creates a lock file located at */var/lock/subsys/dbora* in the start section of the *dbora* script.

5. Perform the *chkconfig* command to set up the proper run level of the *dbora* script.

6. Verify that the stop and start of the database is working properly.

In order to perform an automatic stop and start of Oracle under Linux, it is necessary to have the file */etc/oratab* on the system that should contain information about the instance system identifier (*ORACLE_SID*), the home of Oracle (*$ORACLE_HOME*) and the automatic stop and start flag with the value *y* or *n* depending on what needs to be achieved. Use the example with the database newdb that can be automatically stopped and started. Observe that the arguments are separated with the colon character (:) and that comments can be added with # as prefix. The file */etc/oratab* contains the following line.

```
newdb:/u01/app/oracle/product/10.2.0/db_1:Y
```

Stop and Start Script *dbora*

It is important in Linux to have a file created in the directory */var/lock/subsys/* as it is an additional control to see if the product, service or application is running on the Linux server. Its status can be controlled with the service command *service <initscript> status.* The command returns the different states if the service is running, stopped or dead.

```
[root@orion ~]# service syslog status
syslogd (pid 3005) is running...
klogd (pid 3009) is running...
[root@orion ~]#
```

Create a script owned by root in the directory */etc/rc.d/init.d/dbora* that contains the following lines:

```
#!/bin/sh
# oracle Start/Stop the Databases...
#
# chkconfig: 2345 99 10
# description: stop and starts your Oracle databases instances
# processname: oracle
# config: /etc/oratab
# pidfile: /var/run/oracle.pid

oracle_home=/u01/app/oracle/product/10.2.0/db_1
```

```
oracle_owner=oracle

if [ ! -f $oracle_home/bin/dbstart ]
then
    echo "Oracle startup: Can't be started"
    exit
fi

case "$1" in
    'start')
        # Start the Oracle databases:
        su - $ORACLE_OWNER -c "$ORACLE_HOME/bin/dbstart $ORACLE_HOME"
        touch /var/lock/subsys/dbora
        ;;
    'stop')
        # Stop the Oracle databases:
        su - $ORACLE_OWNER -c "$ORACLE_HOME/bin/dbshut $ORACLE_HOME"
        rm -f /var/lock/subsys/dbora
        ;;

*)
        echo "usage: $0 {start|stop}"
        exit
        ;;

esac

exit
```

Note: The Oracle listener that has its password set cannot be stopped automatically. The listener that uses a different name other than the default name (*LISTENER*) can be stopped and started in the section stop/start; in this example case, by adding the following line:

```
$ORACLE_HOME/bin/lsnrctl {start|stop} your_listener_name
```

In the script *dbstart* in the release 10.2.0.1, an error can be corrected manually with the variable *ORACLE_HOME_LISTENER=*. It contains the *$ORACLE_HOME* as value. The Metalink note #336299.1 gives more information about that issue.

The command *dbstart* is starting the listener first, the ASM instance next if used, and at the end, the database instance is started. The Enterprise Manager dbconsole and iSQL*Plus can be added in the script *dbora* to start up and shut down the script.

After the *dbora* script is created, it is necessary to have it linked in the appropriate *init* directories, or by using the Linux utility *chkconfig*, it can be set up as a service. With the command *chkconfig –list*, all the services running on the Linux system can be set and in what *init* mode they are available can be discovered. It is quite important that the lines regarding the *chkconfig* run level and the description are present; otherwise, it is impossible to add the services to the system.

Therefore, the following lines hereunder are mandatory in the *dbora* file.

```
# chkconfig: 2345 99 10
# description: stop and starts the Oracle database instances
```

The *chkconfig* arguments *2345 99 10* concern the run level where the *start* script is present (*init 2, 3, 4 and 5*) and where the *stop* script can be created (*run level 0, 1 and 6*). The script is named *S99dbora* for the *start* script, and for stopping, *K10dbora.*

The *dbora* service can be added by doing:

```
chkconfig --add dbora
```

Make sure that the service is created with the correct *init* modes with the command:

```
[root@orion init.d]# chkconfig --list | grep -i ora
```

```
dbora           0:off    1:off    2:on     3:on     4:on     5:on     6:off
oracleasm       0:off    1:off    2:on     3:on     4:on     5:on     6:off
```

The *oracleasm* is also managed by the *chkconfig* utility.

After the *add* option has been executed on the *chkconfig*, all the links created in the *init* directories should point to the *dbora* script.

```
[root@orion etc]# ls -alR /etc/rc.d/rc?.d/*dbora | grep dbora
```

```
lrwxrwxrwx  1 root root 15 Jun  6 12:08 /etc/rc.d/rc0.d/K10dbora -> ../init.d/dbora
lrwxrwxrwx  1 root root 15 Jun  6 12:08 /etc/rc.d/rc1.d/K10dbora -> ../init.d/dbora
lrwxrwxrwx  1 root root 15 Jun  6 12:08 /etc/rc.d/rc2.d/S99dbora -> ../init.d/dbora
lrwxrwxrwx  1 root root 15 Jun  6 12:08 /etc/rc.d/rc3.d/S99dbora -> ../init.d/dbora
lrwxrwxrwx  1 root root 15 Jun  6 12:08 /etc/rc.d/rc4.d/S99dbora -> ../init.d/dbora
lrwxrwxrwx  1 root root 15 Jun  6 12:08 /etc/rc.d/rc5.d/S99dbora -> ../init.d/dbora
lrwxrwxrwx  1 root root 15 Jun  6 12:08 /etc/rc.d/rc6.d/K10dbora -> ../init.d/dbora
```

In the *dbora* script, it is possible to add more lines to start other Oracle services like the Oracle EM dbconsole in the stop and start sections.

```
$oracle_home/bin/emctl {stop| start} dbconsole &"

#!/bin/sh
```

```
# oracle Start/Stop the Databases...
#
# chkconfig: 2345 99 10
# description: stop and starts your Oracle databases instances
# processname: oracle
# config: /etc/oratab
# pidfile: /var/run/oracle.pid

oracle_home=/u01/app/oracle/product/10.2.0/db_1
oracle_owner=oracle

if [ ! -f $oracle_home/bin/dbstart ]
then
    echo "Oracle startup: Can't be started"
    exit
fi

case "$1" in
    'start')
        # Start the Oracle databases:
        su - $oracle_owner -c "$oracle_home/bin/dbstart $oracle_home"
        touch /var/lock/subsys/dbora
        su - $oracle_owner -c "$oracle_home/bin/emctl start dbconsole"
        ;;
    'stop')
        # Stop the Oracle databases:
        su - $oracle_owner -c "$oracle_home/bin/dbshut $oracle_home"
        su - $oracle_owner -c "$oracle_home/bin/emctl stop dbconsole"
        rm -f /var/lock/subsys/dbora
        ;;

*)
        echo "usage: $0 {start|stop}"
        exit
        ;;

esac

exit
```

> Exam Advice: Be able to explain all the steps to make an automatic startup of the Oracle services and what are the files used and created during those actions.

Oracle EM Dbconsole Scheduling Possibilities

With the Oracle Enterprise Manager, it is also possible to schedule tasks that can be *rman* scripts, SQL and PL/SQL scripts, stored procedures, Linux OS commands and *perl* scripts. It is possible to see those scheduled tasks in the dictionary view *dbms_scheduler*. In the Enterprise Manager console, the scheduled tasks can be found in the administration page in the section Database Scheduler.

Figure 11.1A: *Database Scheduler*

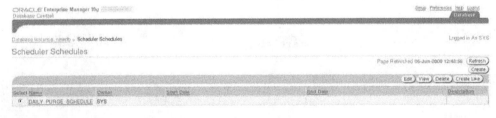

Figure 11.1B: *Database Scheduler*

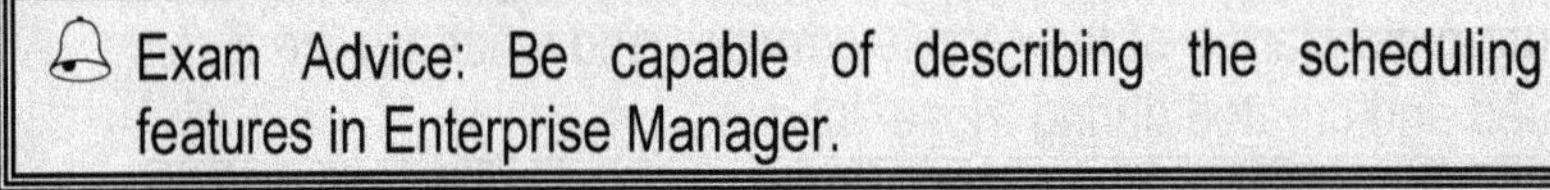

Exam Advice: Be capable of describing the scheduling features in Enterprise Manager.

Customization of Oracle Initialization Parameters

The parameters in Oracle can be managed and customized with *pfile*, *spfile* and the *alter system set* commands. Oracle recommends using the *spfile* as dynamic parameters can be modified dynamically without stopping and starting the instance and *spfile* makes it possible for the DBA's database to auto-tune. When using the *pfile* (*init<sid>.ora*) that is a text-based file, it is not possible to maintain it within Oracle. This means that the changes have to be performed by editing in the file and performing a restart of the instance. In ASM, *spfile* is located in *<diskgroup>*/*<sid>*/ by default.

Summary

This short chapter dealt with customizing Oracle under Linux is order to be able to start up and shut down Oracle database services. One way this is accomplished is within the initilizations parameters of Oracle. Next, how to start up or shut down the database manually or automatically was shown.

Also, use of the Enterprise Manager dbconsole was covered in more detail in regards to automating scheduling tasks.

Exercises

1. Configure Oracle installation on the Linux server to shut down and start up automatically.
2. Modify the shutdown and startup script to include iSQL*Plus and the Enterprise Manager dbconsole.

Q&A

Questions

1. An Oracle database instance can be started... (Choose all that apply)

A. Semi-automatically
B. Manually
C. Automatically
D. Only manually

2. What are the actions listed below that are mandatory to start an Oracle instance automatically? (Choose all that apply)

A. Create a *startup* script, i.e. called *dbora*
B. Use the *dbstart* and *dbstop* in the *startup* script

C. Use the *dbstart* and *dbshut* in the *startup* script
D. Run the command *checkconfig* to have the *startup* script linked in the different *init* directories
E. Run the command *chckconfig* to have the *startup* script linked in the different *init* directories
F. Link manually the script *dbora* in all the */etc/rc.d/rc*.d* directories

3. What are the Oracle standard stop and start scripts to start/stop an Oracle instance? (Choose all that apply)

A. *dbstop*
B. *dbstartup*
C. *dbshut*
D. *dbstart*

4. What is the file used by the Oracle standard script to start and stop a database instance? (Choose the correct answer)

A. */etc/oracle_std*
B. */etc/ora_installation*
C. */etc/oratab*
D. */var/opt/oracle/oratab*

5. Where can a *spfile* be stored on an Oracle database that is using the following instance? (see the exhibit) Choose all the possible locations.

```
[oracle@orion bin]$ ps -efd | grep pmon | grep -v grep
oracle    1103     1  0 13:48 ?         00:00:01 ora_pmon_newdb
oracle   31614     1  0 13:23 ?         00:00:02 asm_pmon_+ASM
```

A. Only in *$ORACLE_HOME/dbs*
B. Only in *+ASM*
C. In *+ASM* but as *pfile*
D. In *+ASM /<diskgroup>/<oracle_sid>* and *$ORACLE_HOME/dbs*

Answers

1. The correct answers are: B. Manually and C. Automatically.

HINT: Read again the section "Automatic vs. Manual Oracle Stop and Start".

2. The correct answers are: A. Create a *startup* script, i.e. called *dbora*; C. Use the *dbstart* and *dbshut* in the *startup* script; and E. Run the command *chckconfig* to have the *startup* script linked in the different *init* directories.

HINT: Consult again the section "Stop and Start Script *dbora*".

3. The correct answers are C. *dbshut* and D. *dbstart.*

HINT: Read again the section on stopping and starting script *dbora.*

4. The correct answer is C. */etc/oratab.*

HINT: Consult again "Script to Perform Stop and Start of an Oracle Database" section.

5. The correct answer is D. In +ASM /<diskgroup>/<oracle_sid> and $ORACLE_HOME/dbs.

HINT: Study again the section "Customization of Oracle Initialization Parameters".

Solutions to the Exercises

1. Configure Oracle installation on the Linux server to shut down and start up automatically.

a) Prerequisite: Have a */etc/oratab* filled properly with the flag *y.*
b) Create a script, i.e. *dbora*, that will call the *dbstart* and *dbshut* script that is located in the */etc/rc.d/init.d* directory.
c) Have the correct permission set on the *dbora* file (ideally 750).
d) Make sure that the script creates a lock file located at */var/lock/subsys/dbora* in the start section of the *dbora* script.
e) Perform the *chkconfig* command to set up the proper run level of the *dbora* script.
f) Verify that the stop and start of the database is working properly.

2. Modify the shutdown and startup script to include iSQL*Plus and the Enterprise Manager dbconsole.

The *dbora* script includes the stop/start of the *emctl* and *isqlplusctl.* They are in bold.

```
#!/bin/sh
# oracle Start/Stop the Databases...
#
# chkconfig: 2345 99 10
# description: stop and starts your Oracle databases instances
# processname: oracle
# config: /etc/oratab
# pidfile: /var/run/oracle.pid

ORACLE_HOME=/u01/app/oracle/product/10.2.0/db_1
ORACLE_OWNER=oracle
```

```
if [ ! -f $ORACLE_HOME/bin/dbstart ]
then
    echo "Oracle startup: Can't be started"
    exit
fi

case "$1" in
    'start')
        # Start the Oracle databases:
        su - $ORACLE_OWNER -c "$ORACLE_HOME/bin/dbstart $oracle_home"
        touch /var/lock/subsys/dbora
        su - $ORACLE_OWNER -c "$ORACLE_HOME/bin/emctl start dbconsole"
        su - $ORACLE_OWNER -c "$ORACLE_HOME/bin/isqlplusctl start"
        ;;
    'stop')
        # Stop the Oracle databases:
        su - $ORACLE_OWNER -c "$ORACLE_HOME/bin/dbshut $oracle_home"
        su - $ORACLE_OWNER -c "$ORACLE_HOME/bin/emctl stop dbconsole"
        su - $ORACLE_OWNER -c "$ORACLE_HOME/bin/isqlplusctl stop"
        rm -f /var/lock/subsys/dbora
        ;;
*)
        echo "usage: $0 {start|stop}"
        exit
        ;;

esac

exit
```

Memory Management

CHAPTER 12

This chapter covers the following exam objectives:

8. Managing Memory
8.1. List the memory models available in Linux kernels
8.2. Implement hugepages
8.4. List the implications of Linux memory configuration on Oracle Database
8.5. Identify the issues regarding 32-bit OS versus 64-bit OS

Memory Models Available in Linux Kernels

As has been seen in the previous chapter, the Linux operating system is quite flexible and for memory management, it is possible to configure and customize the memory usage. Since the Linux kernel 2.6, there are manageability features such as hugepages, memory file systems and techniques like page addressing extensions.

A page table is a structure of data that is mapped from a physical address to a virtual address. The page is the smallest unit for data on memory allocation and swap operations. The CPU has a dedicated cache area, for performance reasons, that stores the TLB (Translation Look-aside Buffer) of a page table. The *hugetlb* is an entry in the TLB that is pointing to a hugepage. *Hugetlbfs* is a memory management option that enables Linux to use a large virtual address space as it is based on a file system. It is possible to make sure that the kernel is supporting the hugepages with the command *grep -i huge /proc/meminfo* if it is built in the kernel hugespages. The result is shown below.

```
[oracle@orion bin]$ grep -i huge /proc/meminfo

HugePages_Total:      0
HugePages_Free:       0
Hugepagesize:      4096 kB
```

The PAE (Page Address Extension) is a feature available in the x86 and x86-64 processors' architecture that enables the DBA's operating system to use more than four gigabytes of physical memory. For x86 32-bit machines, they can handle from 4 GB up to 64 GB. This kind of memory is called VLM (Very Large Memory).

This is possible as the hardware has additional memory addresses that are increased from 32 bits to 36 bits, so it goes from 232 = 4,294,967,296 (4 GB) to 236 = 68,719,476,736 (64 GB). VLM can be used by Oracle under Linux without having performances issues related to that usage. CPU x86-64 bit processors can handle up to 16 exabytes (1018 bytes) memory.

Exam Advice: Be sure to know the memory concept described previously.

Swap in Linux

The purpose of the swap in Linux, like in other operating systems, is to provide more memory than physically available on the hardware. In order to avoid issues with the memory left on the Linux servers, the swap space on disk will keep some contents from the physical memory when the processes do not have enough RAM memory rather than failing the process with the error "no memory left". So Linux makes a copy of some content of the RAM in the swap area on disk by having the content of the swap space continually monitored and, if necessary, sorting the swap data to the ram data and vice-versa. By doing the update of the RAM and swap memory data, Linux is efficiently handling the free memory for the DBA's applications and processes.

With the intention of helping the swap to be more effective, a swap cache area that is stored in the RAM tracks the memory pages that are sorted out to the disk swap. By doing this operation, it reduces unnecessary I/O. The page-in operation is sending a memory page from disk to the RAM; however, it is the page-out operation making a transfer of the memory pages from RAM to the disk.

In Chapter 6, *Preparing Linux for Oracle*, the section on hardware requirements shows the details related to the swap configuration depending on the memory size.

 Exam Advice: Be able to describe the purpose of the swap and how to size the swap in the function of the available memory.

Memory Report Tools

It is possible to get reports of the free, used and cached memory in Linux with the utilities *top* and *free* that can be used in the shell sessions. The command *free* shows the amount of free and used memory both physical and in the swap. Switches like *-k*, *-m* and *-g* can be used to display kilo, mega, and gigabytes. The output below shows that there is 47 MB free and 276 that are cached.

```
[oracle@orion bin]$ free -m

             total       used       free     shared    buffers     cached
Mem:           582        535         47          0         28        276
-/+ buffers/cache:        230        352
Swap:         2047        136       1910
```

With the *top* command, the process ID (PID), memory usage, load on the server, number of users and more that is periodically updated can be seen. *top* gives many more details about the physical and virtual (swap) memory, as shown next:

```
top - 14:21:55 up  5:24,  5 users,  load average: 4.61, 4.63, 3.83
Tasks: 141 total,   1 running, 139 sleeping,   0 stopped,   1 zombie
Cpu(s):  9.0% us,  7.1% sy,  0.0% ni, 80.6% id,  0.3% wa,  2.9% hi,  0.0% si
Mem:    596764k total,   585904k used,    10860k free,    28092k buffers
Swap:  2096472k total,   140892k used,  1955580k free,   256328k cached

  PID USER      PR  NI  VIRT  RES  SHR S %CPU %MEM    TIME+  COMMAND
 4997 root      15   0 48676  18m 5188 S  6.8  3.1  10:03.30 X
 9631 oracle    15   0 41264  14m 7616 S  6.1  2.5   1:08.89 gnome-terminal
12658 root      15   0  2192  928  784 S  0.6  0.2   0:54.75 vmware-guestd
12664 oracle    15   0  8652 2104 1776 S  0.6  0.4   1:44.40 vmware-user
  467 root      15   0     0    0    0 S  0.3  0.0   0:23.20 kjournald
 1113 oracle    16   0  329m  21m  18m S  0.3  3.7   0:05.99 oracle
 5416 root      16   0  2780  560  504 S  0.3  0.1   0:04.52 pam_timestamp_c
12517 oracle    16   0  574m  84m  24m S  0.3 14.5   0:27.32 java
12610 oracle    16   0  329m  41m  37m S  0.3  7.1   0:01.13 oracle
    1 root      16   0  2844  508  456 S  0.0  0.1   0:02.53 init
```

 Exam Advice: Be able to enumerate the previous commands that display the memory information.

Hugepages

The support of the hugepages in Linux started with the kernel release 2.6 with the standard size of 4 KB as regular page size. With the hugepages, it is possible to increase the page size to 4 MB without having any performance issues as the page table entries are still allocating the same information about the pages. The performance might also be enhanced since the hugepages are not swapped out because they are still in the RAM.

Configuration of Hugepages

Hugepages can be configured on a 32-bit Linux system. Below, the details to perform in order to be able to use hugepages with Oracle under Linux are found. The operations are performed as the Linux super user root.

Get the *ramfs* mounted when the system boots. Edit the file */etc/rc.local* and add the following lines:

```
umount /dev/shm
mount -t ramfs ramfs /dev/shm
chmod 640 /dev/shm
chown oracle:dba /dev/shm
```

After these lines are added, reboot the server. When the server is up again, log on as the super user *root*.

Make sure that the device */dev/shm* is mounted with the type *ramfs* and that the permissions given are correct.

```
root@orion vmware-tools-distrib]# mount | grep shm
ramfs on /dev/shm type ramfs (rw)
root@orion vmware-tools-distrib]# ls -lad /dev/shm
drw-r-----  2 oracle dba 0 Jun 13 15:01 /dev/shm
```

Modify the memory limit settings in the file */etc/security/limits.conf* to the following values:

```
*               soft    memlock                 3145728
*               hard    memlock                 3145728
```

Connect as the user oracle and verify the maximum lock memory limits with the command *ulimit –l*. The result is the same value that was configured previously.

```
[oracle@orion ~]$ ulimit -l
3145728
```

Now it is necessary to configure the Oracle instance to use the VLM (Very Large Memory) that is configured in Linux with the following information. After that, readapt the size of the SGA and restart the instance. In case the parameter *sga_target* is being used, it should be removed. Use the parameter *db_block_buffers* instead of *db_cache_size* or *db_xK_cache_size*.

Control the memory usage after the instance is restarted by doing this:

```
ls -l /dev/shm
ipcs -m
```

To get the hugepages working on the Linux server, the size of the hugepages can be obtained by doing a *grep -i hugepagesize /proc/meminfo.*

Use the following formula to get the number of hugepages with the value of the *hugepagesize:*

$$Number\ of\ huge\ pages = \frac{max(ipcs - m)}{(hugepagesize * 1024) + 1}$$

Get the *hugepage* values added to the Linux server with the value from the formula:

```
sysctl -w wm.nr_hugepages=<Number of huge pages>
```

It can also be added in the file */etc/sysctl.conf.* After that has been done, restart the Oracle instance or the server and make sure that the values of *hugepages* are in the file */proc/meminfo*. There should be some pages free.

Note: If it is discovered that the hugepages are not working, it is advisable to reboot the Linux server and see that the hugepages are working after performing this changes.

> Exam Advice: Know how to perform the configuration and the benefits of using the hugepages.

SGA Relocation Operations

The Oracle SGA (System Global Area) has two memory limitations under Linux. The first limitation is about the memory space allocated to the Oracle and user processes and the second is about the kernel limitation. Linux kernels under 32-bit architecture are not able to access more memory than 4 GB (232 bytes) by using PAE described previously in the section concerning memory models available in Linux kernels that can go over the 32-bit limitations. Once again, Linux OS shows its flexibility by making it possible to change the memory allocation addresses. The next paragraphs give the method to enable and disable the memory relocation.

It is possible to relocate the database buffer cache to use up to 60 GB in theory, but feasible limits are about 20 GB. The Linux memory map can also be relocated so the SGA can be increased from 1.7 GB up to 2.6 GB.

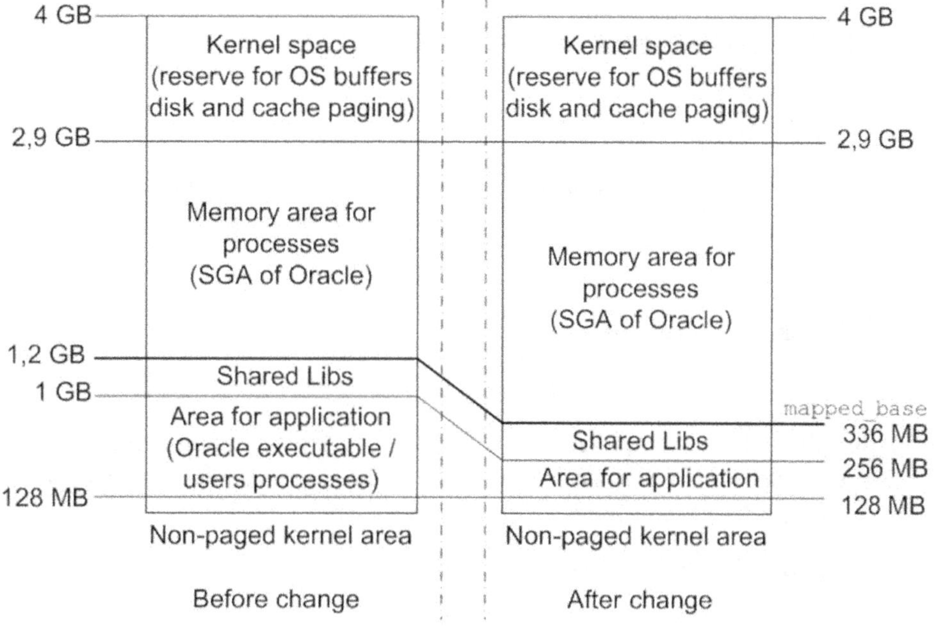

Figure 12.1: *Before and After Memory Relocation on 4 GB*

As shown in Figure 12.1, it is possible to reduce the size of the memory area for the application and for the shared libraries. By doing that operation, it is possible to get a bigger memory area for the user's Oracle SGA. The memory mappings can be controlled in the file */proc/<the process pid>/maps*. The operations can be performed on releases other than Oracle 10g; it is possible to use the procedures from Oracle 8.1.7 up to 11g. Unfortunately, the operation also has negative consequences on the PGA and sorting procedures and Oracle can only be started from a shell that has its *mapped_based* relocated.

First, the area used by the Oracle processes needs to be reduced to 0x15000000 by performing the operations described here:

1. As the user oracle or the Oracle software owner, shut down all instances of Oracle and make sure that there are no Oracle background or listener processes running:

```
cd $ORACLE_HOME/lib
```

2. Make a backup of the library.

```
cp libserver10.a libserver10.a.orginal
```

```
cd $oracle_home/bin
```

3. Make a backup of the executable Oracle.

```
cp oracle oracle.orginal
cd $oracle_home/rdbms/lib
cp ksms.s ksms.s.orignal
```

4. Get the SGA down to *0x15000000 genksms -s 0x15000000 >ksms.s.*

5. Recompile the relocated SGA.

```
make -f ins_rdbms.mk ksms.o
```

6. Relink the Oracle binaries.

```
make -f ins_rdbms.mk ioracle
```

After the relocation of the SGA, it is necessary to change the value of the *mapped_base.* To do this, two terminals will be needed: one with a root session and a second with an Oracle Linux user session.

7. Get the Oracle Linux session PID.

8. From the Linux Oracle terminal, do an *echo $$.*

9. Change the value of the *mapped_base 0x10000000* (decimal value 268435456).

10. *oracle_pid* is the value received from *echo $$ echo 268435456 >/proc/<oracle_pid>/mapped_base*

11. In the Oracle user Linux shell, the instance can be started up.

If the DBA needs to roll back to the original configuration, do the following:

12. As the user oracle or the Oracle software owner, shut down all instances of Oracle and make sure that there is not any Oracle background or listener processes running.

```
cd $ORACLE_HOME/rdbms/lib
```

13. If there is a copy of the *ksms.s*:

```
cp ksms.s.orignal ksms.s
```

14. Only in the case that there is not the original file:

```
genksms >ksms.s
```

15. Recompile the relocated SGA.

```
make -f ins_rdbms.mk ksms.o
```

16. Relink the Oracle binaries.

```
make -f ins_rdbms.mk ioracle
```

The extension of the database buffer cache can be performed with the following steps:

17. Increase the *shmmax* value for the entire SGA from a root session by doing an echo *3000000000 >/proc/sys/kernel/shmmax*. This is for 3 GB. If this value needs to be kept, change the value *kernel.shmmax* in the file */etc/sysctl.conf*.
18. Activate the hugepages (consult the section on configuration of hugepages).
19. Set up the shared memory file system SHMFS (SHared Memory File System), i.e. with a 4 GB file system, as root of the root user: *mount -t shm shmfs -o size=4g /dev/shm.*
20. The shared memory file system can be mounted automatically by adding the following line into the */etc/fstab* file: *shmfs /dev/shm shm size=4g 0 0.*
21. Get the initialization parameters updated for using the SHMFS by setting the Oracle *init* parameters *use_indirect_data_buffers=true* and *db_block_buffers=524288.* For a file system of 4 GB with a *db_block_size* of 8 KB, the formula is *db_block_buffers = (size_of the SHMFS disk * 1024 * 1024) / db_block_size.*

It is important that none of the following parameters are set:

- *db_cache_size*
- *db_2k_cache_size*
- *db_4k_cache_size*
- *db_8k_cache_size*
- *db_16k_cache_size*
- *db_32k_cache_size*
- *sga_target*

22. Restart the instance(s).

Note: The application area is reduced, so it is necessary to make sure that the Oracle users are still able to create new sessions. Therefore, it is advisable to perform some tests after the changes and tune the value of the *mapped_base*. If ORA-3113 errors are showing up during the test, it will be necessary to increase the *mapped_base* value.

> Exam Advice: Know how to enable and disable the SGA relocation on Linux systems.

Kernel with Huge Memory

The *kernel-hugemem* package provides a lot of benefits. It makes it possible to allocate much more RAM (up to 64 GB), it uses the PAE, allows up to 4 GB per process, provides an available size for the SGA of 3.42 GB without implementing the VLM and supports multiple processors.

Note: This chapter covers the exam requirements. If more details on that topic are desired, refer to the Metalink White paper note: Doc ID: 260152.1 Subject: Linux Big SGA, Large Memory, VLM - White Paper.

>  Exam Advice: Be capable of enumerating the purpose and benefits of using the hugemen on the kernel of the Linux servers.

Summary

Chapter 12 described all the possibilities with Oracle under a 32-bit Linux system that are required for passing the OCE exam. It started with a description of what is possible under Linux, the swap concept was reviewed, and memory commands and tools were also described. After that, it presented the hugepage concepts and the SGA relocation operations. Then the chapter concluded with the benefits of the huge memory package.

Exercises

1. Get the outputs of the memory commands to evaluate the free memory on the Linux server.
2. Perform all the operations to get the system configured with the hugepages, then recompile and re-link the Oracle binaries.

Q&A

Questions

1. What are the commands that can help to evaluate the memory usage? Choose all that apply:

A. *topas*
B. *top*
C. *free*
D. *mem*

2. What is the swap cache used for on Linux? Choose the correct answer.

A. The swap cache exists only on Windows systems, so it is not supported by Linux OS
B. It helps to get the swap much more effective with a swap area cache, but has no effect on the I/O
C. It helps to get the swap much more effective with a swap area cache and increases I/O
D. It helps to get the swap much more effective with a swap area cache and reduces I/O

3. Choose the correct combination for the acronyms and the definitions:

A. PAE
B. TLB
C. hugetlb
D. hugetlbfs

a. Is the memory management option that enables Linux to use a large virtual address space since it is based on a file system

b. Is an entry in the Translation Look-aside Buffer that is pointing to a hugepage
c. Is a feature available in the x86 and x86-64 processors architecture that enables the operating system to use more than 4 GB physical memory
d. Is Buffer Look-aside that is a translation of a page table

4. What are the benefits of using PAE? Choose all that apply.

A. Enables the use of more than 4 gigabytes of ROM
B. Enables the use of more than 4 gigabytes of RAM
C. It enables access up to 64 GB of memory on 32-bit machines
D. PAE under Linux brings no benefits as it can only be used by WINTEL platforms

5. What is possible with hugepages? Choose all that apply.

A. With hugepages, it is possible to increase the page size from 4 B up to 4 KB
B. With hugepages, it is possible to increase the page size from 4 KB up to 4 MB
C. Hugepages are swapped out as they are still in the RAM
D. Hugepages are not swapped out as they are still in the RAM

6. In the following exhibit, what is missing or wrong?

```
su - oracle
vi /etc/rc.local
umount /dev/shm
mount -t ramfs ramfs /dev/shm
chmod 640 /dev/shm
chown oracle:dba /dev/shm
```

A. The *su – oracle* cannot be performed on Linux
B. The privileges for the */dev/shm* file must be 770
C. It is only root that can perform that operation
D. It is correct that no errors are in the exhibit

7. The command *genksms –s* is used for?

A. Relocating the PGA
B. Relocating the SGA
C. Relocating the *shmmax* value
D. Relinking Oracle binaries

8. When are the *ramfs* being used?

A. During the relink of Oracle binaries
B. During the change of the *shmmax* kernel value
C. During the maintenance mode of the server
D. During the configuration of the hugepages

9. What are the correct commands to execute after doing a *genksms -s 0x15000000 >ksms.s*? Choose all that apply and set the question in the proper order.

A. *relink –f ins_rdbms.mk ioracle*
B. *make -f ins_rdbms.mk ioracle*
C. *make -f ins_rdbms.mk ksms.o*
D. *relink –f ins_rdbms.mk ksms.o*

10. On question 9, the relink was performed, but the customer would like to get the previous values. Unfortunately, the original files were not kept. What can be done?

A. Nothing can be done - the Oracle binaries need to be reinstalled
B. Nothing can be done - the Oracle binaries need to be restored from the last backup
C. *genksms >ksms.s*
D. *genksms –s 0x000000000 >ksms.s*

Answers

1. B. *top* and C. *free* are the proper commands to evaluate the memory usage.

HINT: Consult the section on memory report tools in this chapter.

2. Correct answer is D. It helps to get the swap much more effective with a swap area cache and reduces I/O.

HINT: Reread the section "Swap in Linux".

3. Correct combination is A. c., D. a., C. b. and B. d.

HINT: Consult again the section Memory models available in Linux kernels

4. Correct answers are B. Enables the use of more than four gigabytes of RAM and C. It enables access up to 64 GB of memory on 32-bit machines.

HINT: Review the section "Memory Models Available in Linux Kernels".

5. B. With hugepages, it is possible to increase the page size from 4KB up to 4MB and D. Hugepages are not swapped out as they are still in the RAM are the correct answers.

HINT: Study again the section “Hugepages”.

6. C. It is only root that can perform that operation is the only correct answer.

HINT: Read again the section on configuration of hugepages.

7. Only B. Relocating the SGA is correct.

HINT: Go over to the section “SGA Relocation Operations”.

8. D. During the configuration of the hugepages is the correct answer.

HINT: Review the configuration of hugepages again.

9. First do C. *make -f ins_rdbms.mk ksms.o* and then B. *make -f ins_rdbms.mk ioracle* as correct answers and order.

HINT: Read again “SGA Relocation Operations”.

10. C. *genksms >ksms.s* is the only correct answer.

HINT: Study again the section on SGA relocation operations.

Solutions for Exercises

1. Get the outputs of the memory commands to evaluate the free memory on the Linux server.

Use the Linux commands *top* and *free*.

2. Perform all the operations to get the system configured with the hugepages, then recompile and relink the Oracle binaries.

Follow up the operations that are described in the section about the configuration of hugepages and SGA relocation operations.

Measurement, Tuning and Debugging

CHAPTER

This chapter covers the following exam objectives:

9. Using Linux Measurement Tools
9.1. Use Linux monitoring tools
9.2. Interpret memory measurements
9.3. Interpret I/O measurements

10. Tuning Performance
10.1. Evaluate file systems
10.2. Tune supported file systems
10.3. Configure initialization parameters
10.4. Implement asynchronous input/output (I/O)
10.5. Implement advanced memory management techniques

11. Debugging Oracle 10g on Linux
11.1. Install and configure OS Watcher
11.2. Use Oracle Support's Remote Diagnostics Agent
11.3. Trace programs and processes with strace
11.4. Gather required information for resolving *ORA-600* and *ORA-7445* errors

Introduction

This is the last exam objective chapter that will divulge the measurement tools available in Linux and Oracle as well as the tools for tuning the performances and debugging Oracle. The tuning operations are a continuous process that analyzes the performance of the hardware for the database and vice-versa.

Linux Measurement Tools

The measurement tools under Linux cover the memory area, swap area, disk and network Input/Output. In the next section, the areas to be tuned that are required for passing the exam will be covered.

Memory Consideration and Tuning Tools

When memory utilization and paging measurement is being performed, it is important that the statistics include the pages in/out, memory demand rate, inactive pages, context switches and total memory. The Linux commands that can be used to perform the monitoring of memory are *free*, *top*, *sar*, *vmstat* and viewing the file */proc/meminfo* that can give information about the memory.

By using the *free* command, it is possible to get information on the swap and the total memory available. The section with -/+ buffers/cache indicates the alterations on the free and used memory by the kernel cache pages and disks buffers.

```
[oracle@orion]$ free

             total       used       free     shared    buffers     cached
Mem:        763408     697356      66052          0      57288     432660
-/+ buffers/cache:     207408     556000
Swap:      1164672          4    1164668
```

With the SAR (System Activity Reporter), it is possible to get system activity reports. By using the *-B* option, the pages in and out will be shown in seconds (*pgpgin/s*, *pgpgout/s*) as well as the inactive pages that are dirty (*inadtypg*), clean (*inaclnpg*) and the target pages (*inatarpg*).

```
[oracle@orion]$ sar -B 2 3

Linux 2.6.9-78.0.17.ELsmp (orion)      07/18/2009

14:54:42 PM pgpgin/s  pgpgout/s activepg inadtypg inaclnpg inatarpg
14:54:45 PM 26112.33  94.33       186898    56296     3362    49311
14:54:48 PM 24086.00  30.33       185125    61120     3363    49921
14:54:51 PM 20554.00  125.33      182891    67445     3362    50739
```

On the newer release of *sar –B*, it will give only the *pgpgin/s*, *pgpgout/s* and after that, *fault/s* and *majflt/s* that are about the number of page faults.

The *sar* also has the switch *-R* that shows the number of pages free in seconds (*frmpg/s*) and shared memory pages (*shmpg/s*), the buffer pages (*bufpg/s*) and cached pages (*campg/s*).

```
[oracle@orion]$ sar -R 4 5

Linux 2.6.9-78.0.17.ELsmp (orion)      07/18/2009

15:20:22 AM    frmpg/s    shmpg/s    bufpg/s    campg/s
15:20:26 AM      -0.10       0.00       0.12      -0.07
15:20:30 AM       0.02       0.00       0.19      -0.07
(…)
```

Depending on whether the shared memory is used or not, the *sar –R* results are given with or without the *shmpg/s*.

With the command *vmstat,* it is possible to make statistics reports about the virtual memory usage. The swap paging is represented with "si" for the page-in and "so" for the page-out.

```
[oracle@orion]$ vmstat 5 7

procs -----------memory---------- ---swap-- -----io---- -system-- ----cpu----
 r  b   swpd   free   buff  cache   si   so    bi    bo   in    cs us sy id wa
 2  1     12  11352  53816 469800    0    0   278   178  253 3920 24 58 14  5
 1  0     12   9740  53932 470816    0    0   142   568  265  328 46 25  0 29
 1  0     12   8980  54120 471884    0    0   163   453  282  321 54 25  0 21
 1  0     12   8280  54116 469936    0    0   148   183  277  230 67 26  0  8
 1  0     12   7944  54432 470876    0    0   153   369  279  222 56 33  0 11
 1  0     12   9052  54492 470388    0    0   137   595  293  245 63 27  0  9
 1  0     12   8420  54664 469940    0    0   170   210  281  252 63 24  0 13
```

In order to reduce the memory issues, two possibilities can be suggested to decrease the memory demand. They are to reduce the size of the PGA or SGA or increase the memory on the server. To get the best system measurement on memory, a large collection of information can be made. In particular, observe the swap area in the case of high memory swap usage, the high values of the paging in /out and the low activity of the unused/inactive pages.

I/O Consideration and Tuning Tools

The Linux commands that will help to evaluate the usage of the I/O are *sar -d, iostat -d* and *-p*, *wmstat*, *osview* and the files in the virtual file *system /proc.*

Measurement statistics are possible with *iostat* on the I/O. Activity can be displayed by partitions with the *-p* option or by devices *–x*. When using the *–d* option, it does not show the CPU statitics.

```
[oracle@orion]$ iostat -d -p

Linux 2.6.9-78.0.17.ELsmp (orion)      07/18/2009

Device:            tps   Blk_read/s   Blk_wrtn/s   Blk_read   Blk_wrtn
sda               1.24         6.08        19.16    5846646   18408342
sda1              0.00         0.00         0.00       2010        262
sda2              0.00         0.00         0.00       1248        816
sda3              1.24         6.08        19.15    5842396   18407264
sdb               0.13         3.20         1.41    3070678    1355928
```

```
[oracle@orion ~]$ iostat -d -x

Linux 2.6.9-78.0.17.ELsmp (orion)      07/18/2009

Device:    rrqm/s wrqm/s   r/s   w/s  rsec/s  wsec/s    rkB/s    wkB/s
avgrq-sz avgqu-sz   await  svctm  %util

sda          0.01   1.53  0.38  0.86    6.08   19.16     3.04     9.58
20.29     0.00    2.40    1.41   0.18

sda1         0.00   0.00  0.00  0.00    0.00    0.00     0.00     0.00     5.40     0.00     2.20
2.10   0.00

sda2         0.00   0.00  0.00  0.00    0.00    0.00     0.00     0.00    30.35     0.00     3.15
2.82   0.00
```

With the *sar -d* command, it is possible to display the transfer rates/blocks in seconds per devices.

```
[oracle@orion]$ sar -d 1 1

Linux 2.6.9-78.0.17.ELsmp (orion)      07/18/2009

02:44:29 PM    DEV            tps   rd_sec/s   wr_sec/s
02:44:30 PM    dev1-0       11.00      12.00      10.00
02:44:30 PM    dev1-1        6.50       4.00       9.50
02:44:30 PM    dev1-2        3.00       6.50       6.00
```

With the command *vmstat*, statistics reports about the I/O usage are able to be made, the blocks are represented with "bo" for the block sent and "bi" for the block received.

```
[oracle@orion]$ vmstat 5 7

procs -----------memory---------- ---swap-- -----io---- -system-- ----cpu----
 r  b   swpd   free   buff  cache   si   so    bi    bo   in   cs us sy id wa
 2  1     12  11352  53816 469800    0    0   278   178  253 3920 24 58 14  5
 1  0     12   9740  53932 470816    0    0   142   568  265  328 46 25  0 29
 1  0     12   8980  54120 471884    0    0   163   453  282  321 54 25  0 21
```

When working with the I/O measurement, the focus is set on speed and volume of data transferred to the read/write I/O operations, the queue sizes, wait/service times and transfer rates. If the I/O is the source of the limitations on the system's performance, then it should be evaluated if the system gets multiple disks, controllers and HBAs (Host Bus Adapters) in order to spread the loads. Remember that the Oracle binaries, redologs, data and index datafiles can be on different devices.

CPU Consideration and Tuning Tools

Linux also includes commands to perform the monitoring of the CPU usage; those commands are *top*, *vmstat*, *mpstat –P ALL* (*P* means CPU), *sar -u* (reports CPU utilization), *sar –q* (report the queue's length and load average), *xload* and *xosview*. In the */proc*, there is *cpuinfo*, *stat* and *loadavg* that can also provide information about the CPU usage.

When CPU is analyzed, the focus should be set on the number of CPU available, load average and the load factor. The average of the load is given in the *top* command in the section "load average:". The load factor can be obtained with the formula:

load factor = load average / Number of CPU

The run queue size can be evaluated with the *sar -q* command (*runq-sz* is the value of the run queue size):

```
[oracle@orion ~]$ sar -q 1 3

Linux 2.6.9-78.0.17.ELsmp (orion)       07/18/2009
03:26:50 PM   runq-sz  plist-sz   ldavg-1   ldavg-5  ldavg-15
03:26:51 PM         1       110      1.11      1.23      0.99
03:26:52 PM         2       110      1.31      1.53      0.99
03:26:53 PM         1       110      1.31      1.43      0.99
Average:            1       110      1.11      1.23      0.99
```

For the *vmstat,* the CPU measurements are in the column *CPU* and the other sections *procs* and *system* provide information about the processes and the system context switches and interrupts.

If the load average is lower than one, then the CPU is not a limitation. When between one and two, it could be an issue, but when the value is higher then two, the CPU should be investigated. So when the system has poor response time with high idle times, uses too much time on system or user codes, or has run queue size values higher than the number of CPUs, a re-evaluation of the number of CPUs should be made.

Areas Linux Commands	CPU	Disk I/O	Network I/O	Memory	Process	History Log
/proc/cpu_info /proc/stat /proc/loadavg	✓					
/proc/meminfo				✓		
/var/log/messages						✓
free				✓		
iostat		✓ -p -d				
meminfo				✓		
mpstat	✓ -P ALL					
netstat			✓			
pstree					✓ Process hierarchy list	
sar (system activity reporter)	✓	✓		✓		✓ in /var/log/sa/
top	✓ cpu load			✓ usage	✓ Process list	
vmstat	✓	✓		✓	✓	
xload	✓					
xosview	✓	✓	✓	✓	✓	✓ limited

Table 13.1: *List of the Tuning Commands*

> 🔔 Exam Advice: Know the aspects discussed in the previous section and include the commands and options given previously.

Tuning Performance

In the tuning part, the basic tuning operations for both Linux and Oracle RDBMS are examined in order to get better performances on the Oracle databases and perform basic optimization operations.

To get proper performances on Linux, first be aware about kernel release choice. As criteria, choose a kernel that supports the server's hardware and the one that is the latest supported kernel. This means that if there is more than 4 GB on a 32-bit hardware, choose an enterprise or huge-mem kernel (consult Chapter 12 for more details). If the server has multiple CPUs, choose a smp (symmetric multiprocessing) kernel that enables the usage of more than one CPU. It is possible to use both kernels on single CPU machines but no advantages of those technologies can be taken since the hardware is not supporting it, and bad performances will be the result as the overhead cannot be handled. Therefore, make sure that the Linux release in use and the hardware of the hosting server are set up as recommended by the Linux editor.

The tuning operations are a continuous process as the usage of the database can increase or decrease and the way users are working with the application can influence the databases. Therefore, it is important for the DBA to collect information about the performances with both the Linux and Oracle tools described in this chapter.

Evaluate and Tune Supported File Systems

When the file system is being used as OCFS2 (release 1.4.1), ext2 or ext3 to store the Oracle database files, it is possible to tell the Linux OS to reduce the number of I/O by disabling the time-read attribute. This is not important for Oracle database files since this statistic is not used by the database. The time-read attribute is recorded information that can be used by root to get statistics about the file access and can help the administrator to implement some improvements on the most accessed files.

It is possible to set the attribute on a file with the command *chattr +A <file name>*:

```
[oracle@orion]$ chattr +A sqlplus
```

It is also possible to set it on a whole directory tree by using the following options:

```
[oracle@orion]$ chattr +R +A /var/spool
```

The changes can also be made persistent by editing the files */etc/fstab* and setting the attribute *noatime* in the fourth column. The following example shows the database files stored in */u02/oradata/* on the disk */dev/sdc5.*

```
/dev/sdc5 /u02/oradata/ ext3 rw,noatime 1 1
```

Elementary Oracle Database Optimizations

In the next sections of the tuning topic, the basic optimization rules and settings that are possible within Oracle database are introduced.

For the Oracle database tablespaces, create them by using the LMT (Locally Managed Tablespace). This option is set by default on the release 10g, but this can be used on older databases than 9i that were migrated to Oracle 10g. The LMT option reduces the I/O by having the datafiles managed within the tablespace and not by the Oracle dictionary, also called DMT (Dictionary Managed Tablespace). On some databases, it can increase the performance up to 15%. It is possible to control how the tablespaces are managed in the database by running the following query.

```
SELECT tablespace_name, extent_management FROM dba_tablespaces;
```

```
TABLESPACE_NAME                EXTENT_MAN
------------------------------ ----------
SYSTEM                         LOCAL
SYSAUX                         LOCAL
TEMP                           LOCAL
UNDOTBS01                      LOCAL
USERS                          LOCAL
```

It is also important to choose the proper size of the database blocks depending on the usage of the Oracle database. As a basic rule, the file system block size and the database block size should always be of the same size or be a multiple. It is also important that the block size matches the memory page size by being an equal or a multiple, i.e. for ext3, if the default file system size is 4 KB, the page size on the memory can be 4 KB and then choose a *db_block_size* of 4 KB (*db_block_size* =4096).

Depending on the usage of the databases, it is possible to optimize the performances by choosing the proper value of the *db_block_size*. The databases can be classified in two principal types: the OLTP (On Line Transaction Processing) and DSS (Decision Support System/DWH (DataWareHouse) databases.

On the OLTP, there are normally a lot of users that are accessing the database at the same time with small transactions, so the risk of users accessing the same blocks is higher. This leads to a *buffer_busy wait* situation as more than one user is accessing the same block; therefore, it is quite important to reduce the number of rows in the blocks. This can be obtained by making a smaller block size. As a best practice, a block size of 4 KB should be used on OLTP-like databases.

For the DSS/DWH, the transaction data sizes are much bigger than on OLTP. Due to this large size of data sets, it would be preferable to set the block size from 8 KB up to 32 KB depending on the Linux release as the maximum value on a Linux 32-bit is about 16 KB.

Note: The indexes are also concerned by the block size changes. Therefore, it is recommended that every new production system should have an evaluation phase of the database block sizing.

The database buffer cache should also be a part of the tuning optimizations since it holds the most recent block used by the Oracle instance. In Oracle 10g, it is possible to set the parameter value *db_cache_advice=on* to get advice about the database buffer cache in Enterprise Manager or in the view *v$db_cache_advice*. It is also important that the *statistics_level* is set to *typical* or *all.*

Another place for tuning and optimization are the redologs in an Oracle database because the Data Manipulation Language statements are producing a large amount of data in the redolog files. It is important that the sizes of the redolog files are optimal because when the files are full, the redolog file switching occurs and this should not occur too often. The proper redolog file switching time should be every 20 to 30 minutes. The performances of the redologs can be monitored with the STATSPACK report, especially the wait event *log_buffer_space.*

It is also possible to increase the size of the *log_buffer* that enables the user to do memory buffering of the redolog entries to reduce disk I/O. The values given for this parameter are in bytes. The ideal value of the *log_buffer* should be about 65536 or higher. It can also be calculated with the following formula: *log_buffer=max (0.5M, (128K * number of cpus).* It is also possible to do a monitoring of the values with the following query:

```
select name, value
  from v$sysstat
 where name = 'redo buffer allocation retries';
```

Another improvement that can be tried is on the log writer (LGWR) performances by moving the online redolog files on faster devices or by optimizing the performances of the checkpoints or archiving process, also on the disk I/O.

Note: When an Oracle database is being tuned, use the Automatic Workload repository included in the licensed database tuning package or statistics package that is free of charge. The "How to" Metalink note 394937.1 Subject: Statistics Package (STATSPACK) Guide provides much more information on that.

Configure Initialization Parameters and Asynchronous Input/Output (I/O)

It was shown that the previously described *db_block_size*, *db_cache_advice* and *log_buffer* initialization parameters can be modified to perform basic optimizations.

In the next section, the initialization parameters *db_cache_size*, *db_writer_processes* about the database writer background process, *pre_page_sgq* related to the Shared Global Area and *dbwr_io_slaves* can be configured to get better performances.

On databases that are handling high volumes of data, the standard configuration of the background process database writer (DBWR) may not be enough to provide sufficient writing throughput with the consequence that the memory buffer pool is also affected. As a first optimization step, it would be wise to increase the values of the initialization parameter *db_cache_size* since that is the default buffer pool. The value for the *db_cache_size* should be at least set with the following formula *db_cache_size=4m x number of cpus x granule size*.

The granule size can be obtained by doing this query:

```
select name, bytes from v$sgainfo where name = 'Granule Size';
```

After having the cache size set, it is possible to increase the number of database writer background processes with the initialization parameter *db_writer_processes.* The default value can be obtained with the formula *db_writer_processes=Number of CPU +7 / 8.* The value can be set up to 20. It will help to distribute the write work, but it is mandatory to have more than one CPU and asynchronous I/O to get the benefits of this feature. In case the parameter is set too high, there might be disk I/O contentions.

The *dbwr_io_slaves* can simulate asynchronous I/O when the file system used does not have that feature available. The initialization parameter should not be higher than two times the number of disks where the database is located. On the other hand, it is not possible to combine the *dbwr_io_slaves* that has a non-zero value with the *db_writer_processes* as the *dbwr_io_slaves* forces the *db_writer_processes* to the value 1. When the *dbwr_io_slaves* is set, the server processes ARCH and LGWR are set to the value 4 and on some platforms, the *disk_asynch_io* is set to the value *false.*

SGA behavior can be changed by using the initialization parameter *pre_page_sga* with the value *true* or *false*. The benefits of getting the *pre_page_sga=true* set is to have a SGA memory mapped on the physical memory with the fully capacity available after the startup, avoiding having this phase later on when the memory is needed. However, this has consequences on the startup time and the connection processing that might be slower. The parameter *pre_page_sga* should only be used on systems having sufficient physical memory to hold the entire SGA; otherwise, the system will suffer on unnecessary swapping operations.

Implement Advanced Memory Management Techniques

In Oracle 10g RDBMS, it is possible to use the feature Automatic Shared Memory Management (ASMM) to resize the SGA memory areas such as the buffer cache (*db_cache_size*), shared pool (*shared_pool_size*), large pool (*large_pool_size*), Java pool (*java_pool_size*) and Streams pool (*streams_pool_size*). The *log_buffer*, *keep* and *recycle* buffers are not automatically tuned. On an OLTP or DWH system that has online users during the day and batch or backup jobs during the nights, the *sga_target* provides a quite flexible solution as it will not require stopping the database in order to resize the pools to perform the required operations.

In order to enable this feature, the *sga_target* has to be set to a non-zero value, i.e. with a 3 GB memory dedicated for the SGA, the *sga_target=3g*. By default, the value is 0, meaning that this feature is disabled. The view *v$sga_target_advice* will provide some advice about the size of that parameter.

 Exam Advice: Be able to describe all the changes that can be applied on Linux and Oracle to get better performances on the databases.

Debugging

The next section describes the tools available to perform the debugging of Oracle under Linux.

RDA

The RDA (Remote Diagnostics Agent) tool is able to collect all the information for the Oracle support. The information collected can include installation, configuration, linking, upgrade, patching errors and performance issues. The collection of the RDA information is stored in a HTML format and collected in a zip file. The RDA package can be downloaded from Metalink. After the RDA package dedicated for a particular operating system has been downloaded, it is necessary to install it this way with the Oracle Linux user. To have RDA running, there needs to be *perl 5.005* installed on the Linux system.

Uncompress the RDA package in *$ORACLE_HOME*:

```
[oracle@orion]$ gunzip p8548777_416_LINUX.zip
```

Perform the setup of the RDA:

```
[oracle@orion]$ cd $ORACLE_HOME/rda
[oracle@orion]$ ./rda.sh -S
```

The results of the configuration performed are stored in the file *setup.cfg*. If that configuration needs to be changed, delete that file and run the setup of the RDA again.

Collect diagnostic data:

```
[oracle@orion]$ ./rda.sh -v
```

To consult the data collected by RDA, read the index HTML file located in *$ORACLE_HOME/rda/output/* from a web browser and choose the topics that are desired.

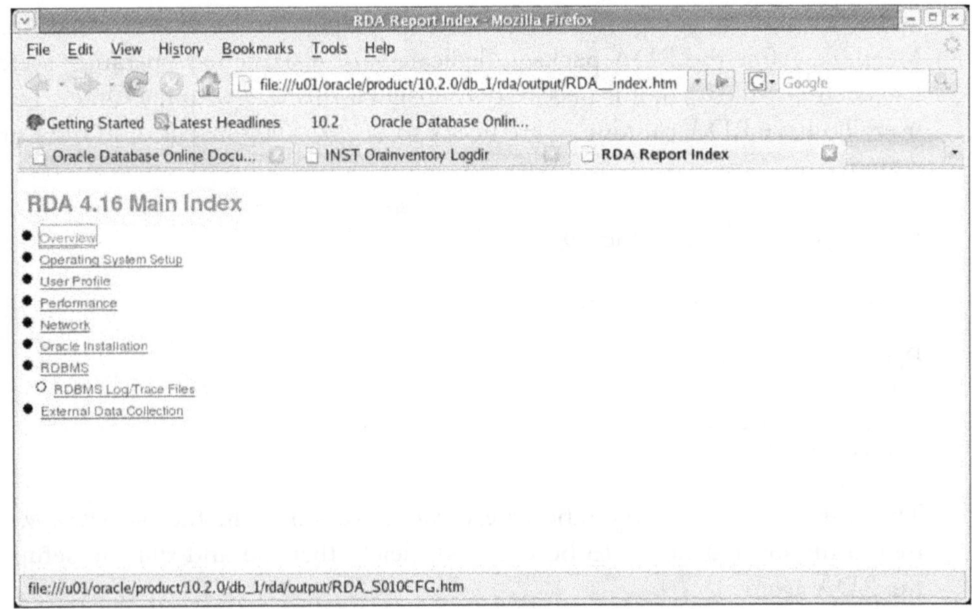

Figure 13.1: *Main RDA Screen*

> Exam Advice: Be capable of explaining the purpose of the RDA tool with all the related details of the tool.

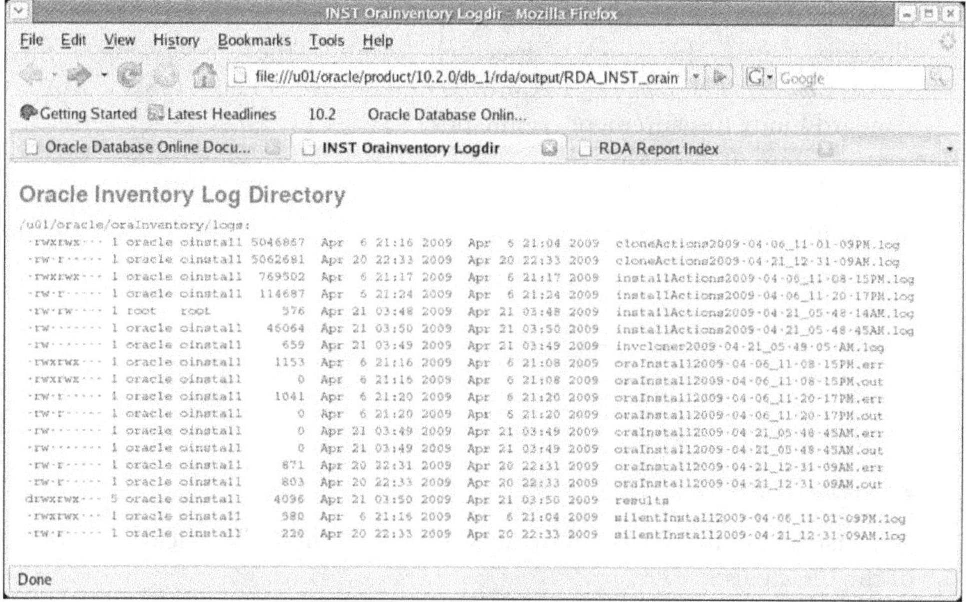

Figure 13.2: *Details Regarding the Oracle Inventory Directory*

Note: More details regarding RDA are available on the following Metalink:

- Note ID 314422.1 subject: Remote Diagnostic Agent (RDA) 4 - Getting Started

- Note ID 330363.1 subject: Remote Diagnostic Agent (RDA) 4 - FAQ.

OS Watcher

OSW (Operating System Watcher) is a collection of Linux scripts whose purpose is to collect information about the performances of the Linux OS. OSW collects data on the processes, the I/O, network and memory with the tools covered in the previous sections. This tool can be downloaded from the Oracle Metalink website.

The installation of the tool is quite simple as it is only necessary to untar the tarball containing the *osw* utility. The untar creates an *osw* directory that contains all the scripts. It is important that the OSW is installed on every node that is running an Oracle database instance and that only one installation of the

OSW is done. OSW is creating snapshots that are stored in an archive directory in the *osw* directory with the following format: *<node_name>_<OS_utility>_YY.MM.DD.HH24.dat.* The OSW uses the standard Linux measurement commands:

- *iostat*
- *mpstat*
- *netstat*
- *ps*
- *top*
- *traceroute*
- *vmstat*

The installation is performed by uncompressing the OSW package in *$HOME* of the Oracle user:

```
[oracle@orion]$ tar -xvf osw212.tar
```

To do the de-installation, just delete the created directory *osw*.

```
[oracle@orion]$ rm -fr osw
```

The startup of the OSW tool is done with the command *./startOSW.sh <snapshot interval in seconds> <number of hours to archive>*. If no value is specified, the default values will be every 30 seconds and it stores the last 48 hours of data in archive files:

```
[oracle@orion]$ cd osw
[oracle@orion]$ ./startOSW.sh 15 48

Testing for discovery of OS Utilities...

VMSTAT found on your system.
IOSTAT found on your system.
MPSTAT found on your system.
NETSTAT found on your system.
TOP found on your system.
Discovery completed.

Starting OSWatcher V2.1.2 on Thu Jun 18 07:47:28 CEST 2009
With SnapshotInterval = 15
With ArchiveInterval = 48

OSWatcher - Written by Carl Davis, Center of Expertise, Oracle Corporation
```

```
Starting Data Collection...
osw heartbeat:Thu Jun 18 07:47:28 CEST 2009
```

In the previous example, a snapshot is being run every 15 seconds and the data stored from the last 48 hours will be kept.

If there is a need to log out, execute it with the *nohup* and the multi-tasking option:

```
[oracle@orion]$ nohup ./startOSW.sh 15 48 &
```

The OSW can be stopped manually with the following command:

```
[oracle@orion]$ ./stopOSW.sh
```

It is possible to configure the OSW with the configuration section of the script *OSWatcher.sh* that contains all the commands used. The commands used can be easily changed or the switches and arguments of the commands can be modified, i.e. the *iostat* could be changed to monitor a disk partition by substituting the *-x* with *-p* and the name of the partition, so the *iostat* command will be *iostat -p /dev/sda2.*

```
##########################################################
# CONFIGURATION  Determine Host Platform
##########################################################
case $platform in
  Linux)
##########################################################
#The parameters for linux iostat are now configured in #file
# oswlnxxio.sh and supercede the following value for #iostat
######################################################################
    IOSTAT='iostat -x 1 3'
    VMSTAT='vmstat 1 3'
##########################################################
#   The parameters for linux top are now configured in #file
#   oswlnxxtop.sh and supercede the following value for #top
##########################################################
    TOP='eval top -b -n 1 | head -50'
    PSELF='ps -elf'
    MPSTAT='mpstat 1 3'
    MEMINFO='cat /proc/meminfo'
    SLABINFO='cat /proc/slabinfo'
    ;;
```

It is possible to consult the results of the OSW in the archive directory under the following directories that contain **.dat* files of the snapshot results:

```
[oracle@orion osw]$ cd archive/
```

```
[oracle@orion archive]$ ls -alrt

total 44
drwxr-xr-x  11 oracle oinstall 4096 Jun 18 07:47 .
drwxr-xr-x   2 oracle oinstall 4096 Jun 18 07:47 oswvmstat
drwxr-xr-x   2 oracle oinstall 4096 Jun 18 07:47 oswtop
drwxr-xr-x   2 oracle oinstall 4096 Jun 18 07:47 oswps
drwxr-xr-x   2 oracle oinstall 4096 Jun 18 07:47 oswnetstat
drwxr-xr-x   2 oracle oinstall 4096 Jun 18 07:47 oswmpstat
drwxr-xr-x   2 oracle oinstall 4096 Jun 18 07:47 oswiostat
drwxr-xr-x   2 oracle oinstall 4096 Jun 18 07:47 oswslabinfo
drwxr-xr-x   2 oracle oinstall 4096 Jun 18 07:47 oswprvtnet
drwxr-xr-x   2 oracle oinstall 4096 Jun 18 07:47 oswmeminfo
```

```
[oracle@orion oswvmstat]$ head orion.hal.dk_vmstat_09.06.18.0700.dat
Linux    OSW v2.1.2    orion.hal.dk
zzz ***Thu Jun 18 07:47:28 CEST 2009
procs -----------memory---------- ---swap-- -----io---- --system-- ----cpu----
 r  b   swpd   free   buff  cache   si   so    bi    bo   in    cs us sy id wa
 6  0      0 159896  27400 630140    0    0   166   115 1052   227  7 18 72  3
 3  0      0 158600  27408 630132    0    0     0   368 1014   130  2 98  0  0
 0  0      0 158856  27408 630392    0    0    24    88 1051   171  5 78 17  1
zzz ***Thu Jun 18 07:47:44 CEST 2009
```

Note: More details can be found in the Metalink note 301137.1 Subject: OS Watcher User Guide.

The release v2.0.0 or higher of OSW is bundled with a data parsing and graphical tool. More details are available on the note id 461053.1 Subject: OS Watcher Graph (OSWg) User Guide.

strace

Linux has a debugging tool that is used to monitor the system calls and signals used by a program. This tool is called *strace* under Linux, and on other UNIX distributions, it is called *truss*. The Linux kernel has a feature called *ptrace* that makes it possible to trace processes. With the *stace* tool, the system calls can be recorded in a file, diagnostics can be made and both commands and running processes can be traced. Make sure that the *strace rpm* package is installed on the system by using this command:

```
[oracle@orion]]$ rpm -aq | grep strace
strace-4.5.18-2.el5_3.3
```

Syntax for tracing a *pmon* process with the *pid 5881*:

```
[oracle@orion]$ strace -p 5881 -o /tmp/pmon_trace.txt
```

Syntax for tracing a command:

```
[oracle@orion]$ strace -o /tmp/ls.out ls
```

The result of the *strace on ls* command is the following:

```
[oracle@orion]$ head /tmp/ls_trace.out
execve("/bin/ls", ["ls"], [/* 21 vars */]) = 0
brk(0)                                  = 0x8d49000
access("/etc/ld.so.preload", R_OK)      = -1 ENOENT (No such file or directory)
open("/etc/ld.so.cache", O_RDONLY)      = 3
fstat64(3, {st_mode=S_IFREG|0644, st_size=37653, ...}) = 0
mmap2(NULL, 37653, PROT_READ, MAP_PRIVATE, 3, 0) = 0xb7f66000
close(3)                                = 0
open("/lib/librt.so.1", O_RDONLY)       = 3
read(3, "\177ELF\1\1\1\0\0\0\0\0\0\0\0\0\3\0\3\0\1\0\0\0\200\230\203\0004\0\0\0"..., 512) = 512
fstat64(3, {st_mode=S_IFREG|0755, st_size=44060, ...}) = 0
```

ORA Errors

When errors occur on the Oracle software, an ORA-****** is produced and stored in the log's files. In the next paragraph, the errors *ORA-00600* and *ORA-07445* are covered since they need to be known for passing the certification.

ORA-00600 is produced when the kernel code of the Oracle RDBMS catches an inconsistency or an unexpected condition occurred. It could be an issue with the OS, hardware failure or missing resources and not necessarily a software bug. The *ORA-00600* comes with a list of arguments stored in square brackets; use the first argument to find out where in the code the error is produced as this helps to find out what the error could be. The information in the first bracket can be numbers or a character string. The other arguments give the values of internal variables. i.e.: *ORA-00600: internal error code, arguments: [12333], [14], [0], [68],* `[], [], [], []`.

Trace files are generated when an *ORA-00600* occurs that can be located in *user_dump_dest* or *background_dump_dest* if the error is a user process or a background process that was failing. The information is also written in the *alert<ORACLE_SID>.log* of the database with the location of the trace file.

ORA-07445 is produced when the Oracle server process gets a fatal signal from the OS. Depending on the type of error, traces are produced in *user_dump_dest* or *background_dump_dest* and a core dump is produced in *core_dump_dest.* The process is also written in the *alert<ORACLE_SID>.log.* The errors can be raised by the background or foreground processes. *ORA-*

07445 can be a generic error in the Oracle code with the traces. It is possible to identify where the location of the error is. A Linux system can trap many illegal operations such as a process that is writing to an invalid memory location; as a result, a fatal signal will be sent to protect the system. The signal in question can be *SIGSEGV* (signal 11, segmentation violation), *SIGBUS* (signal 10, bus error), and such. As for the *ORA-00600,* the trace files indicate what exactly happened. See the following example of an error.

```
ORA-07445: exception encountered: core dump [kgghstfel()+4] [SIGSEGV]
[Address not mapped to object] [0x000000018] [] [] found in
/app/oracle/testdb/bdump/alert_testdb.log
```

Note: On the Metalink website, it is possible to retrieve the details on the errors by using the ORA-600 Argument Lookup Tool that can be found with the Note ID 153788.1 Subject: Troubleshoot an ORA-600 or ORA-7445 Error Using the Error Lookup Tool.

Additional information can be found regarding the errors on the Note 18485.1 - OERR: ORA 600 "internal error code, arguments: [%s],[%s],[%s], [%s], [%s], and Note 1038055.6. Subject : List Of UNIX Signals And Explanations.

Solving the *ORA-00600* & *ORA-07445* Errors

The Oracle errors *ORA-00600* and *ORA-07445* can be solved by using the Argument Lookup Tool in Metalink or by opening a Service Request on Metalink Oracle Support. It will be necessary to provide the following information:

- The *alert<ORACLE_SID>.log* of the database having the errors that is located in *BACKGROUND_DUMP_DEST*
- the trace files mentioned in the *alert<ORACLE_SID>.log*
- Information about the system regarding system environment changes that could be new hardware, new OS patches or other failures
- A fresh RDA containing the ORA errors

Be sure that the information provided in the trace file contains a stack trace that could be in that format:

```
*** 2009-05-29 06:48:06.511
ksedmp: internal or fatal error
ORA-00600: internal error code, arguments: [12333], [14], [0], [68], [], [], [], []
----- Call Stack Trace -----
calling              call     entry                argument values in hex
location             type     point                (? means dubious value)
-------------------- -------- -------------------- ----------------------------
ksedst+001c          bl       ksedst1              088444844 ? 041144844 ?
ksedmp+0290          bl       ksedst               1044D3850 ?
ksfdmp+0018          bl       03EDCE44
kgeriv+0108          bl       _ptrgl
kgesiv+0080          bl       kgeriv               000000013 ? 1100D9218 ?
                                                   000000000 ? 00000000A ?
                                                   1100DB6B0 ?
ksesic3+0060         bl       kgesiv               104B86ED0 ? 000000003 ?
                                                   1102267B8 ?
                                                   800000000000F0B2 ?
                                                   000000000 ?
opitsk+0edc          bl       01F43CAC
opiino+0990          bl       opitsk               1E00000000 ? 000000000 ?
opiodr+0ae0          bl       _ptrgl
opidrv+0484          bl       01F451F4
sou2o+0090           bl       opidrv               3C02D4903C ? 4A00D7928 ?
                                                   FFFFFFFFFFFF070 ?
opimai_real+01bc     bl       01F42DD4
main+0098            bl       opimai_real          000000000 ? 000000000 ?
__start+0098         bl       main                 000000000 ? 000000000 ?
```

With all this information, Oracle Support should be able to provide a workaround or a patch to solve the issue.

> Exam Advice: Be able to describe all the debugging tools and *ORA-00600* & *ORA-07445* error messages available under Linux for Oracle databases.

Summary

Chapter 13 described the Linux measurement tools including those dealing with memory, tuning and debugging. For instance, the commands *free*, *top*, *sar*, and *vmstat* were explained in regards to monitoring memory.

The next section covered the commands used to analyze CPU usage and then much attention was giving to the tuning performance of the database with details about the changes that can be made to improve performance. Finally, the tools used to aid in debugging Oracle and Linux databases such as the Operating System Watcher (OSW) and *strace* were examined.

Exercises

1. Use all the commands and options to perform measurements.
2. Use the utilities RDA, OSWatcher and *strace*.

Q&A

Questions

1. What are the differences between DWH/DSS databases and a classical OLTP database?

A. DWH/DSS have smaller blocksizes than the OLTP
B. DWH/DSS have bigger blocksizes than the OLTP
C. DWH/DSS have small transactions and OLTP have big transactions
D. DWH/DSS have big transactions and OLTP have small transactions

2. What kind of modification can be performed in order to do the tuning of the redolog files? (Choose all that apply with the described situation)

A. Resizing the redologs by making them bigger as the database has too many log switches
B. Resizing the redologs by making them smaller as the database has too many log switches
C. Control the wait on the redologs
D. Decrease the size of the *log_buffer* parameter

3. In the following list, what parameter can affect the performance on an Oracle database? (Choose all that apply)

A. *db_writer_processes*
B. *dbwr_io_stat*
C. *db_block_size*
D. *pre_page_sga*

4. In the following list, what is the parameter that can slow the connection processes but makes the SGA map all of the memory on the instance startup? (Choose the correct answer)

A. *sga_max_size*
B. *mem_sga*

C. *pre_page_sga*
D. *post_page_sga*

5. A junior DBA needs to know what is the advantage of using Automatic Shared Memory Management (ASMM)? (Choose the correct answer)

A. ASMM manages the tablespace sizes
B. ASMM manages the redologs
C. ASMM manages the PGA size
D. ASMM manages the memory areas and resizes the SGA depending on the memory demand

6. A colleague asks why the file */etc/fstab* now contains *noatime* only on the file system that has the Oracle datafiles. Explain why this was set. (Choose the correct answer)

A. Reduces the memory usage of the SGA
B. Increases the memory usage of the SGA
C. Decreases the disk I/O by disabling the *atime* statistics
D. Increases the disk I/O by enabling the *atime* statistics

7. A colleague has two databases (OLTP and DWH) to configure on two different Linux servers. He needs to know what should be considered for the *db_block_size* parameters. (Select the adapted block size for the database usage)

A. DWH database should have the smallest value available for the *db_block_size*
B. DWH database should have the biggest value available for the *db_block_size*
C. OLTP database should have the biggest value available for the *db_block_size*
D. OLTP database should have the smallest value available for the *db_block_size*

8. A Linux expert would like to use both *db_writer_processes* and *dbwr_io_slaves* parameters together on the same database. What are the recommendations? (Choose the correct answer)

A. *dbwr_io_slaves* and *db_writer_processes* can be combined
B. It is possible to combine the *dbwr_io_slaves* having a non-zero value with the *db_writer_processes*
C. Is not possible to combine the *dbwr_io_slaves* having a non-zero value with the *db_writer_processes*
D. *dbwr_io_slaves* and *db_writer_processes* can be combined with zero values on both

9. A colleague is learning Linux and she needs to know what is covered by the Linux command *sar*. (Choose all the correct usages that apply to the *sar* command)

A. *sar* can perform statistics on the Oracle SMON process
B. *sar* is a Linux command that enables the system's activity reporter
C. *sar* can make reports on the CPU
D. *sar* can write reports on the location */var/log/sa/*

10. What are the commands to monitor CPU load? (Choose the correct answers)

A. *top*
B. *topas*
C. */proc/cpuinform*
D. *mpstat*
E. *sar*
F. *xload*
G. *xosview*

11. Can *sar, mpstat* and *vmstat* be used for tuning the memory? (Choose the correct answers)

A. The *sar* command can only be used with the CPU tuning
B. The *sar* command can be used for tuning the memory, but not only for that
C. *mpstat* cannot be used to tune CPU
D. *vmstat* is producing tuning information also for the CPU

12. What is the Linux command *strace* used for? (Choose the correct answers)

A. *strace* does not exist under Linux, just under UNIX
B. *strace* cannot be used by Oracle under Linux
C. It is a debugging tool that is able to monitor the system calls used by a program
D. It is a debugging tool that is able to monitor the signals used by a program

13. What are the tools that can be used to debug Oracle? (Choose the correct answers)

A. RDA
B. *strace*
C. OSW
D. *startOSW.sh*

14. What are the differences between the errors *ORA-00600* and *ORA-07445*?

A. *ORA-00600* is produced with the kernel code of the Oracle RDBMS
B. *ORA-00600* is produced when the Oracle server process has a fatal signal from the OS
C. *ORA-07445* is produced with the kernel code of the Oracle RDBMS
D. *ORA-07445* is produced when the Oracle server process has a fatal signal from the OS

15. The database received an error:

```
"ORA-07445: exception encountered: core dump [strlen()+56] [SIGSEGV]
[Address not mapped to object] [0x86DA07010E] [] []"
```

What can the first argument under brackets *[strlen()+56]* be used for?

A. The second can be used, but not the first argument
B. The first argument is just an information field without any usage
C. Use the first argument to find out where in the code the error is produced
D. Use the first argument to get a new parameter setting

16. How can the collection of OSW be started with 30-second intervals between the snapshots that are kept in 24 hours? (Choose the correct answer)

A. cd osw nohup ./startOSW.sh 30 24 &
B. cd ostw ;nohup ./startOSW.sh 30 48 &
C. cd osw ; nohup ./startOSW.sh 30 24 &
D. cd osw; nohurp ./startOSW.sh 30 24 &

17. A Junior DBA is asking about the differences between the option –*x* and –*p* of *iostat*. Select the correct answer that explains what the differences are between those two options.

A. The option -*x* is collecting extra information
B. The option -*x* is showing I/O information by devices
C. The option -*p* is showing I/O information by partitions
D. The option -*p* is showing parallel processes information

18. The installation of the RDA is done on a Linux server. How can the RDA be configured and the information collected? (Choose the correct answer)

A. cd $TNS_NAMES/rda ; ./rda.sh -S
B. cd $ORACLE_LIB/rda ; ./rda.sh -S
C. cd $ORACLE_BASE/rda ; ./rda.sh -S
D. cd $ORACLE_HOME/rda ; ./rda.sh -S

19. Which of the following commands show the system calls? (Choose the correct answer)

A. *truss*
B. *tron*
C. *strace*
D. *troff*

20. What can be done to fix the Oracle error *ORA-00600*? (Select all answers that apply)

A. See the *alert<$ORACLE_SID>.log* file and the file referenced in the error
B. Nothing must be done because this is not an error
C. Get the first argument analyzed in the Metalink lookup tool
D. Open a service request that will contain the *ORA-00600* error, the file describing the error and a RDA file generated after the error occurred

Answers

1. The correct answers are: B. DWH/DSS have bigger blocksize than the OLTP; and D. DWH/DSS have big transactions and OLTP have small transactions.

HINT: Consult the section "Elementary Oracle Database Optimizations" in this chapter.

2. A. Resizing the redologs by making them bigger as the database has too many log switches; and C. Control the wait on the redologs are right answers.

HINT: Read again the section on elementary Oracle database optimizations.

3. Correct answers are A. *db_writer_processes* C. *db_block_size* and D. *pre_page_sga.*

HINT: Consult again the sections "Elementary Oracle Database Optimizations" and Configure Initialization Parameters and Asynchronous Input/Output (I/O)".

4. The correct answer is C. *pre_page_sga.*

HINT: Study again the section "Configure Initialization Parameters and Asynchronous Input/Output (I/O)".

5. Answer D. ASMM manages the memory areas and resizes the SGA depending on the memory demand is the only correct answer.

HINT: Read the section "Implement Advanced Memory Management Techniques".

6. The correct answer is C. Decreases the disk I/O by disabling the *atime* statistics.

HINT: Read again the section "Evaluate and Tune Supported File Systems".

7. B. DWH database should have the biggest value available for the *db_block_size* and D. OLTP database should have the smallest value available for the *db_block_size* are correct.

HINT: Study the section "Elementary Oracle Database Optimizations" again.

8. The answer C. Is not possible to combine the *dbwr_io_slaves* having a non-zero value with the *db_writer_processes.*

HINT: Consult the section "Configure Initialization Parameters and Asynchronous Input/Output (I/O)".

9. The Linux command *sar* is capable of making measurements and reports on the CPU, memory and I/O usage, so the correct answers are B. *sar* is a Linux command that enables the system's activity reporter, C. *sar* can make reports on the CPU and D. *sar* can write reports on the location */var/log/sa/.*

HINT: Read again the sections about "Tuning Performance".

10. The tools to monitor CPU load are A. *top*, D. *mpstat*, E. *sar*, F. *xload* and G. *xosview.*

HINT: Study the sections about tuning.

11. The correct answers are B. The *sar* command can be used for tuning the memory, but not only for that; and D. *vmstat* is producing tuning information also for the CPU.

HINT: Read again the sections about "Tuning Performance".

12. C. It is a debugging tool that is able to monitor the system calls used by a program; and D. It is a debugging tool that is able to monitor the signals used by a program are the only correct answers.

HINT: Study again the section strace.

13. The correct answers are A. RDA, C. OSW and D. *startOSW.sh.*

HINT: Consult the sections on RDA, strace and OS Watcher.

14. A. *ORA-00600* is produced with the kernel code of the Oracle RDBMS and D. *ORA-07445* is produced when the Oracle server process has a fatal signal from the OS are the correct answers.

HINT: Study again the section "ORA Errors".

15. C. Use the first argument to find out where in the code the error is produced is the only correct answer.

HINT: Read again the section "ORA Errors".

16. The only correct answer is C. cd osw ; nohup ./startOSW.sh 30 24 &.

HINT: Study again the section "OS Watcher".

17. B. The option *-x* is showing I/O information by devices; and C. The option *-p* is showing I/O information by partitions are the correct answers.

HINT: Consult the section "I/O Consideration and Tuning Tools".

18. The only correct answer in D. *cd $ORACLE_HOME/rda; ./rda.sh -S.*

HINT: read again the section RDA.

19. C. *strace* is the only correct answer.

HINT: Study the section *strace* again.

20. The correct answers are A. See the *alert<$ORACLE_SID>.log* file and the file referenced in the error; C. Get the first argument analyzed in the Metalink lookup tool; and D. Open a service request that will contain the *ORA-00600* error, the file describing the error and a RDA file generated after the error occurred.

HINT: Consult again the section "ORA Errors".

Solutions for Exercises

1. Use all the commands and options to perform measurements.

Use all the Linux commands listed in the sections related to the measurements.

2. Use the utilities RDA, OSWatcher and *strace.*

Follow up the operations that are described in the RDA, *strace* and OSWatcher sections.

Post Certification Information

CHAPTER

Read this post certification chapter when the exam is passed.

Congratulations!

Congratulations on passing the Oracle Certified Expert exam about Managing Oracle under Linux!

Here is some advice for the next steps as the certification process is a part of the career with additional information related to the work of DBA and Linux system administrators. This chapter also gives a couple of on-the-job scripts on important topics not covered by the exam and other exams that could be taken to improve the knowledge on Linux and Oracle. The information provided might be interesting depending on one's job experience.

DBA and Linux System Administrator Jobs

Database administrators and Linux system administrators do have specific tasks and duties to do on the customer's IT systems. In some companies, DBAs and system administrators are the same people, but in other companies those jobs are in different departments. Therefore, it is important to know who is in charge of what. As common activity in both jobs, the DBA should keep informed and up-to-date by reading books, manuals and being active in user forums. DBAs and Linux system administrators can be consultants or employees in a company, and it will be necessary to choose between those two kinds of employment or combine both.

DBA Tasks

Below is a non-exhaustive list of the tasks database administrators are given. DBAs are responsible for:

1. Design, prepare and implement the Linux environments for Oracle: Ideally, the DBA should use the Optimal Flexible Architecture recommendation to build the database server's structure with the naming conventions recommended by Oracle.
2. Download, configure, install and maintain Oracle database software with defined standards of installation: The management of patches, features enabled on the databases and version controls are also a part of the DBA activities.
3. Monitoring and managing database performances: This can be made with Oracle Enterprise Manager Database Console or Grid controller to ensure that the availability of the database corresponds to the Service Level Agreement and avoids long downtime of the databases. Therefore, it is important that the DBA is informed quickly if a database is defective or down and needs monitoring.
4. Scheduling and automating jobs: It is imperative to get the most out of the administration tasks, batches and application-related operations automatically so the DBA can concentrate on other issues.
5. Designing database storage: It is important that the DBA works with the storage to get a stable and effective storage area for the databases.
6. Performing users and security administration: On databases that contain sensible information, make sure that the user administration is performed and that the data is secured both against failures and hacking. Ideally, the DBA should create and maintain users and roles to assign privileges.
7. Managing schema objects: It is quite important that the schema objects are still valid and built properly. The DBA should also make scripts that are reporting issues with invalid objects.
8. Performing backup and recovery: Backup and recovery policies and procedures are the most important topics of database administration since without having backups of the databases, it is impossible to recover the database services. As DBA, it is essential to test or at least get the backups validated.
9. Monitor and tune performances of the database: On databases with high SLA, it is important that the DBA takes care of the performances and keeps an eye on the performances.

10. Writing and maintaining the documentation of the installation, standards and the database: The documentation of the database is important in order to perform.

11. Evaluating and planning the database growth and changes on all the databases is also a task the DBA can take care of in order to have a capacity planning of the IT systems.

12. In implementation and upgrade projects, give an evaluation of the new features and Oracle products and help development teams to get familiar with the features. DBAs can also give some consultation to the development team on database design and index creations.

13. DBAs working 7x24 in BAU (Business As Usual) teams are efficient team members and have planned preventive actions so the SLA are not broken.

14. DBAs are also in charge of maintaining the database and are the single point of contact with Oracle.

15. Network, cluster and other specific settings related to the database are also taken in charge by the DBA.

System Administrator Tasks

As DBA, the Linux system administrators are also responsible for several tasks and activities to be performed. The Linux system administrators are in charge of:

1. Installing the hardware and software of the Linux systems.

2. Performing the configuration of the network, startup and stop of services, applications, file systems and all other OS aspects.

3. The security of the systems and the data by setting up the backups and performing restore tests. Applying control scripts of weak passwords, firewall controls, and such.

4. Doing the system administration of the Linux systems by scheduling scripts to control the system and having monitoring activities. It will also be necessary to maintain the users' accounts, system stability, upgrade the rpm packages and control the performances of the system.

5. Development of scripts and maintenance routines in order to automate and simplify the administration works.

6. Writing the documentation of the Linux system and ensuring that the specific operations performed by the servers are also documented.
7. Having communication with the users about the performances, account creations and business needs.
8. Solving issues on the Linux systems and making sure that the SLA about availability is not too bad.
9. Participating in projects, meetings and other activities when the expertise of a Linux system administrator is required.
10. Being proactive on issues and having preventive operations set.

Skills Required

The skills required to do the job as a DBA are to have knowledge about the physical database design, have operating system skills to do scripting and know what is going on with the system. But the job as administrator requires also knowing how Oracle manages the data integrity, the backup and recovery scenarios depending on the situation and a solid idea of how to handle performance and tuning issues. The administrators must also have excellent communication skills as they are in touch with management, vendors, development and other teams in the organization. The DBA should also be able to give his point of view on the strategies for the different databases in the organization and be able to juggle with multiple projects that are delivered on time by respecting the deadlines.

Different Types of DBAs

As an Oracle IT specialist, it is possible to choose different jobs as database administrator in different areas. The different types of DBAs are:

1. The classical RDBMS administrative DBA that performs all the tasks related to the databases by doing backups, restores, patching upgrade, replication and all other administrative activities on a RDBMS database.
2. Oracle application DBA must have a good knowledge of the core DBA jobs, but also have skills on the database design, application server (including Oracle application server) and excellent skills on Oracle eBusiness Suite (Oracle Financials).

3. Oracle ERP consultant is in charge of doing the implementations of products like General Ledger, Accounts Payables, Accounts Receivables, Purchasing and Inventory, Financials, HR, Material Management and must have a good insight into the business knowledge of the customers. His knowledge must also include ERP and MRP (Material Resource Planning).
4. Oracle Developers create applications, procedures, functions, and triggers to meet the customer requirements on the applications part. They essentially work with PL/SQL and sometimes do scripting with Linux and other scripting languages.
5. Architect DBAs work to design the databases and the schemas (tables, indexes, partitions, FK and PK) that meet the business requirements and needs of the customers. After that, the design is done and the developers and the DBA will use the work to create the databases.
6. Data warehouse DBA is a newer role that takes care of merging different data from different sources into the company data warehouse. This DBA designs standardized operations to clean and handle the data before they are loaded into the DWH.
7. OLAP DBA is in charge of building multi-dimensional cubes for OLAP and decisions systems.
8. RAC DBA is responsible for the implementation of Real Application Clusters (RAC) to ensure that the database has a high availability. Sometimes this also includes dataguard databases in the designed solutions.
9. The replication DBA is in charge of doing data replications with Advanced replication or Streams; he ensures that all data is properly replicated without any conflicts.
10. All-in-One DBA is the database administrator that performs all the tasks in this list and sometimes does additional work as a system administrator.

Other Certifications Paths

After passing the exam, a question will come up: what is next?

It would be wise to get 'one's life back' after passing the exam and use the spare time with friends and family. Earning that exam required a lot of study hours and before starting with a new certification, use time to celebrate the achievement and meet again with other people.

After having that time off, it could be an advantage to take other certifications related to this certification or to the job, so it is possible to get the other skills validated by a certification. The possible certifications that can be taken to achieve recognition on other IT related topics will now be covered. Oracle offers other certifications; it is also possible to upgrade the earned certifications when a new release is published.

Additional certifications with the topic Linux that could also be chosen are the Linux+ from Comptia, RHCT/ RHCE/ RHCA from Redhat, Linux Professional Institute Certified (LPIC) with LPCI level I, II and III and many others Linux or UNIX certifications that are available on the Operating System topic.

Sometimes having other certifications that are complementary to the specialty can be an advantage, so try to seek other certifications in areas like development, security, methodologies and such. When working with customers who require Information Technology Infrastructure Library (ITIL), it is important to get the knowledge validated by a certification. The major ITIL certification providers are Information Systems Examinations Board (ISEB- http://www.bcs.org/iseb) and the Dutch company EXIN (http://www.exin-exams.com/).

DBA Tools

As a DBA, it is important to have a set of SQL scripts to perform the administration tasks. In this section, a couple of scripts are included in order to help get those script collections. It is also important in maintenance situations late at night or after long working hours to have a set of scripts in order to control, restore and recover from crashes. In BAU situations, it is also necessary as DBA to have preventive operations.

SQL Scripts

This section gives a couple of scripts in the following areas:

- Database and tablespace usage in gigabytes
- Find the invalid objects
- Find the invalid indexes

- Get a list of the sessions in the database
- Have a list of the session waits
- Ongoing tasks on the database
- View what the ongoing tasks are doing
- Size of the redologs in gigabytes
- Get an overview of the redologs switching
- Details of the redolog threads
- List of the privileges
- Status of the various operations in the database
- Know the operations listed in the status and what they are doing
- I/O statistics
- Who makes the I/O in the database
- Index count usage
- Full index scan queries
- Top SQL waits
- Wait time of users
- Wait time details
- SQL by CPU usage
- List of the database users
- List of all data dictionary tables
- Size and free space of the database tablespace
- Get the log information
- Execution details by user
- Get details of a view structure
- Open cursors count
- OS users' details
- Kill them all

- List the Oracle parameters
- Resource limits list
- Schema size
- Summary of *v_$sqlarea* and *dba_users*
- Users' SQL area memory use
- Create a grant privilege of database users
- Variable length columns
- Get the index creation scripts
- Usage of the temporary tablespace
- Usage of the undo tablespace
- Usage of the redo logs
- Preparation of the undo tablespace size
- Full table scan information
- Redo space request
- Redo statistics
- Compilation of entire schema

Database and tablespace usage in gigabytes:

```
ttitle "Database and tablespace usage in gigabytes"

select total.name "tablespace name",
       nvl(free_space, 0) space_free,
       nvl(total_space-free_space, 0) space_used,
       total_space
from
  (select tablespace_name, sum(bytes/1024/1024/1024) free_space from
sys.dba_free_space group by tablespace_name) free,
  (select b.name,  sum(bytes/1024/1024) total_space
     from sys.v_$datafile a, sys.v_$tablespace b
    where a.ts# = b.ts#
    group by b.name
  ) total
where
    free.tablespace_name(+) = total.name
order by
    total.name
/
```

Find the invalid objects:

```
select
     owner, object_type, object_name
from
     dba_objects where status <> 'VALID'
```

Grouped by the owner and type:

```
select
     count(*),owner,object_type from dba_objects
where
     status<>'VALID'
group by
     owner,object_type;
```

Find the invalid indexes:

```
select
     owner, index_name, index_type, status
from
     dba_indexes
where
     status <> 'VALID'
```

Get a list of the sessions in the database:

```
select
       sid,
       serial#,
       USERNAME,
       osuser,
       program
from
       v$session
/
```

Have a list of the session waits:

```
select
     count(*),decode(wait_time,0,event,'Active')
from
     v$session_wait
group by
     decode(wait_time,0,event,'Active');
```

Ongoing tasks on the database:

```
select
     sid, serial#, context, sofar, totalwork,
```

```
     round(sofar/totalwork*100,2) "%_complete"
from
     v$session_longops
where
     totalwork != 0
and
     sofar <> totalwork;
```

View what the ongoing tasks are doing (the ongoing session has the *sid 99*, just substitute that number with the sid number):

```
select
     username,sid,serial# from v$session where sid=99;
```

Size of the redologs in gigabytes:

```
select
     group#, bytes/1024/1024/1024 from v$log;
```

Get an overview of the redologs switching:

```
set linesize 180;
set pagesize 200;
SELECT *
  FROM (
SELECT *
  FROM (
SELECT
  TO_CHAR(FIRST_TIME, 'DD/MM') AS "DAY"
, TO_CHAR(SUM(DECODE(TO_CHAR(FIRST_TIME, 'HH24'), '00', 1, 0)), '999') "00:00"
, TO_CHAR(SUM(DECODE(TO_CHAR(FIRST_TIME, 'HH24'), '01', 1, 0)), '999') "01:00"
, TO_CHAR(SUM(DECODE(TO_CHAR(FIRST_TIME, 'HH24'), '02', 1, 0)), '999') "02:00"
, TO_CHAR(SUM(DECODE(TO_CHAR(FIRST_TIME, 'HH24'), '03', 1, 0)), '999') "03:00"
, TO_CHAR(SUM(DECODE(TO_CHAR(FIRST_TIME, 'HH24'), '04', 1, 0)), '999') "04:00"
, TO_CHAR(SUM(DECODE(TO_CHAR(FIRST_TIME, 'HH24'), '05', 1, 0)), '999') "05:00"
, TO_CHAR(SUM(DECODE(TO_CHAR(FIRST_TIME, 'HH24'), '06', 1, 0)), '999') "06:00"
, TO_CHAR(SUM(DECODE(TO_CHAR(FIRST_TIME, 'HH24'), '07', 1, 0)), '999') "07:00"
, TO_CHAR(SUM(DECODE(TO_CHAR(FIRST_TIME, 'HH24'), '08', 1, 0)), '999') "08:00"
, TO_CHAR(SUM(DECODE(TO_CHAR(FIRST_TIME, 'HH24'), '09', 1, 0)), '999') "09:00"
, TO_CHAR(SUM(DECODE(TO_CHAR(FIRST_TIME, 'HH24'), '10', 1, 0)), '999') "10:00"
, TO_CHAR(SUM(DECODE(TO_CHAR(FIRST_TIME, 'HH24'), '11', 1, 0)), '999') "11:00"
, TO_CHAR(SUM(DECODE(TO_CHAR(FIRST_TIME, 'HH24'), '12', 1, 0)), '999') "12:00"
, TO_CHAR(SUM(DECODE(TO_CHAR(FIRST_TIME, 'HH24'), '13', 1, 0)), '999') "13:00"
, TO_CHAR(SUM(DECODE(TO_CHAR(FIRST_TIME, 'HH24'), '14', 1, 0)), '999') "14:00"
, TO_CHAR(SUM(DECODE(TO_CHAR(FIRST_TIME, 'HH24'), '15', 1, 0)), '999') "15:00"
, TO_CHAR(SUM(DECODE(TO_CHAR(FIRST_TIME, 'HH24'), '16', 1, 0)), '999') "16:00"
, TO_CHAR(SUM(DECODE(TO_CHAR(FIRST_TIME, 'HH24'), '17', 1, 0)), '999') "17:00"
, TO_CHAR(SUM(DECODE(TO_CHAR(FIRST_TIME, 'HH24'), '18', 1, 0)), '999') "18:00"
, TO_CHAR(SUM(DECODE(TO_CHAR(FIRST_TIME, 'HH24'), '19', 1, 0)), '999') "19:00"
, TO_CHAR(SUM(DECODE(TO_CHAR(FIRST_TIME, 'HH24'), '20', 1, 0)), '999') "20:00"
, TO_CHAR(SUM(DECODE(TO_CHAR(FIRST_TIME, 'HH24'), '21', 1, 0)), '999') "21:00"
, TO_CHAR(SUM(DECODE(TO_CHAR(FIRST_TIME, 'HH24'), '22', 1, 0)), '999') "22:00"
, TO_CHAR(SUM(DECODE(TO_CHAR(FIRST_TIME, 'HH24'), '23', 1, 0)), '999') "23:00"
FROM
    V$LOG_HISTORY
WHERE
     extract(year FROM FIRST_TIME) = extract(year FROM sysdate)
GROUP BY
     TO_CHAR(FIRST_TIME, 'DD/MM')
) ORDER BY
     TO_DATE(extract(year FROM sysdate) || DAY, 'YYYY DD/MM') DESC
) WHERE
     ROWNUM < 20;
```

Details of the redolog threads:

```
column current_group#                heading Current|Group#
column Checkpoint_change#      heading Checkpoint|Change#
column checkpoint_time                        heading Checkpoint|Time
column open_time                                 heading Open|Time
column thread#                            heading Thread#
column status                              heading Status
column enabled                                       heading Enabled
column groups                             heading Groups
column Instance                                      heading Instance
column sequence#                                  heading Sequence#
set lines 132 pages 59
start title132 'Redo Thread Report'

select *
from
            sys.v_$thread
order by
            thread#;
```

List of the privileges:

```
set
     linesize 121
     col username format a10
     col profile format a10
     col "tmp tbs" format a10
select
     u.username, u.default_tablespace, u.temporary_tablespace "TMP    TBS",
u.profile, r.granted_role, r.admin_option, r.default_role
from
     sys.dba_users u, sys.dba_role_privs r
where
     u.username = r.grantee (+)
group by
     u.username,   u.default_tablespace, u.temporary_tablespace, u.profile,
r.granted_role, r.admin_option, r.default_role;
```

I/O statistics:

```
/* Copyright © 2004, 2008 by Rampant TechPress Inc.*/
col file_id heading 'File|ID' format 9999
col file_name heading 'File|Name'
col begin_time heading 'Begin Time'
col end_time heading 'End Time'
col physical_block_reads heading 'Physical|Block|Reads'
col physical_block_writes heading 'Physical|Block|Writes'
col average_read_time heading 'Average|Read|Time'
col average_write_time heading 'Average_write_time'
col average_write_time heading 'Average|Write|Time'
col physical_reads heading 'Physical|Reads'
col physical_writes heading 'Physical|Writes'
```

```
set lines 200 pages 55
ttitle '10g File IO Statistics'
spool
        10g_io
select
        to_char(begin_time,'dd-MON-yy hh:mi') begin_time,
        to_char(end_time,'dd-MON-yy hh:mi') end_time,
        a.file_id,
        file_name,
        average_read_time,
        average_write_time,
        physical_reads,
        physical_writes,
        physical_block_reads,
        physical_block_writes
from
        sys.v_$filemetric_history a,
        sys.dba_data_files b
where
        a.file_id = b.file_id
order by
        1,3
/
spool off
ttitle off
set lines 80 pages 22
```

Who makes the I/O in the database:

```
/* Copyright © 2004, 2008 by Rampant TechPress Inc.*/
-- ******************************************************************
--   Copyright © 2004, 2008 by Rampant TechPress Inc.
--   Free for non-commercial use!  To license, e-mail info@rampant.cc
-- ******************************************************************
prompt
prompt  This will identify any single file who's write I/O
prompt  is more than 25% of the total write I/O of the database.
prompt

set
      pages 999

break on snap_time skip 2

col filename       format a40
col phywrts        format 999,999,999
col snap_time      format a20

select
   to_char(begin_interval_time,'yyyy-mm-dd hh24:mi') snap_time,
   filename,
   phywrts
from
   dba_hist_filestatxs
   natural join
   dba_hist_snapshot
where
```

```
   phywrts > 0
and
   phywrts * 4 >
(
select
   avg(value)                 all_phys_writes
from
   dba_hist_sysstat
   natural join
   dba_hist_snapshot
where
   stat_name = 'physical writes'
and
  value > 0
)
order by
   to_char(begin_interval_time,'yyyy-mm-dd hh24:mi'),
   phywrts desc
;
```

Index count usage:

```
ttitle 'Invocation Counts for index|&idxname'

select
   to_char(sn.begin_interval_time,'yy-mm-dd hh24')  c1,
   p.search_columns                                 c2,
   count(*)                                         c3
from
   dba_hist_snapshot  sn,
   dba_hist_sql_plan   p,
   dba_hist_sqlstat   st
where
   st.sql_id = p.sql_id
and
   sn.snap_id = st.snap_id
and
   p.object_name = 'YOUR_INDEX_NAME'
group by
   begin_interval_time,search_columns
;
```

Full index scan queries:

```
column nbr_scans  format 999,999,999
column num_rows   format 999,999,999
column tbl_blocks format 999,999,999
column owner      format a9;
column table_name format a20;
column index_name format a20;

ttitle 'Index full scans and counts'
select
   to_char(sn.end_interval_time,'mm/dd/rr hh24') time,
   p.owner,
   d.table_name,
```

```
   p.name index_name,
   seg.blocks tbl_blocks,
   sum(s.executions_delta) nbr_scans
from
   dba_segments seg,
   dba_indexes d,
   dba_hist_sqlstat    s,
   dba_hist_snapshot sn,
  (select distinct
     pl.sql_id,
     object_owner owner,
     object_name name
   from
      dba_hist_sql_plan pl
   where
      operation = 'INDEX'
      and
      options = 'FULL SCAN') p
where
   d.index_name = p.name
   and
   s.snap_id = sn.snap_id
   and
   s.sql_id = p.sql_id
   and
   d.table_name = seg.segment_name
   and
   seg.owner = p.owner
having
   sum(s.executions_delta) > 9
group by
   to_char(sn.end_interval_time,'mm/dd/rr hh24'),p.owner, d.table_name,
p.name, seg.blocks
order by
   1 asc;
```

```
ttitle 'Index range scans and counts'
select
   to_char(sn.end_interval_time,'mm/dd/rr hh24') time,
   p.owner,
   d.table_name,
   p.name index_name,
   seg.blocks tbl_blocks,
   sum(s.executions_delta) nbr_scans
from
   dba_segments seg,
   dba_hist_sqlstat    s,
   dba_hist_snapshot sn,
   dba_indexes d,
  (select distinct
     pl.sql_id,
     object_owner owner,
     object_name name
   from
      dba_hist_sql_plan pl
   where
      operation = 'INDEX'
      and
```

```
      options = 'RANGE SCAN') p
where
   d.index_name = p.name
   and
   s.snap_id = sn.snap_id
   and
   s.sql_id = p.sql_id
   and
   d.table_name = seg.segment_name
   and
   seg.owner = p.owner
having
   sum(s.executions_delta) > 9
group by
   to_char(sn.end_interval_time,'mm/dd/rr hh24'),p.owner, d.table_name,
p.name, seg.blocks
order by
   1 asc;
```

```
ttitle 'Index unique scans and counts'
select
   to_char(sn.end_interval_time,'mm/dd/rr hh24') time,
   p.owner,
   d.table_name,
   p.name index_name,
   sum(s.executions_delta) nbr_scans
from
   dba_hist_sqlstat    s,
   dba_hist_snapshot sn,
   dba_indexes d,
  (select distinct
     pl.sql_id,
     object_owner owner,
     object_name name
   from
      dba_hist_sql_plan pl
   where
      operation = 'INDEX'
      and
      options = 'UNIQUE SCAN') p
where
   d.index_name = p.name
   and
   s.snap_id = sn.snap_id
   and
   s.sql_id = p.sql_id
having
   sum(s.executions_delta) > 9
group by
   to_char(sn.end_interval_time,'mm/dd/rr hh24'),p.owner, d.table_name,
p.name
order by
   1 asc;
```

Top SQL waits:

```
select
```

```
   ash.user_id,
   u.username,
   sqla.sql_text,
   sum(ash.wait_time + ash.time_waited) wait_time
from
   v$active_session_history ash,
   v$sqlarea                sqla,
   dba_users                u
where
   ash.sample_time > sysdate-1
and
   ash.sql_id = sqla.sql_id
and
   ash.user_id = u.user_id
group by
   ash.user_id,
   sqla.sql_text,
   u.username
order by 4;
```

Wait time of users:

```
select
   sess.sid,
   sess.username,
   sum(ash.wait_time + ash.time_waited) wait_time
from
   v$active_session_history ash,
   v$session sess
where
   ash.sample_time > sysdate-1
and
   ash.session_id = sess.sid
group by
   sess.sid,
   sess.username
order by 3;
```

Wait time details:

```
prompt
prompt  This will compare values from dba_hist_waitstat with
prompt  detail information from dba_hist_active_sess_history.
prompt

set
    pages 999
set
    lines 80

break on snap_time skip 2

col snap_time      heading 'Snap|Time'    format a20
col file_name      heading 'File|Name'    format a40
col object_type    heading 'Object|Type'  format a10
col object_name    heading 'Object|Name'  format a20
```

```
col wait_count    heading 'Wait|Count'  format 999,999
col time          heading 'Time'        format 999,999

select
   to_char(begin_interval_time,'yyyy-mm-dd hh24:mi') snap_time,
--   file_name,
   object_type,
   object_name,
   wait_count,
   time
from
   dba_hist_waitstat            wait,
   dba_hist_snapshot            snap,
   dba_hist_active_sess_history ash,
   dba_data_files               df,
   dba_objects                  obj
where
   wait.snap_id = snap.snap_id
and
   wait.snap_id = ash.snap_id
and
   df.file_id = ash.current_file#
and
   obj.object_id = ash.current_obj#
and
   wait_count > 50
order by
   to_char(begin_interval_time,'yyyy-mm-dd hh24:mi'),
   file_name
;
```

SQL by CPU usage:

```
column sql_text format a40 word_wrapped heading 'SQL|Text'
column cpu_time heading 'CPU|Time'
column elapsed_time heading 'Elapsed|Time'
column disk_reads heading 'Disk|Reads'
column buffer_gets heading 'Buffer|Gets'
column rows_processed heading 'Rows|Processed'
set
     pages 55 lines 132
@title132 'SQL by CPU Usage'
spool
    rep_out\&db\cpu
select *
    from
    (select sql_text,cpu_time/1000000000    cpu_time,elapsed_time/1000000000
elapsed_time,
     disk_reads, buffer_gets, rows_processed
from
     v$sqlarea order by cpu_time desc, disk_reads desc)
where
     rownum<21
/
spool off
set pages 22 lines 80
ttitle off
```

List of the database users:

```
select a.username,
       a.account_status,
       TO_CHAR(a.lock_date,'dd-mon-yyyy hh24:mi') lock_date,
       TO_CHAR(a.expiry_date,'dd-mon-yyyy hh24:mi') expiry_date,
       a.default_tablespace,
       a.temporary_tablespace,
       a.profile,
       b.granted_role,
       b.admin_option,
       b.default_role,
       a.initial_rsrc_consumer_group
from
       sys.dba_users a,
       sys.dba_role_privs b
where
       a.username = b.grantee
order by
       username,
       default_tablespace,
       temporary_tablespace,
       profile,
       granted_role;
```

List of all data dictionary tables:

```
/* Copyright © 2004, 2008 by Rampant TechPress Inc.*/
column table_name format a25 heading 'View Name'
column tab_comments format a37 word_wrapped heading 'Table Commnet'
column column_name format a25 heading 'Column Name'
column col_comments format a37 word_wrapped heading 'Column Comment'
break on table_name on tab_comments
set
     lines 131 feedback off verify off pages 47
start
     title132 'Dictionary Documentation'
spool
     rep_out\&db\dict_doc
select
     distinct a.table_name,a.comments tab_comments,b.column_name,
     b.comments col_comments
from
     dba_tab_comments a, dba_col_comments b
where
     a.owner=b.owner and
     a.table_name=b.table_name and
    (a.table_name like 'DBA_%' or
     a.table_name like '%$')
order by
     table_name
/
spool off
clear columns
clear breaks
```

```
set lines 80 pages 22 feedback on verify on
ttitle off
```

Size and free space of the database tablespace:

```
select tablespace_name,
       total_space,
       total_space-free_space,
       free_space,
       (free_space/total_space)*100,
       ((total_space-free_space)/total_space)*100,
       num_files
  from (select tablespace_name,
               sum(bytes/1024) total_space,
               count(*) num_files
          from sys.dba_data_files
        group by tablespace_name),
       (select tablespace_name TS_NAME,
               sum(bytes/1024) free_space
          from sys.dba_free_space
        group by tablespace_name)
 where
        tablespace_name = ts_name
 order by
        6,1
/
```

Get the log information:

```
column log_id format 999999
column filename format A45
column low_scn  format 9999999
column high_scn format 9999999
set
     lines 132 pages 45
@title132 'Log Miner Log Files'
spool
     rep_out\&&db\log_miner
select
     log_id,filename,low_time,high_time,low_scn,next_scn
from
     v$logmnr_logs
/
spool off
set
     lines 80 pages 22
```

Execution details by user:

```
col sql_text format a40 word_wrapped heading 'SQL|Text'
col executions heading 'Executions'
col ave_cpu_time heading 'AVE|CPU|TIME'
col ave_elapsed_time heading 'AVE|ELAP|TIME'
col ave_disk_reads heading 'AVE|Disk|Reads'
```

```
col per_mem heading 'Per.|Mem'
col run_mem heading 'Run.|Mem'
col ave_sorts heading 'AVE|Sorts'
col ave_parse_calls heading 'AVE|Parse|Calls'
col ave_buffer_gets heading 'AVE|Buff|Gets'
col ave_row_proc heading 'AVE|Row|Proc.'
set
     lines 132 pages 1000
select
     sql_text, executions,
     ceil(cpu_time/greatest(executions,1)) ave_cpu_time,
     ceil(elapsed_time/greatest(executions,1)) ave_elapsed_time,
     ceil(disk_reads/greatest(executions,1)) ave_disk_reads,
     persistent_mem per_mem, runtime_mem run_mem,
     ceil(sorts/greatest(executions,1)) ave_sorts,
     ceil(parse_calls/greatest(executions,1)) ave_parse_calls,
     ceil(Buffer_gets/greatest(executions,1)) ave_buffer_gets,
     ceil(rows_processed/greatest(executions,1)) ave_row_proc
from
     v$sqlarea
where
     Sql_text like '%&sub_str%'
/
```

Get details of a view structure:

```
set
     long 1000000
select
     text
from
     dba_views
where
     owner = 'youruser'
and
     view_name  = 'yourtable';
```

Open cursor's count:

```
select
     user_name, count(*) num
from
     sys.v_$open_cursor
group by
     user_name;
```

OS users' details:

```
rem
rem Name: OSUSER.SQL
rem
rem Function: Provide list of SID, System PID and username for
rem Function: current oralce users
rem
```

```
start
     title132 'Oracle System Users'
set
     lines 132 pages 0
select
     a.sid,b.spid,a.username,a.osuser
from
     v$session a, v$process b
where
     a.paddr=b.addr (+)
/
```

Kill them all:

```
/* Copyright © 2004, 2008 by Rampant TechPress Inc.*/
rem
rem ora_kill.sql
rem function: Kills non-essential Oracle sessions (those that aren't owned
rem: by SYS or "NULL"
rem dependencies: Depends on kill_session procedure
rem mra 9/12/96
rem
set
     heading off termout off verify off echo off
spool
     kill_all.sql
select
     'execute kill_session('||chr(39)||sid||chr(39)||','||
chr(39)||serial#||chr(39)||');'
from
     v$session
where
     username is not null
     or username <> 'SYS'
     /
spool off
rem start kill_all.sql
```

List of the Oracle parameters:

```
select
     name, value, isses_modifiable ses, issys_modifiable sys, description
from
     v$parameter
order by
     name;
```

Resource limits list:

```
select *
     from v$resource_limit
/
```

Schema size:

```
select
     owner,sum(bytes)/1024/1024/1024
from
     dba_segments
group by
     owner;
```

Summary of *v_$sqlarea* and *dba_users*:

```
select
     username, sharable_mem, persistent_mem, runtime_mem
from
     sys.v_$sqlarea a, dba_users b
where
     a.parsing_user_id = b.user_id
order by
     2;
```

Users' SQL area memory use:

```
select
     username users, sql_text, Executions, loads, users_executing,
sharable_mem, persistent_mem
from
     sys.v_$sqlarea a, dba_users b
where
     a.parsing_user_id = b.user_id
and
     b.username like upper('youruser')
order by
     3 desc,1;
```

Create a grant privilege of database users:

```
select
     'grant ' || rpad(lower(privilege),30) || ' TO ' || lower(grantee) ||
      decode(admin_option,'yes',' with admin option;',';')
  from
      sys.dba_sys_privs
  where
      grantee not in ('connect','resource','dba',
                      'exp_full_database','imp_full_database')
order by
      grantee
/
```

Variable length columns:

```
col owner format a10 heading 'Owner'
col table_name format a30 heading 'Table Name'
```

```
col column_name format a25 heading 'Column Nmae'
col data_type format a10 heading 'Data Type'
col data_length heading 'Data Length'
set
     lines 132 pages 47
     @title132 'Variable Length Columns'

select
     owner, table_name, column_name, data_type, data_length
from
     dba_tab_columns
where
     owner=upper('&owner') and data_type in ('varchar2','number')
order by
     1,2,column_id
/
```

Get the index creation scripts:

```
set
     pagesize 0
set
     long 90000
set
     feedback off
set
     echo off
col out form a200
set
     linesize 300

spool stasys_indexes.sql
--- connect as user
conn SAMI/SAMI
select
     dbms_metadata.get_ddl('TABLE',u.table_name
from
     user_tables u;
select
     dbms_metadata.get_ddl('INDEX',u.index_name) out
from
     user_indexes u;
spool off;
```

Usage of temporary tablespace in gigabytes:

```
select
      A.tablespace_name tablespace, D.gb_total,
      sum (A.used_blocks * D.block_size) / 1024 / 1024 /1024  gb_used,
         D.gb_total - SUM (A.used_blocks * D.block_size) / 1024 / 1024 /1024
gb_free
from
     v$sort_segment A,
     (
select
     B.name, C.block_size, SUM (C.bytes) / 1024 / 1024 /1024 gb_total
```

```
        from      v$tablespace B, v$tempfile C
        where     B.ts#= C.ts#
        group by B.name, C.block_size
        ) D
where
     A.tablespace_name = D.name
group by
     A.tablespace_name, D.gb_total;
```

Usage of the undo tablespace:

```
--- Usage of undo tablespace
select
     to_char(s.sid)||','||to_char(s.serial#) sid_serial,
     NVL(s.username, 'None') orauser,
     s.program,
     r.name undoseg,
     t.used_ublk * to_number(x.value)/1024||'K' "Undo"
from
     sys.v_$rollname    r,
     sys.v_$session     s,
     sys.v_$transaction t,
     sys.v_$parameter   x
where
     s.taddr = t.addr
and
     r.usn   = t.xidusn(+)
and
     x.name  = 'db_block_size';
```

Usage of the redologs:

```
select
      le.leseq  "Current log sequence No",
      100*cp.cpodr_bno/le.lesiz "Percent Full",
      cp.cpodr_bno              "Current Block No",
      le.lesiz                  "Size of Log in Blocks"
from
      x$kcccp cp, x$kccle le
where
      le.leseq =CP.cpodr_seq
and
      bitand(le.leflg,24) = 8
/
```

Preparation of the undo tablespace size:

```
select d.undo_size/(1024*1024) "actual undo size [MByte]",
       substr(e.value,1,25) "undo retention [Sec]",
       (to_number(e.value) * to_number(f.value) *
       g.undo_block_per_sec) / (1024*1024)
       "needed undo size [MByte]"
  from (
       select sum(a.bytes) undo_size
```

```
          from v$datafile a,
               v$tablespace b,
               dba_tablespaces c
         where c.contents = 'undo'
           and c.status = 'online'
           and b.name = c.tablespace_name
           and a.ts# = b.ts#
       ) d,
       v$parameter e,
       v$parameter f,
       (
select
       max(undoblks/((end_time-begin_time)*3600*24))
       undo_block_per_sec
from
       v$undostat
       ) g
 where
       e.name = 'undo_retention'
  and
       f.name = 'db_block_size'
/
```

Full table scan information:

```
select
     object_owner, object_name, hash_value
from
     v$sql_plan where operation='table access'
and
     options = 'FULL';
select
     name, value
from
     v$sysstat where name like 'table scan%';
```

Redo space request:

```
select
     name, value
from
     v$sysstat
where
     name = 'redo log space requests';
```

Redo statistics:

```
select
     name,
     value
from
     v$sysstat
where
     name like '%redo%'
```

```
order by
     statistic#;
```

Compilation of entire schema:

```
exec dbms_utility.compile_schema(schema => 'my_schema');
```

Backup and Restore

The backup and restore with Recovery Manager (RMAN) topic is one of the most important a DBA should be aware of since it is crucial to get a database restored. The Managing Oracle under Linux certification exam is not covering that topic, but it is highly recommended to study more on that topic. Here are some scripts:

RMAN backup to disk:

```
RMAN target /

RMAN> run {
 allocate channel d1 device type disk
 format '/u01/oradata/backup/%u';
 backup database plus archivelog;
release channel;
}
```

Restore validations of the backup:

```
RMAN> run {
     allocate channel d1 device type disk
     restore database validate;
     release channel dev1;
}
```

Restore from RMAN backup:

```
RMAN> run {
     allocate channel d1 device type disk
     set until time 'May 1 2010 01:01:00';
     sql "alter database mount" ;
     restore database;
     recover database;
     sql "alter database open resetlogs";
     release channel dev1;
}
```

How far is the RMAN backup:

```
select
     sid, serial#, context, sofar, totalwork,
     round(sofar/totalwork*100,2) "%_complete"
from
     v$session_longops
where
     opname like 'RMAN%'
```

and:

```
     opname not like '%aggregate%'
and
     totalwork != 0
and
     sofar <> totalwork;
```

List the backups:

```
RMAN> list backup summary;
```

List the backups of archive logs:

```
RMAN> list backup of archivelog from time 'sysdate-1';
```

Monitoring

As a backup and restore topic, monitoring is important to get information when the database is failing or crashed. However, the actual monitoring tools like Tivoli will not be covered here.

With the scripts given previously, it is possible to have them executed by the crontab or internally by Oracle with *dbms_scheduler*.

Objects accessed by schema names:

```
set
     linesize 255
set
     verify off

column object format A30

select
     a.object,
```

```
     a.type,
     a.sid,
     b.username,
     b.osuser,
     b.program
from
     v$access a,
     v$session b
where
     a.sid   = b.sid
and
     a.owner = upper('&1')
order by
     a.object
/
```

Actual SQL statements that are running currently:

```
set
     linesize 500
set
     pagesize 1000
set
     feedback off

select
     s.sid,
     s.status "Status",
     p.spid "Process",
     s.schemaname "Schema Name",
     s.osuser "OS User",
     Substr(a.sql_text,1,120) "SQL Text",
     s.program "Program"
from
     v$session s,
     v$sqlarea a,
     v$process p
where
     s.sql_hash_value = a.hash_value (+)
and
     s.sql_address    = a.address (+)
and
     s.paddr          = p.addr;

set
     pagesize 14
set
     feedback on
```

Monitor the memory:

```
set      linesize 200

column username format A20
column module format A20
```

```
select
       NVL(a.username,'(oracle)') AS username,
       a.module,
       a.program,
       Trunc(b.value/1024) AS memory_kb
from
       v$session a,
       v$sesstat b,
       v$statname c
where
       a.sid = b.sid
and
       b.statistic# = c.statistic#
and
       c.name = 'session pga memory'
and
       a.program IS NOT NULL
order by
       b.value DESC;
```

Display the jobs in Oracle database:

```
set
       linesize 200

column
       owner FORMAT A20
column
       next_run_date FORMAT A35

select
       owner,
       job_name,
       enabled,
       job_class,
       next_run_date
from
       dba_scheduler_jobs
order by
       owner, job_name;
```

For upgraded database (from 7.3.4. and up to 9i):

```
select
       r.sid, r.job, r.this_date, r.this_sec, substr(what,1,40) what
from
       dba_jobs_running r,dba_jobs j
where
       r.job = j.job;
```

Mandatory Readings

As an Oracle DBA, it is necessary to keep updated with the latest technology and procedures, so here is a collection of mandatory readings that all DBAs should go through.

Books:

- *Oracle 11g New Features*, John Garmany, Steve Karam, Lutz Hartmann, V.J. Jain, Brian Carr ISBN 978-0-9797951-0-7
- Oracle Shell Scripting Linux and UNIX Programming for Oracle, Jon Emmons
- Personal Oracle RAC Clusters Create Oracle 10g Grid Computing at Home, Edward Stoever ISBN: 0-9761573-8-1
- Easy Oracle Automation: Oracle10g Automatic Storage, Memory and Diagnostic Features, Dr. Arun Kumar R.

Also, other Oracle documentations are available at http://www.oracle.com/pls/db111/portal.portal_db?selected=16&frame=#essentials and for 11g and for 10g, http://www.oracle.com/pls/db102/homepage.

In addition, there are books related to whatever DBA job specialty is chosen, and the list is available at http://www.rampant-books.com/menu_oracle.htm.

Forums and Websites

It would also be beneficial to be an active member on the following forums. It is possible to get and give help on a variety of issues.

Forums:

- http://www.dbaforums.org/oracle/
- http://www.dbasupport.com/forums
- http://forums.oracle.com
- http://www.orafaq.com/forum/
- http://www.club-oracle.com/

Magazines:

- http://www.dbazine.com/
- http://www.oracle.com/oramag/index.html

And also about a million Oracle blogs:

- http://blogs.oracle.com/
- http://wiki.oracle.com/page/List+of+Oracle-related+blogs

Good readings!

Book Conclusion

This book is written to help people passing the exam '1Z0-046 : Oracle Database 10g: Managing Oracle on Linux Certified Expert' to cover the need of IT professional to get help on passing the exam. Use this book for the study of the exam and get well prepared on the exam. The meaning of getting certified is not only having a additional diploma, but get the work, knowledge and experience rewarded and recognized. The Oracle exam is not covering all the real life situations that a DBA will face of the book isn't written to cover it either, but a lot of useful queries and commands that are worth knowing. Best of Luck on getting that exam passed.

A book conclusion would be a restatement of the beginning of the book showing that what needed to be accomplished was indeed accomplished, i.e. this is what the book intends to do in the beginning and the book conclusion would state that this actually occurred. So for your book, the emphasis is on giving the reader what they would need to pass the Linux OCE exam and that because they read the book, took the sample exams, etc., they should be successful in passing the exam.

Index

About the Author

Hubert Savio

Hubert is a senior IT specialist currently employed as a Senior Database Administrator at IBM Denmark. Hubert has worked with Oracle since late 1996 as far back as releases 6 and 7.3.4. Before working at IBM, he worked in several companies as a Linux/UNIX system engineer and IT consultant. Hubert holds a Masters degree in IT from the Centre d'études Supérieures Industrielles of Strasbourg in France.

Hubert is a specialist in Oracle Real Application Clusters, Oracle under UNIX and Linux. He works on implementation projects for IBM. He holds several Oracle certifications including OCP on 10g, OCE on both RAC and Oracle under Linux and is also certified on Linux. Hubert also passed the ITIL and the Open Group Master Certified IT specialist program. Hubert is a regular contributor on the Oracle Forum. Hubert lives in Lyngby north of Copenhagen in Denmark.

Need more
horsepower?
Call the Oracle Experts.
Expert Oracle Support
• Remote DBA Services
• Remote Oracle Health Checks
• Oracle Tuning
• RAC & Grid Support
On-Site Oracle Training
• Oracle RAC and Grid Training
• Oracle Tuning Expert Secrets
• Customized Oracle Training
• Follow-up Mentoring
Slow Oracle
Performance?
BC is a leading provider of Remote
Oracle Database Healthchecks
Help!
BURLESON
Consulting
BC
BURLESON
CONSULTING
800.766.1884
www.dba-oracle.com

www.ingramcontent.com/pod-product-compliance
Lightning Source LLC
Chambersburg PA
CBHW062047050326
40690CB00016B/3012
* 9 7 8 0 9 8 4 4 2 8 2 1 2 *